IN SEARCH OF
ANTI-SEMITISM

IN SEARCH OF ANTI-SEMITISM

William F. Buckley, Jr.

• • •

CONTINUUM • NEW YORK

1992
The Continuum Publishing Company
370 Lexington Avenue, New York, NY 10017

Printed in the United States of America

Library of Congress Cataloging-in-Publication Data

Buckley, William F. (William Frank), 1925–
    In search of anti-Semitism / William F. Buckley, Jr. ; foreword by
John O'Sullivan.
        p. cm.
    Reprint of the author's original essay from National review, with
responses from commentators and epilogue added.
    ISBN 0-8264-0619-X (hardcover : acid-free)
    1. Antisemitism—United States. 2. Antisemitism in the press-
-United States. 3. United States—Ethnic relations. I. Title.
DS146.U6B83   1992
305.892'4073—dc20
                                              92-16268
                                                  CIP

In memory of Will Herberg (1909–1977), author of *Protestant, Catholic, Jew*, beloved friend and mentor.

Contents

Acknowledgments ix

Foreword by John O'Sullivan xi

Part One 1

1. Joe Sobran 3
2. Pat Buchanan 26
3. The Dartmouth Review 45
4. The Nation 59
5. Conclusions 76

Part Two 89

(*Much of the following appears with commentary by the author.*)

1. An Essay by Joseph Sobran 93
2. An Interrogatory from Ronald R. Stockton 108
3. An Open Letter to William F. Buckley, Jr.,
   from Norman Podhoretz 111
4. A Letter from William Pfaff 122
5. A Letter from Irving Kristol 124
6. An Editorial by James M. Wall 127
7. A Letter and Column by A. M. Rosenthal 129
8. A Letter from Alan M. Dershowitz 132

9, A Letter from David Frum 133

10. A Letter from Robert D. Novak 134

11. A Letter from Hugh Kenner 137

12. A Letter from Edwin M. Yoder, Jr. 137

13. A Letter from Murray Reswick 138

14. A Letter from Eliot A. Cohen 140

15. An Essay by Manfred Weidhorn 142

16. The Political Scene: From a Speech by Murray Rothbard 152

17. Excerpts from Miscellaneous Letters and Columns 156

Part Three 161

1. Further Reflections, and Commentary 163

2. Epilogue 189

Index 199

Acknowledgments

Inasmuch as the first two sections of this book were published (in *National Review* December 1991, March 1992) there was a great deal of commentary, some of it appearing in other publications, some of it written in letters to the author. The letters (and articles and columns and editorals) came in such profusion as to make it impossible even routinely to acknowledge most of it, or even to thank everyone whose advice, insights, and criticisms helped directly to mold the third section. However, I must acknowledge gratefully the invaluable suggestions made before the publication of the first essay, by Father John Richard Neuhaus, editor of *First Things*; Professor Thomas Wendel of San Jose State University; and my colleague John O'Sullivan, who speaks eloquently for himself in the foreword to this book.

I am as ever indebted to Dorothy McCartney, *National Review*'s research director, for her resourceful and diligent work. Without the help of my assistant, Frances Bronson, I would undertake no editorial project, let alone one of this complexity. Tony Savage helped with the organization and did the typing, and Evander Lomke of Continuum made some very useful suggestions. Because the publishing schedule did not permit me to work with my usual team, I turned gratefully to Alice Manning for valuable copy-editing help.

And, finally, I thank the dozens—hundreds—of people, the majority of them unknown to me, who undertook to send me their own thoughts on the elusive subject I have sought to pursue. I deeply regret that space did not permit including even more commentary. It has all been kept, and will be filed for the benefit of scholars and researchers, at the Yale University Library.

W. F. B.
Stamford, Connecticut
July 1992

Foreword

William F. Buckley is no fool, but in the essay that opens this book, he strolled in where angels fear to tread. Mr. Buckley's essay tackles the topic of anti-Semitism at its most uncomfortable. It is not a history of anti-Semitism, nor a social-psychological definition of anti-Semitism, nor a survey of anti-Semitism in the world today—any of which might have been attempted with minimum controversy—but an examination of how anti-Semitism is treated when it appears, or is alleged to appear, in the limited but influential milieu in which he happens to live: opinion magazines, op-ed pages, syndicated columns, television talk shows. And because Mr. Buckley is incapable of being dull, he has written an essay that treats a recalcitrant topic with some wit as well as perception.

When I saw the first draft, my immediate reaction was that it was a "great read." But it was also about ten times as long as the average cover story in *National Review*. While I reread it to select the best passages for publication, I sent it to my senior colleagues for their comments. We reached the same conclusion: it was not an easy book to excerpt. Either one cut whole chapters and incidents, inviting charges of selective coverage and partiality; or one cut evenly throughout—which would risk distorting what are often finely balanced conclusions and a complicated message. The upshot was that the senior editors and the publisher of *National Review* unanimously agreed to publish the entire essay as a special issue of the magazine, to invite responses from those mentioned in the text, and to publish a special supplement to *National Review* containing these responses with Mr. Buckley's rejoinder. The original essay, the replies, the rejoinder, and, finally, a substantial afterword by Mr. Buckley reflecting on the wider public debate which his essay evoked form the contents of this book.

My motives in devoting such space to the original essay were inevitably mixed. One motive was, I hope, public-spirited. On a number of occasions since its foundation, *National Review* has quietly played the role of conscience of the Right. As Mr. Buckley parenthetically records, this magazine pushed both the cranks of the John Birch Society and the anti-Semites associated with *The American Mercury* (in its decline) from the ranks of respectable conservatism. At the time I received Mr. Buckley's manuscript, however, we had not dealt in anything like detail with what were then recent and highly publicized allegations of anti-Semitism. And we felt the need to do so. But there was another motive at work as well. I knew that Mr. Buckley's essay would arouse controversy, and that is always good for a magazine. Just how much controversy it would arouse, however, I had no idea. Nor could I have guessed the roller-coaster route that the controversy would take, transforming critics into allies, allies into critics, and restoring both to their original identities again as we hurtled along. The reason for the high-decibel level of the controversy was, of course, that most of the criticism in the original essay was directed at writers who appear in our pages or who are associated with conservative causes dear to the magazine's heart. Indeed, except for the episode of Gore Vidal and *The Nation*, all the instances of alleged anti-Semitism examined here— and the adjective "alleged" should be understood to accompany the noun "anti-Semitism" for the rest of this introduction—were cases of anti-Semitism among conservatives. The suspects were Joseph Sobran, *The Dartmouth Review*, and, above all, Patrick J. Buchanan. As if that were not enough, Mr. Buchanan announced his candidacy for the Presidency in the very week that the issue of *National Review* containing the essay hit the newsstands. That was the purest coincidence, since the issue had been in preparation for several months. But it was a coincidence that provided the liberal media with what it likes most: a family quarrel among conservatives in which a favorite son was thought to be showing signs of a hereditary ideological taint. An enormous public row ensued that has yet to run its course.

Yet, in one respect at least, the controversy was an odd and misleading one. For it implied that anti-Semitism was mainly a sin of the Right when in fact it is now found there only rarely. Indeed, those conservative groups in the United States traditionally suspected of harboring anti-Semitic opinions (e.g., rural fundamentalists) have consciously abandoned such prejudice and embraced a thoroughgoing philo-Semitism, based in some cases on Biblical prophecies about Israel's role in Armageddon and in others on repentance for what is seen as Christian complicity in the Holocaust. It is remarkable, as Mr. Buckley points out, that two of the strongest supporters of Israel in America today are the Reverend Jerry Falwell, for mainly religious reasons, and Senator Jesse Helms, for mainly strategic ones. Their forebears, both ideological and genetic, in the 1930s and before would very likely have been suspicious or even hostile toward the Jews they seldom actually met.

When anti-Semitism appears today outside the "restricted" confines of the country club (which is seen as right-wing by the Left and as "establishment" by the Right), it is almost invariably a left-wing phenomenon. Mr. Buckley's chapter on *The Nation* and Gore Vidal deals with one variant of this. But there is also the anti-Semitism of radical black consciousness as exhibited by Professor Leonard Jeffries and the Reverend Al Sharpton; the anti-Semitism of radical Arab or Palestinian nationalism (yes, I realize that the Arabs are themselves Semites); and the anti-Semitism that blends the two in a rainbow coalition of radical leftism and Third-Worldery as exhibited by the Reverend Louis Farrakhan and, on occasion, by the Reverend Jesse Jackson.

What is disturbing about these varieties of anti-Semitism is the spread of their appeal. They enjoy the complicity of tenured opinion in the university, the nervous tolerance of big-city politicians, the collusion of respectable black organizations, and the willingness of the establishment media to report such matters in a context of social excuses (the tabloids are significantly more critical). At the same time they arouse the enthusiasm of thugs in the street and help to recruit young people for terrorist training camps. Today it is the anti-Semitism of the Left that, in its extreme and revolutionary forms, actually leads to the killing of Jews, whether in Jerusalem, Paris, or Crown Heights. Yet it receives much less criticism from the surrounding culture than do expressions of anti-Semitism from conservatives.

One of the most striking illustrations of this public mood is that, until very recently, the institutions of organized anti-anti-Semitism have been somewhat diffident in tackling black or left-wing anti-Semitism. This is humanly understandable. Older leaders of such organizations remember only too well when anti-Semitism of the most horrifying kind was overwhelmingly a crime of the Right. The organizations are themselves part of a society which, until the collapse of Communism, was generally inclined to interpret the Left's sins in the light of its professed humanitarianism, and the sins of racial minorities in the light of past injustices done to them. Finally, the leaders of such organizations have generally emerged, or not emerged, from the Left, misdirected there (as it seems to me) by the liberal Jewish conscience. And we are all inclined to be tender to the lapses of our friends.

Still, the indulgent willingness to forget the Reverend Jesse Jackson's remark about "Hymietown" in the 1988 New York primary (when Mayor Edward Koch was heartily denounced as divisive for bringing it up) was in sharp contrast to the willingness of both the media and such organizations to treat Mr. Buckley's nuanced judgment of Mr. Buchanan as an unqualified condemnation. That may now be changing, perhaps as a result of the controversy Mr. Buckley provoked. Five months after the publication of his essay, we saw an upsurge of criticism of Governor Jerry Brown during the 1992 New York primary because he was considering Reverend Jackson as his vice-presidential running mate. As well as drawing an eloquent apology from Mr. Jackson for the Hymietown remark four years earlier—which should perhaps be accepted as finally settling his debt in this matter—this suggested that the Left's immunity no longer holds and that anti-Semitism is to be condemned, no matter where it comes from.

But was right-wing anti-Semitism demonstrated beyond any question in the cases discussed in the original essay? Mr. Buckley establishes that, in some instances, there is at least a case to answer. But without anticipating his full verdicts, which would oversimplify a subtle argument and spoil the reader's suspense, it is worth asking how we should weigh a few instances of suspected anti-Semitism from a writer's large output. What if he can point also to philo-Semitic writings? Or what if he can cite the testimony of friends as to his personal decency in the matter? What, in particular, if those friends are Jewish? The claim "Some of my best friends are Jews" is often derided as the classic excuse of the social anti-Semite. But that is apt only if the excuse is manifestly insincere. If his best friends really are Jews, then either his Jewish friends are extremely odd or he is not an anti-Semite.

Norman Podhoretz is quoted later in these pages as saying, in effect, that only God can know the secrets of the human heart. That is so, but we may reasonably speculate all the same. There are several possible reasons why a man might give vent to anti-Semitic remarks. He might, of course, be an anti-Semite. One should never neglect the obvious. Or he might make anti-Semitic remarks in the heat of an argument in order to deliberately wound a Jewish adversary. That would show an unpleasant character; it would demonstrate his grasp of the anti-Semitic vocabulary; and, other things being equal, it would create a reasonable supposition of anti-Semitism. But it would not in the end convict him of a general anti-Semitism, any more than the arguments of most wives in domestic rows would convict them of a general hostility to husbands. And if he could cite Jewish friendships or other signs of philo-Semitism, he might well persuade us of his goodwill. A third possibility is that because of an exaggeratedly polemical writing style, he might take criticism of Israel, or of American supporters of Israel, over that invisible line separating legitimate anti-Zionism from culpable anti-Semitism. (In that case, he would be the more vulnerable to misunderstanding because much anti-Zionism is in fact a disguised form of anti-Semitism.)

This third possibility is my own explanation of how both Mr. Sobran and Mr. Buchanan first began to be suspected of harboring anti-Semitic feelings. In effect, both men were denounced in severe terms for first or uncertain offenses that represented folly rather than bigotry. But they compounded the folly by their failure to issue simple apologies then and there (and indeed since), and by their subsequent reactions to criticism. Mr. Sobran, unable to believe that anyone could sincerely think him seriously ill-natured, declared himself the victim of political persecution and froze in a posture of heroic defiance. Since the defiance is of Jewish pressure, it produces effects that are sometimes hard to distinguish from anti-Semitism, as Mr. Buckley documents. Mr. Buchanan, displaying that instinctive pugnacity he has put to excellent use on a thousand other occasions, delivered a column straight to the jaw of his first major critic, A. M. Rosenthal, and "moved on" unapologetically, refusing to reply to later attacks. Given that the opening line of his response was: "There goes the B'nai B'rith Man of the Year award," he was certainly not turning the other cheek. And it was this obduracy, as much as the original remarks about the "amen corner" and so on, that hardened the impression that Mr. Buchanan had, as someone said, "a problem with the Jews."

In the main, the press reporting of Mr. Buckley's essay did not bother with these or other subtleties in his argument. What it carried, in effect, was a headline: Buchanan Anti-Semitic, Says Buckley. And since Mr. Buchanan again refused to respond directly, that would have remained the lasting public impression but for two further developments. The first was part two. We had promised to publish full replies from those criticized; we also sought comments from people whose comments we thought likely to prove illuminating; and we received a vast mailbag of letters, some of which were worthy of publication. These replies *did* deal with the subtleties of Mr. Buckley's argument; indeed, they added some subtleties of their own.

Some columnists and respondents, like A. M. Rosenthal in the *New York Times,* felt both that Mr. Buchanan was anti-Semitic and that Mr. Buckley might have said so with greater forthrightness and fewer qualifications. Others, notably Irving Kristol, shrank from that verdict but thought that Mr. Buchanan was guilty of something—"political anti-Semitism," thought Mr. Kristol; folly and mischief, thought the editors of *National Review.* On the other side of the ledger, however, those criticized plainly felt a genuine sense of indignation about the charges leveled against them. In the absence of Mr. Buchanan, Mr. Sobran expressed this outrage most sharply and effectively in an essay which, whatever fault may be found with its stance, is a fine example of the polemicist's art. The friends of Buchanan and Sobran—some of them Jewish—were hardly less indignant. Robert Novak, for instance, wrote, in a letter quoted in part two, that "Buchanan is no anti-Semite, as anybody who knows him well will avow. Nor does the body of his writing support the indictment." And there were, finally, some correspondents whose arguments cannot be easily assigned to one side or the other of the divide, but who had important and imaginative things to say on Jewish life and religion, Christian–Jewish relations, and so forth. No one could deny, having read part two, that every decent opinion on the topic had been given a fair hearing.

Then the second development occurred: *National Review* and Mr. Buckley both issued tactical endorsements of Pat Buchanan in the New Hampshire primary in the hope of drawing President Bush back toward a more conservative politics. Those endorsements came accompanied by strong criticisms of Mr. Buchanan's general and specific political programs; by the proviso that they would not have been given if the magazine had believed Mr. Buchanan to be anti-Semitic; by the commentary that his campaign was appealing too much to people's resentments and not enough to their optimism and idealism; and finally by the request, subsequently repeated, that he should apologize for the remarks that had given rise to the suspicion that he was anti-Semitic. No one could have mistaken this qualified and tactical approval for an endorsement of everything Mr. Buchanan had ever said, still less a sympathy for what he had been accused of saying. But it evoked a reaction that made sense only on those grounds.

Mr. Rosenthal in the *New York Times* accused "conservatives," naming Mr. Buckley and me as examples, of failing to distinguish between "political good and political evil." (When Mr. Rosenthal expressed doubt that I disapproved of "some of Mr. Buchanan's visceral viciousness," I pointed out in a letter to the *Times* that I had called on Mr. Buchanan to apologize in the very article of mine that Mr. Rosenthal had quoted; but the *Times* in its large liberal way decided not to publish this correction.) There was an almost equally severe reproof in *Commentary* from its editor, Norman Podhoretz, who had given an almost unqualified welcome to Mr. Buckley's initial essay. (*Commentary*, however, generously invited me to reply.) Finally, 13 distinguished conservatives wrote a letter to *National Review* regretting our endorsement in similar terms. All three documents argued, in essence, that our endorsement of Mr. Buchanan, however qualified, was incompatible with Mr. Buckley's original criticisms.

In the third section of this book, Mr. Buckley gives a full and lively account of these final twists in the controversy. He replies point by point to his critics; he refines his own criticisms of Pat Buchanan; and, responding to the claims of some respondents in part two that he was navigating without a compass, he forges his own definition of what anti-Semitism means in today's politics. And that tour de force brings to an end this remarkable dialectical exercise.

To quote Little Peterkin, however, what good came of it at last? I have gone through several reactions since I received Bill Buckley's first draft of

In Search of Anti-Semitism a year ago. My first impulse, as I wrote above, was to publish something that both was a "good read" and would establish a clear conservative "line" on anti-Semitism. As the controversy developed and subtleties were condensed into headlines, however, I wondered whether we were not putting reputations at risk unfairly. It was some comfort to me that we had offered the right of reply to people criticized. Then, when we came to publish part two, I began to fear that our very fairness in publishing such a wide range of viewpoints would create a Babel drowning out the principles we had originally hoped to establish. And this anxiety intensified with the rows over *National Review*'s endorsement of Mr. Buchanan in New Hampshire. But with the exercise finally completed by Mr. Buckley in part three, I believe that *In Search of Anti-Semitism* has achieved something very worthwhile. It has given the reader all the material needed to reach one's own judgments, the firm moral principles that should guide the reader toward the right ones, a basis for understanding why others arrive at a different view, and the insight that many otherwise good people can be foolish, stubborn, and just plain unreasonable.

Let me offer three tentative conclusions to which I have been led. First, it cannot be in anyone's interest to drive people into anti-Semitism by accusing them of it peremptorily. If the venial sins of the Right are first equated with more serious left-wing offenses and then punished with still greater severity, they are likely to become mortal: mortal sins, mortal wounds, perhaps both. If so, the result will be needless bitterness, broken friendships, a harsher tone in conservative debate, and the waste of some remarkable talents. We should all try to avoid that. But the greatest responsibility rests upon those tempted to commit venial sins in the first place.

Second, for our society, the wider issue is to lift the standards of public debate so that certain habits of mind and discussion can have no place on either Left or Right. We need a greater sensitivity—not in the corrupt sense of the word that justifies censorship and thought control, but precisely to allow honest discussion of the most delicate topics.

And, finally, *sub specie aeternitatis,* the lasting benefit of this debate, as Irving Kristol has argued elsewhere, may be to remind us all of the nurturing power of religion in our lives at a time when it is increasingly under pressure from the secular Left. And that is an issue on which Jews and Christians are the most natural of allies.

JOHN O'SULLIVAN

PART ONE

1 · Joe Sobran

The letter from Mr. Horan (a stranger) of Fort Smith, Arkansas, came in to the office in June 1991, soon after we had published an article by Joe Sobran to the effect that it was the Earl of Oxford who had written the plays universally attributed to Shakespeare. The writer caught what humor is to be found *In Re Sobran and The Problem*, and touches, however inadvertently, on some of the questions I intend to explore.

Dear Mr. Buckley:

Look, I love the hell out of Joseph Sobran, but I think that he's getting a little kooky. In fact, I think that he's getting *a lot* kooky. I'd like to think that he inhaled a little too much sidestream smoke when he took his boy to see the Rolling Stones, but that was two years ago. If Mr. Sobran is not peddling variants on the Blood Libel, he's schmoozing with the Liberty Lobby, or running on (and on) about the Earl of Oxford, or moaning about how we're gonna get whupped in the Desert . . .

The boy needs a rest.

Mr. Sobran is the best "Aginner" I have ever seen. Down my part of the country, an Aginner is a feller who is "against" most everything in general. By and by, these folks have to tell you what they are *for,* as a way of 'splaining why they are agin something that is going on as they speak. The world has done mostly turned Joe's way in the past three years. Hell, even the universities are getting sick of PC. In five years, Mr. Sobran is going to have nothing which he can legitimately be agin!

Well, who would've thunk and Hallelujah. But there's the rub. Aginners would rather have a silly argument than a nice juicy steak and a roll in the hay with a Genuine Hollywood Star. So now Mr. Sobran is having to go *find* things to ruckus about, and he has picked up a bunch of sure-fire hellraisers: Jews and Shakespeare. Down here in the South, us dum ole dirteaters would say: "Those is issues that deserve a good lettin' alone."

Please impart that little bit of folk wisdom to my Good Buddy. And tell Mr. Sobran that "You should never try to teach a pig to sing: it can't be done, and it annoys the pig." *Robertson v. White,* 633 F. Supp. 954, 959 (W.D. Ark. 1986). After all, it's The Law.*

Yours sincerely,
Matthew Horan

We'll let Shakespeare go, while making the point in passing that Mr. Horan is mistaken in suggesting that Joe is always caught up by something or another. Our association goes back twenty years, and though it is true that he has a high capacity for sustained indignation, it is only Israel and The Jews that seem to have him semi-permanently obsessed; yes, the right word, I think. I propose to inquire into the question by analyzing Joe Sobran (a close friend) to the extent necessary to explore contemporary anti-Semitism. This is not a history of anti-Semitism or of its causes. It is rather a look at it as revealed by the practices of a few journalists and intellectuals, and by the arguments they use. There is a great deal to be learned from the experience of Joe Sobran.

Types of Anti-Semitism

I have some credentials in the area, among them my own father's anti-Semitism. It is probably never too early to distinguish the kinds of anti-Semitism we run into in the world. The apocalyptic kind was, of course: The Holocaust; and I'll be asking whether the shadow of the Holocaust is being made to stretch too far in contemporary polemics. This is different from denying that the Holocaust is, and will always be, one of the great historical ventures in denatured human barbarism. There are Jews who continue to fear that the fires that lit the Holocaust might one day be rekindled. But there are also Jews who, comfortable with the protocols built up around Auschwitz, are disposed, so to speak, to prolong the period of de-Nazification indefinitely. And fierce anti-Semitism of a threatening kind continues, for instance among the Palestinians. Probably a higher percentage of them hate the Jews than ever Germans hated the Jews in the Thirties, and the Holocaust is eloquent testimony to what a very few, moved by intense clinical passions, can accomplish. And then too, every now and again one comes across such as Amos Elon, writing in *The New Yorker* (May 13, 1991):

Anyone with more than a fleeting acquaintance with Vienna knows that

---

*From the opinion of H. Franklin Waters, Chief Judge of the Western District of Arkansas: "However, where the Court is of the opinion that the complaint does not and cannot state a cause of action under state or federal law, then there is no point in passing the matter into discovery. As the saying goes, you should never try to teach a pig to sing: it can't be done, and it annoys the pig."

for every Viennese hatemonger you read about there are many Viennese who are liberal-minded. And yet in a 1980 poll, 20 per cent of the Austrians who responded said they were in favor of legally prohibiting Jews from owning real estate and capital in Austria. A poll taken in 1984 by Vienna University social scientists showed that only 14 per cent of the population was "largely free of prejudice" against Jews. Sixty-four per cent said that Jews were "too powerful" politically and economically. Thirty-four per cent believed that "honest competition" with Jews was impossible. Fifty-seven per cent said that they shouldn't have to be reminded so often of the murder of millions of Jews in the extermination camps. Twenty-one per cent said that the "removal of the Jews from our country [under the Nazis] has also produced positive results." In a more recent poll, 23 per cent said that "Jews should not occupy influential positions in our country," and 6 per cent confessed that they would be physically repelled if they had to shake a Jew's hand.

My impression is that these are tabloidized findings, influenced in part by the national resentment over the (deserved) ostracism of President Kurt Waldheim, and that some of the questions were on the order of, "Do you believe that the experience of slavery benefited the Negro race?" to which question 21 per cent of Americans might answer Yes—reasoning, with Booker T. Washington, that slavery en route to emancipation was preferable to a continuation of the kind of life common in Africa during the eighteenth century.

Apprehensive Jews react in two different ways. On the one hand there is the Jew who, reacting to a remark unfriendly to his cause or his religion, deduces from it a potential to revive the spirit of the Holocaust. There is another reaction, opportunistic in character. There are Americans out there, I think, who would resist a Holocaust as fiercely as Elie Wiesel, who are nevertheless whispered about as anti-Israel and derivatively anti-Semitic, never mind that what they want to talk about or to urge on public policy has nothing to do with approval of anti-Semitism, let alone genocide; which leaves us with some people who don't talk about what they want to talk about for fear of being branded as anti-Semitic.

My father and his generation lived in an age in which anti-Semitism was very widespread. I suppose there is no harm in revealing that it was McGeorge Bundy, former dean of Harvard, former national-security assistant to Presidents Kennedy and Johnson, former president of the Ford Foundation, who told me one day at lunch, à propos of I forget what, that if he were to hear spoken today the kind of thing that was "routinely spoken at [his father's] lunch table," he would leave the room in protest.

I knew exactly what he meant, because at my father's lunch table one heard (I must suppose) the same kind of thing. Interestingly enough, the bias never engaged the enthusiastic attention of any of my father's ten children (any more than of Mr. Bundy's four), except in the attenuated sense that we felt instinctive loyalty to any of Father's opinions, whether about Jews or about tariffs or about Pancho Villa. Seven or eight children in Sharon, Connecticut, among them four of my brothers and sisters, thought it would be a great lark one night in 1937 to burn a cross outside a Jewish resort nearby. That story has been told, and my biographer (John Judis) points out that I was not among that wretched little band. He fails to point out that I wept tears of frustration at being forbidden by senior siblings to go out on that adventure, on the grounds that (at age 11) I was considered too young. Suffice it to say that children as old as 15 or 16 who wouldn't intentionally threaten anyone could, in 1937, do that kind of thing lightheartedly. Thoughtless, yes, but motivated only by the desire to have the fun of *scaring adults!* It was the kind of thing we didn't distinguish from a Halloween prank. None of us gave any thought to Kristallnacht, even when it happened (November 9, 1938—I was 12, in a boarding school in England), and certainly not to its implications. But then this is a legitimate grievance of the Jew: Kristallnacht was not held up in the critical media as an international event of the first magnitude, comparable to the initial (1948) laws heralding the formal beginning of apartheid or the triggering episodes of the religious wars of the seventeenth century.

When, a few years before the cross-burning near Sharon, Connecticut, a Jewish student was elected to a fraternity at Yale University, a pig was burned outside its doors that night. Those were the years when Daniel Bell's cousin, Theodore Cohen, freshly graduated from CCNY (the City College of New York), decided to go to Japan to become a Sinologist. Why? Because, he told me, there was no way in which he could achieve a tenured chair at Columbia (his burning ambition) as a mere social scientist: "They just didn't give professorships to Jews," he explained. So his stratagem was to become a Sinologist, who were in such short supply as to permit him the leverage of the seller's market. A world war spared him the effort, and of course he has just retired from a tenured chair at Harvard. But the professor who taught me philosophy was the first Jew to be given tenure at Yale.*

Suffice it to say that anti-Semitism of the kind experienced by such as the above was pervasive in America and that what happened in Germany, Austria, and Poland during the Forties is, in the judgment of many Jews, the hideous result, if not exactly of animus expressed casually at the dining tables of New England and Paris, then of international indifference to such animus.

---

*Contrast: "If someone had predicted earlier this century that the presidents of Princeton, Dartmouth, and Harvard would one day be named Shapiro, Freedman, and Rudenstine (the latter was born half Jewish), he would have been laughed out of town" (*Newsweek,* Oct. 7, 1991).

It is not easy to pin down. There are flashes of memory. I think of the Spanish guide who led us by the great painting in the Prado of the Grand Inquisitor Torquemada, shown hurling the crucifix at the feet of Ferdinand and Isabella. She explained the drama to us: "Torquemada was demanding that the Jews in Spain who continued to deny Christ be expelled—otherwise, said Torquemada, throwing a crucifix down on the floor at the feet of his sovereigns, *¡Crucifiquenlo de nuevo!'* (Crucify him yet again!)" Their sovereign majesties signed the expulsion order, and the Inquisition began.

Yes, 1492. The Jews were formally readmitted to Spain in 1869. Much can be written about the cultural and ethical meaning of those four hundred years of expulsion, but most Catholics would reasonably consider it a quirk of anti-Catholicism to link any present-day Catholic practice to the Inquisition. Anyone who preached that to yield to current Catholic political doctrine on, say, abortion would catapult us back onto the road to the Inquisition would be smiled at, or should be; raising the question whether certain kinds of statements about American Jews, or about Israel, are responsibly interpreted as early-bird signs of a remobilization toward Auschwitz.

And then too, in the immediate shadow of the Holocaust, a number of fragile formulations became modish and, in the general piety brought on by the Holocaust, were inadequately explored. I remember Gregory Peck in the movie *Gentleman's Agreement*. He fought bravely for the right of Jews to buy property in a suburban area previously restricted, informing the judge (jury? newspaperman? congregation?—I forget) *that there was no such thing as a Jewish "race," there was only a Jewish religion.* A valid taxonomic point which, however, should not be used to strip probably the majority of American Jews, who (like their Protestant counterparts) are not actively religious, of their ethnic pedigrees. The famous answer to the question, Who is a Jew? is of course, "Anyone who says he is a Jew." Jewish Orthodoxy has a more formal answer to that question, but we are not talking about doctrinal definitions. A Catholic who does not do his Easter Duty has committed a mortal sin, and until relieved through confession is a spiritual expatriate, but is nevertheless thought by his neighbors, who in any case tend not to notice Sunday parietals, to be "a Catholic," and the census takers formally put him down as one. Many Americans who consider themselves Jewish rest their claims on ethnic origins rather than on religious credenda.

And then another memory. As the editor of the daily newspaper at Yale, I would spend one hour every week (it was a tradition) with the president, in those days a relatively inaccessible figure. Charles Seymour, historian and curator of the Colonel House collection, was an urbane New Englander, and one day he was reflecting, during our weekly colloquy, on the effort being made by the legislature at Hartford (this was 1949) to enact a Fair Educational Practices Act that would require all colleges in the state to strip from questionnaires sent to applicants any question as to their religion, and to stop asking applicants for photographs. President Seymour was greatly irked by this statist imposition. The legislators *do not realize*, he said to me, that among the functions of a university is to act as a collector of materials. "We are in the business of amassing data, and what the religious affiliation of a student is we have legitimate reasons for wanting to know."

I remember taking it for granted that Mr. Seymour was not being disingenuous, though the Catholic chaplain of the university winked at me when I told him about it and divulged that each year a virtually identical percentage of Jews and of Catholics was admitted to the freshman class. A book on the general subject has been published (*Joining the Club*, by Dan A. Oren), and it is certainly true that, at Yale as elsewhere, there was an unspoken racial-religious quota system.

But in that same conversation Charles Seymour went on to say that there were certain taboos that had crystallized in the last generation, among them that one could no longer speak of the Jews as having any "group characteristics." Of course that is nonsense, he said. They do have group characteristics. "So do we Protestants. So do you Catholics. But you aren't supposed to say it." Many years later I repeated this conversation to an urbane Jewish friend, a journalist and author, who said that it was true that you can't ascribe group characteristics to Jews. But a little while later he was telling me that, as a Jew, he was proud of two traits common among Jews, the first a true thirst for justice, the second a "sense of the book," by which he meant a desire to learn; conversely, he disliked what he saw as a tendency to self-imposed tribalism and a tendency of some to violate their ethical precepts by a vulnerability to greed.

This exercise is not for the purpose of attempting a social profile of the American Jew; the intention is much more modest, namely to build some context within which it becomes possible to evaluate what can defensibly be thought of as *anti-Semitism* and, at the same time, what is *wrongfully* thought of as anti-Semitic. If it is anti-Semitic to believe that there are group characteristics among Jews, then anti-Semitism indeed lingers.

What about Joe Sobran?

Joe Sobran was born in 1946 in Detroit, and I came across him when he was doing graduate work in English at Eastern Michigan University. My host showed me a letter Joe had written to a professor who had volubly objected, in the student newspaper, to my having been invited to speak in the first place. I spotted in that letter an extraordinary polemical skill, as also a capacity to arrange thought with lucidity and wit. I approached him. Soon after, he began flying to New York from Detroit every fortnight to do editorials for *National Review*. A year or so later he emigrated to New York to work full time for the magazine; in due course he went to Washington, reducing his commitments to regular editorials and criticism, and coming in to New York once every month.

Meanwhile, he had begun publishing a syndicated column.

Early in 1986 I scheduled a private dinner with him at which I told him that I thought he should know that in his syndicated column he was gradually giving his readers the impression that he was obsessed on the subject of Israel. More, I told him that unlike obsessions with, say, Nicaragua or China or even Russia, an obsession with Israel at the expense of Israel gives rise to suspicions of an awakening anti-Semitism. Anti-Semitism, I told him, is a mortal disease in his profession. I even joked about it a little. William Scranton (I remember saying) had for a generation been among the two or three most influential Republicans in the country. Then President-elect Nixon sent him to the Middle East to survey the scene. He returned to say he thought the Nixon Administration should be "more even-handed" in managing the problems of the Middle East, "and he has never been heard from since!" We both laughed. One does laugh when acknowledging inordinate power, even as one deplores it. It would not have occurred to me, that evening, to suggest to Joe that he avoid *anti-Semitism*. Because to do so would have sounded as patronizing and unnecessary as to warn him against contracting syphilis.

But six months later I judged it to be crisis time. I called the senior staff of *National Review* together. We met three times, twice with Joe. What led to those meetings, and what issued from them, is compactly explained in the editorial note I published in the issue of July 4, 1986:

In Re Joe Sobran and Anti-Semitism

Complaints have reached us concerning a series of columns written by my colleague Joseph Sobran under the aegis of his newspaper syndicate. It is charged that these columns constitute anti-Semitism. In the columns, Mr. Sobran, among other things, has declared that Israel is not an ally to be trusted; surmised that the *New York Times* endorsed the military strike against Libya only because it served its Zionist editorial line; and ruminated that the visit of the Pope to a synagogue had the effect of muting historical persecutions of Christians by Jews. In that last column, Mr. Sobran, exasperated, wrote, "But it has become customary recently to ascribe all Jewish–Christian friction to Christians. If a Jew complains about Christians, Christians must be persecuting him. If a Christian complains about Jews, he is doing the persecuting—in the very act of complaining. It simply isn't fair." And in his most recent column on the theme, Joe Sobran complains that he is criticized for being anti-Semitic unwarrantedly: "I find that the more I say what I really think, the more I'm accused of thinking something else." Again he says that "the word 'anti-Semite' is more potent than most of the charges of bigotry that are flung around these days. It carries the whiff of Nazism and mass murder. 'It means,' as a friend of mine puts it, 'that you ultimately approve of the gas chambers.'"

It is appropriate, on my own behalf and on that of my other senior colleagues, to comment on what is becoming a public quarrel involving Joe Sobran and those who impute anti-Semitism to him.

What needs to be said first is that those who know him know that Sobran is not anti-Semitic. Neither is he (begin counting) a) anti-black, b) anti-Italian, c) anti-women, nor even d) anti-gay, to list some of the controversies he has got into that have resulted in such allegations. He is against a) some things done by blacks, b) some things done by Italian-Americans, c) some things done by the women's liberation movement, and d) some things done by gays. With learning and eloquence, his acute eye roams the universe day and night in search of paradox and irony. In doing so he finds his quarries; but sometimes, in exposing them, he expresses himself with excessive liberty from accepted conventions.

Now ethnic sensitivities vary. It doesn't much matter what John Cheever or John O'Hara or John Updike or anybody else writes about them—you cannot really succeed, in America, in riling the WASPs. Their sense of security is as solid as Plymouth Rock, and incidentally as insensate. Blacks, yes, are sensitive, but black lobbies are not powerful enough to punish nonpolitical transgressors against such taboos. (A black book-buyers' boycott against a novelist would not impoverish.) If the spoken or written offense is egregious enough, as in the case of the joke told [in 1975] to John Dean by Agriculture Secretary Earl Butz, a Cabinet officer gets fired. If a district attorney is named to a federal judgeship and it is revealed that he once made a pot-valiantly genial reference to the Ku Klux Klan, he can be defeated on the floor of the Senate. And no one running for office in a state in which the black population is significant would consider, post 1965, violating the taboo. On the other hand, there is discussion of such questions as relative black intelligence, sexual promiscuity, and upward mobility that still gets a sober hearing in sober surroundings. About the American Indians one can say most things with impunity; about gays, progressively less as, emerging from the closet, they consolidate and give strength to their retaliatory powers.

In respect of American Jews, the sensitivity is of an extremely high order, and for the best of reasons. The toniest "liberal" universities in America would not, until about the time Joe Sobran was born, give tenure to Jewish professors. To elect a Jewish student to most social fraternities was quite simply unthinkable a generation ago. The designation of Jews as mortal enemies of civilization by the same European power that had given us Bach and Goethe, Kant and Einstein, reminded the Jews (those Jews who survived) that no society, however civilized its pedigree, can complacently be trusted to desist from the most ferocious human activity: genocide.

It is a far cry from Auschwitz to the suggestion (Joe Sobran's) that the Israelis are "frequently duplicitous" in their behavior toward America: but it ought not to surprise Sobran that such charges tend to alarm American Jews. And given Sobran's high intellectual acumen, one wonders that he should, on the one hand, quote with evident concurrence an anonymous friend's warning that the word "anti-Semitic" " . . . means that you ultimately approve of the gas chambers," and yet be surprised—indeed, be deeply hurt—by the intensity of the criticism he has experienced. When, 35 years ago, I wrote that an anti-conservative, anti-Christian consensus prevailed in the Yale faculty, I would not have been justified in registering surprise when conservative Christian scholars at Yale failed to achieve tenure.

My own evaluation of the public question in which Joe Sobran is involved—and here I speak also for the other senior editors—is this:

1. The structure of prevailing taboos respecting Israel and the Jews is welcome. The age calls for hypersensitivity to anti-Semitism, over against a lackadaisical return to the blasé conventions of the pre-war generation, which in one country led to genocidal catastrophe. Needless to say, this is hardly to dignify the preposterous charges of anti-Semitism occasionally leveled, ignorantly and sometimes maliciously, at anyone who takes a position contrary to that of organized Jewish opinion, whether in Israel or elsewhere.

2. Any person who, given the knowledge of the reigning protocols, read and agonized over the half-dozen columns by Joe Sobran might reasonably conclude that those columns were written by a writer inclined to anti-Semitism. A savage entering a Catholic church who absentmindedly chewed on consecrated wafers would not be thought blasphemous. The non-savage, doing the same thing, would. Naïfs cannot commit a black mass; cosmopolitans can, and do.

3. Those who know Joe Sobran know not only that he does not harbor ethnic prejudices, but that he regards such prejudice as sinful, despised by God, and therefore despised by man. But the personal integrity of a private man is a matter adjudicated between him, his family, and his conscience. The integrity of a public figure is public business. If the public establishes a consensus that during the playing of the National Anthem hands should not be placed in one's pants pockets, then to do so from the dais is an affront on the assembly, never mind that the clinical argument can be made that hands in pockets are not intrinsically an act of disrespect. [I once passed by Lenin in his tomb, hands in pockets, and was told to remove them. I did so, understanding.]

4. In the last fifteen or twenty years, under the leadership of the Soviet Union, it became plain that institutional anti-Semitism was consolidating around the political Left, where, ideologically, class hatreds belong. A scholar, recently commenting on the drift away from Communism by the American Left, acutely observed that their disillusion with Communism was rather a reaction against Communism's "ungainly" cultural performance in literature and the arts, than against human depravity. In England, anti-

Semitism (disguised as anti-Zionism) is the property of the political Left. So does the animus move in the United States, where *The Nation* magazine exhibits the same kind of toleration toward anti-Semitism (witness the recent essay there by Gore Vidal, in which neoconservatives are dismissed as Zionist imperialists) that it shows to Fidel Castro, the Sandinistas, and Alger Hiss. The movement of anti-Semitism from unexamined prejudice of the political Right to inchoate agenda of the political Left is of epochal significance. The call, on the Right, fully to excrete its old prejudices is, accordingly, of first strategic and tactical importance.

5. *National Review* has, since its inception, declined association with anti-Semites, and indeed on one occasion went a generic step further. When it became clear, in 1957, that the direction *The American Mercury* was headed was anti-Semitic, I ruled, with the enthusiastic approval of my colleagues, that no writer appearing on the *Mercury's* masthead, notwithstanding his own innocence on the subject, could also appear on *National Review's*.

The relationship of this journal toward our highly esteemed and beloved colleague, Joe Sobran, is one that will ultimately reflect a mature and civilized resolution of our commitment to these positions. We know him not to be what he is thought by some to have become; but what they suspect is not, under the circumstances, unreasonable. Accordingly, I here dissociate myself and my colleagues from what we view as the obstinate tendentiousness of Joe Sobran's recent columns. We are confident that in the weeks and months to come, he will charitably and rationally acknowledge the right reason behind the crystallization of the present structure of taboos, and that he will accordingly argue his positions in such fashion as to avoid affronting our natural allies.

How They Reacted

My handling of the Sobran crisis, as it turned out, didn't satisfy all our readers, didn't satisfy all our critics, and didn't satisfy Joe Sobran. He and I arrived at a private covenant: Whenever Joe set out to write about the Mideast, he would call and read me his column in draft form. The assumption here was that I was by experience better equipped than he to detect the formulation that was unwarrantedly provocative. Joe abided for a while by that covenant and read me two columns in the ensuing two or three months. He then stopped doing so, writing infrequently about the Mideast. But in the spring of 1990 he went back to the subject with, well, a vengeance. Meanwhile he had written me a long letter.

Back in February of 1987 I had from my colleague Jeffrey Hart—a senior editor of *National Review*, a professor of English at Dartmouth, a syndicated columnist, and an occasional contributor to *Commentary*—a letter in which he relayed detailed complaints from Norman Podhoretz.

Podhoretz is, of course, the editor of *Commentary*, and a principal figure in the neoconservative movement. Beginning twenty years ago he took *Commentary* from a position of highbrow flatulence on the problem of Soviet imperialism and turned it into one of the most sophisticated and formidable weapons of the West in the cold war. *Commentary* is, officially, a publication of the American Jewish Committee, which body, however, has never interfered with Podhoretz's authority, any more than it had with that of the magazine's distinguished founder, Eliot Cohen.

Podhoretz now wrote to Hart about an article appearing in *National Review* by Sobran criticizing *NR*'s editorial policy on the Mideast.

Mr. Podhoretz reasonably assumed that Jeff Hart would pass the letter on to me, and accordingly I replied to him directly:

You wrote that you were "surprised and dismayed by the fact that *National Review* published such a piece" as Joe Sobran had written, and that my doing so "does damage . . . lending credence to all those like Marty Peretz [the editor-in-chief of *The New Republic*] who have attacked me [Podhoretz] for being too easy on Buckley." The time is clearly overdue for a recapitulation of the relevant data.

1. I deemed Joe Sobran's six columns contextually anti-Semitic. By this I mean that if he had been talking, let us say, about the lobbying interests of the Arabs or of the Chinese, he would not have raised eyebrows as an anti-Arab or an anti-Chinese.

2. I took the initiative in disavowing those columns and in pointing out the contextual danger of such language. In doing so, I proffered my own opinion, which is expert, on the question whether Sobran was in fact anti-Semitic.

3. I advised Joe that if he continued to write such columns, we would need to dissociate ourselves not only from the columns, but from him, on the grounds that he was invincibly ignorant of an ethical–cultural point which I deem critically important in modern discourse.

4. It would appear to me, based on your reaction to my publishing his essay, that you are under the impression that I should have shorn him of his privileges as a senior editor of *National Review*. There is no compelling reason for you to be acquainted with the protocols of this magazine, but for thirty years I have given to any senior editor the privilege of disagreeing with the policy of the magazine through the device of the so-called "Open Question."

5. So convinced is Sobran that the charges of anti-Semitism leveled against him are intellectually and objectively unfair that he asked for space in which to give the reasons why. I did not rescind *National Review*'s policies when I agreed to give him that space, which by organic arrangements he was entitled to. But I did, as an amateur diplomatist, urge him to recast his essay, when I saw the first draft of it, which, had I published it in the form presented, would in turn have required me to reiterate my livid objections to his six columns. He understood my point, substantially reconstructed his essay, and

came up with 1,500 words to only a few sentences of which I have any objection whatever. . . . Moreover, you are strangely insensitive to the point that his essay is much more damaging to me than it is to you, for reasons I shan't patronize you by elucidating. [By this I meant that Joe's scorn for the reasoning by which I and my colleagues were guided was very painful to read from a colleague, published in my magazine.]

6. Your letter to Jeff arrives at the strangest moment, when you profess yourself embarrassed by insufficient docility to Marty Peretz, whose criticisms of *National Review* you [evidently] now feel you must pay more solemn attention to. This notwithstanding an editorial paragraph by Peretz published in the contemporary issue [of *The New Republic*] which is as indefensible as anything ever done by Sobran. [Peretz, reacting to my defense of Cardinal O'Connor when he visited Israel, had written," . . . his abundant ignorance of the Middle East cannot suffice as explanation. The old Catholic Right has always had trouble with the Jewish problem. This explains why Buckley has made things so cozy for an unabashed bigot like columnist Joseph Sobran."] Jeff Hart's covering letter [to me] touches on several subjects, one of them Peretz's attack. "Marty Peretz's remarks in *TNR* are outrageous. Maybe you should take them on in a column—except that it is so disagreeable to get into the ring with someone who can write in the terms Peretz employed." I note that you say that in the next issue of *Commentary* you will apologize for your treatment of me—who took the initiative in respect of Sobran—rather than for Peretz, whose frenzy causes me only to be grateful that he is not a representative of Catholic orthodoxy; he is your problem, not mine. I despise the low level of his polemics, even as I contemplate with genuine pride the invitation I received today to accept the annual award of the Anti-Defamation League.

Norman—of course—replied.

1. For the record, I deemed Joe Sobran's columns anti-Semitic in themselves, and not merely "contextually." On that issue, it seems we disagree.

2. As to whether Sobran himself—as opposed to what he has written—is anti-Semitic, I leave that judgment to God. Your own "expert" opinion carries enormous authority with me, of course. But shouldn't you be entertaining a doubt or two in light of what you say in point 5? [That his original draft had crossed the bearable line.]

3. Might not point 5 also have a bearing here?

4. I do not presume to advise you, or any other editor, on internal procedures. But the rubric under which Sobran's article was published does not absolve the magazine of responsibility for publishing it. [A serious point, worth pondering. Should an editor who traditionally cedes to a dissenting senior editor the space in which to register the reasons for his dissent suspend the convention rather than publish in it material he deems indefensible?]

5. In addition to the comments I have already made on this point, I have to say that I found Sobran's article (as I wrote . . .) "simultaneously disingenuous and unrepentant." Surely you can't disagree with that characterization.

6. What can you mean by saying that Marty Peretz is my problem? That he and I are both Jewish? Why on earth should I apologize for him? He neither works for me nor speaks for me. Indeed, as it happens, I was so outraged by his editorial that I hung up on him when he too remained unrepentant in response to my call of protest. [A resourceful defense. Cowarriors in pro-Israelism don't in fact have to defend, or denounce, one another's tactics. But normally they exercise the right to do so, even if they are not thereby discharging a formal responsibility.]

So that Joe Sobran: Chapter 1 left the concerned public confused. Since anti-Semitism is essentially a moral question, it pays to labor to dissipate at least such confusion as yields to reason.

1. Norman Podhoretz was clearly correct that Joe Sobran was unrepentant.

2. Commentary's editor thought *National Review*'s editor wrong to publish Sobran's defense of himself, on the grounds that it was, inherently, yet another anti-Semitic exercise.

3. Yet another editor (Peretz of *The New Republic*) goes on record as suggesting that Buckley, as a member of the "old Catholic Right," has a "problem" with Jewish questions, which is why he extends hospitality to an "unabashed bigot" like Sobran.

4. Buckley et al., alarmed by Sobran's columns, had dissociated themselves from the sentiments expressed and language used, but were not prepared to sever their links with Sobran.

5. Podhoretz et al. are terminally displeased with Sobran, but only disappointed with Buckley.

6. Peretz is terminally displeased with Sobran and enough displeased with Buckley to denounce him in language that provokes a fellow editor, who is also Jewish, to hang up the telephone on him, while maintaining

7. that although a Jewish editor has no moral mandate publicly to dissociate himself from editorial outlawry committed by a fellow editor who is himself Jewish and is addressing the same questions, a Christian editor who exercises direct editorial control over his own journal should not permit the appearance in it under any dispensation of material deemed indefensible.

Today's Anti-Semitism

In searching out the meaning of contemporary anti-Semitism, it is useful to ask whether in order to qualify as a contemporary anti-Semite one needs to be anti-Israel. The anti-Semitism of days gone by obviously manifested itself in other ways, ranging (with Hitler's awful exception) from exclusion from certain country clubs to immigration barriers. I suppose there are people around who go berserk at the presence of a Jew, as the Vienna poll above suggests, but they cannot be numerous (I have never met one).

In any event, no one is saying that kind of thing about Sobran. "People who call me anti-Semitic haven't the least idea what I'm about," he wrote me. It isn't only that the mere suggestion of such an ethnic allergy *surprises* him. "The fact is that I get bored in most places where there aren't a certain number of Jews, because there are so many really original thinkers among them [group characteristics?]. I need them. Even when I disagree with them I need their challenge."

But Sobran quickly qualifies this, turning it right around. What he calls philo-Semitism, he says, makes inordinate demands on intelligent people with live analytical minds. The people he criticizes, he says, "[feel] victimized even when they have considerable power and aren't using it very creditably." Once again he alights on what Mr. Seymour would have called a group characteristic:

> It's hard to generalize about them, and yet they do have a discernible if not exactly definable character. . . . Philo-Semitism can overgeneralize as preposterously as anti-Semitism. The fact that the one has replaced the other only means that the Jews' corporate fortunes have improved, not that people really appreciate them as they deserve to be appreciated. Real appreciation includes a certain amount of criticism, but even that has to rest on the assumption that they have the same rights as other people . . . But in our time, any criticism that doesn't sound like an after-dinner toast shocks the easy philo-Semitism of people who just don't want any trouble.

Joe then turns (these quotes are from the long personal letter addressed to me) to his reading of history.

> The ancient pagan charge against the Jews was that they were "misanthropes." At any rate, however the Jews now may differ from the Jews then, they've always been aloof debunkers of what they took to be the idolatries of people around them, including Christianity. This naturally irritates the natives—or maybe I should say the nativists. At times it irritates me. But you have to learn to respect that.

Joe was writing during a period when he was so fiercely at odds with Desert Storm that he was attracted to anyone, Left or Right, who opposed the military intervention in Iraq.

> I had to learn that [Noam] Chomsky is as much a native of this country as I am, and that it was silly to call him "anti-American." His integrity and courage show in his willingness to live with that sort of dismissal. He's also been as unsparing of Israel as he has been of the U.S., when he could have made his life a lot easier among the intellectuals by being discreetly selective

in his criticism. To my mind he represents something deeper and more honorable in the Jewish character than the Jewish chauvinists do. He's a true Israelite, in whom there is no guile.

Joe Sobran is convinced that it is only the *policies* of the State of Israel that attract his critical attention, and plague him. Whether it is policies that are distinctively, even uniquely, Israeli that upset him, or whether an anti-Israeli—anti-Semitic?—tropism manipulates his thought, it is an object of this essay to explore.

His criticisms of Israeli policy are adamant, and incessant.

When I talk to a Palestinian for an hour or two, I'm struck at how absolutely *bizarre* it is that an editor of *The New Republic* or *Commentary* can, any time he wishes, buy a plane ticket and, upon landing at Tel Aviv, assume a whole range of "rights" that are denied to the native Arab. . . . Zionism is actually the assertion of some very unusual prerogatives. [Sobran doesn't distinguish here, though he should, between Arabs in the conquered territories, who enjoy virtually no rights, and Arabs within Israel, who have equal rights except that those who do not serve in the military (Jews are required to do so) forfeit some rights, e.g., to government jobs.]

"Anti-Semitism" only seems to show up nowadays in the context of discussion of Israel. Jews aren't beaten in the streets, snubbed, denied entry to Harvard, etc. By every other index, anti-Semitism is defunct. Yet the Zionist Apparat wants to convince us it's raging, "just beneath the surface." It talks about "polite" and "sophisticated" and "thinly veiled" anti-Semitism. For some reason the stuff never gets overt. It always has to be exposed by interpretation. These ostensible qualifiers don't really qualify, either: when you're accused of "polite" anti-Semitism, your accuser is not saying: "Well, he may be an anti-Semite, but at least he's polite." He's saying: "This guy's politeness is phony. Strip away the fake good manners, and he's just another Hitler."

The jury reasonably asks: Is the critic of Israel so possessed to indict as to disfigure what actually goes on in Israel? Is he vulnerable to the charge that selective indignation betrays him? Isn't it fair to point out a historical indifference to the policies of other countries with analogous domestic policies? (Joe Sobran never spent a lot of time blasting apartheid.)

The column most frequently cited by critics of Sobran as dispositive on the matter of whether he is an anti-Semite is the one in which he "praised" the magazine *Instauration,* a wild racist-nativist publication whose deranged editor has a certain aptitude for wit and trenchancy, skills not denied to exhibitionists, as students of Gore Vidal will acknowledge. What Sobran wrote in this column (May 8, 1986) was, "I know of only one magazine in America that faces the harder facts about race: a little magazine called *Instauration.* Its articles are unsigned, and the name of its editor, Wilmot Robertson, is apparently fictitious. . . . *Instauration* is an often brilliant magazine, covering a beat nobody else will touch, and doing so with intelligence, wide-ranging observation, and bitter wit." Now note this carefully: "It is openly and almost unremittingly hostile to blacks, Jews, and Mexican and Oriental immigrants. It is also hostile to Nazism, which makes things confusing. Furthermore, it is hostile to Christianity."

It is characteristic of the critic on the chase that, yelping with glee over the discovery of Sobran on *Instauration,* he is indifferent to the qualifications Sobran entered. That *Instauration* is "hostile to blacks, . . . Mexican and Oriental immigrants . . . [and] Christianity" becomes simply unnoticeable. But even allowing for the qualification, there was no excusing what Sobran said. (The patron wisecrack highlighting the technique of the irrelevant excuse was that of Fr. George Tyrrell, who said of his fellow Jesuits at the turn of the century, "Accuse them of murdering three men and a dog, and they will triumphantly produce the dog alive.") It becomes so-what time that the magazine also hates everybody else. *Instauration* demands of a morally sensible reader simply: denunciation. "It assumes," Joe continued, "a world of Hobbesian conflict at the racial level: every race against every race. Knowing racial harmony is hard, *Instauration* takes a fatal step further and gives up on it." One sees here intellectual curiosity disinterestedly at work, a psychoanalyst probing inquisitively the character of Jack the Ripper. But now Joe Sobran, Explorer, tells us that usually there are grounds for interracial tension. "The liberal bromide tells us that prejudice is the product of ignorance, [but] the truth is that racial antagonism usually comes from personal experience. And yet that same experience produces personal affections for individuals of other races, affections that rule out, for most of us, total racial hostility." This finding is very possibly true, and in any event not uniquely invidious in respect of any particular race or creed.

Sobran, in the end, was respectful enough of public opinion to recognize his mistake. He was writing, after all, as a syndicated columnist, not as a psychologist for the *Parapsychology Review,* in which role he would be as unconcerned for taboos as a computer. "My column," he wrote a few weeks later, "should have denounced *Instauration* more vigorously, and anyone else is certainly welcome to do so. I have since learned, for instance, that it favors abortion as a way of controlling the black population. There you have two ugly positions rolled into one, and I should have had the sense to deduce this from the magazine's general premises. Its racism is serious. What I called its 'bitter wit' is more often cruel sarcasm, compulsively cruel even when it can't be funny."

In conclusion: Sobran made a serious mistake in applauding *Instauration,* whatever the stated qualifications. It is, however, a matter of record, first, that he entered these qualifications, and, second, that he withdrew his praise and publicly regretted having given it. He was nowhere (that I have seen) credited for this act of contrition, any more than for the earlier qualifications.

One Idea at a Time?

The lesson here is important. An editorialist isn't expected to weigh all the pros and cons of an argument or an article or indeed a book that contains outrageous thought or language, *nor is he permitted to do so.* I suppose an analogue would be the columnist who wrote one sentence praising any aspect of Hitler's character. Whatever else he went on to write, he would run the risk, in hostile circles, of being the man who praised Hitler, even as Joe Sobran became the man who praised *Instauration* (as I remain, in some quarters, the man who praised Joe McCarthy). A very strong case can be made, has been made, for evaluating the oeuvre of Ezra Pound without the compunction to critical immobilization upon encountering the anti-Semitic line. Ironically, Pound himself wrote that everyone's ideas should be judged one at a time. A columnist can't reasonably expect such treatment. Politicians, many of whom outlast critical writers, sometimes outpace the black little cloud over their heads. Many Southern segregationists got by, most conspicuously George Wallace, as the passage of time washed away their earlier positions. Churchill had a line or two praising the early Hitler, and Truman said, "I like old Joe Stalin." But they went on to spend most of their public lives fighting totalitarianism, even as columnist James Jackson Kilpatrick, who early on defied the civil-rights laws and their implications, has spent 25 years arguing the contrary position. Joe Sobran hasn't the equivalent opportunity. Having concluded (correctly, I like to think) that anti-Semitism in America is not threatening to American Jews in its shabby old uniform, he is not likely to have the opportunity to do spectacular service for the cause of Judaeo-Christian comity, by emerging as a fighter against a prejudice that no longer threatens. He isn't likely to have any dramatic opportunity to compensate for his isolatable enthusiasm (a single column) for a thoroughly racist screed. I expect it would be quoted against him if he perished on the Golan Heights, planting there the flag of Israel, in the manner of the great tableau on Iwo Jima.

The question naturally then arises whether the gestating anti-Semite has gradually become fixated on the subject of Israel, whose every act at the bargaining table, in the West Bank, in Lebanon, advances the fetal little monster toward untethered life. Sobran has a very difficult time of it. It is a common casualty of the world of polemics that critics don't always have the time, or take it if they do, for patient, detailed inquiry. Such inattentions to detail breed licentiousness. Sobran has written that "Israel is a deeply anti-Christian country; it has even eliminated the plus sign from math textbooks because the plus sign (yes, this: +) looks like a cross! Yet Israel depends on American Christians for tax money and tourism, so it has to mute this theme for foreign consumption." It is true that some hyper-Orthodox Jewish sects oppose the use of the plus sign. But the taboo is not generally exercised in Israel. Besides which, there is the undistributed middle in the syllogistic sequence. American taxpayers who give money to Israel give money for a *Jewish homeland* where it ought not to be expected that Orthodox Jews should respect the cross. For them the identifying profanation is, inevitably, the cross. American Christians who visit Israel do so for the most part as pilgrims going to the Holy Land. Jewish custodians of the Holy Land sites have never interfered with Christians who go to venerate. The distinctions are lost in Sobran's analysis. Israel's "prime minister, Yitzhak Shamir, is the former head of the Stern Gang, an assassin himself; it's rather as if Jimmy Hoffa had been elected President of the United States." The analogy is a Trojan horse, demolishing Joe's point. Hoffa led a movement designed to give him autocratic control of a labor union. Shamir participated in a paramilitary movement, often bloody, designed to realize a great ethnic–religious–historical dream. That they both used guns no more fuses them morally than the Green Berets and John Dillinger become one because both used guns.

In another column, Sobran wrote that Pulitzer Prize–winning Thomas Friedman of the *New York Times* had been suppressed by the editors when he "wrote a path-breaking story describing the massive Israeli bombing of Beirut as 'indiscriminate.'" I found this difficult to believe when I read the column, and called Friedman, who told me hastily (he could not stay long on the telephone, because Rosh Hashanah was closing in) that the allegation was in all important respects incorrect, as recorded in an article he had written for the *Columbia Journalism Review.* He would be glad, he said, to give the whole story to anyone I designated. I wrote to Joe advising him of Friedman's correction and relaying Friedman's invitation. It was a long time before Joe referred to this letter. "When you impugn my 'factual accuracy,' you hit a sore spot. I got my version of Friedman from a couple of conversations, and lazily didn't track the facts down to make sure. I take your word for it; and I'd have called on Friedman if I just hadn't been so damned overwhelmed at the time. Mea culpa." Let's face it, a juror could reasonably conclude that Joe is not industriously curious to uncover refutations of his burgeoning case against Israel.

A week or so earlier, Sobran had cited a book, *By Way of Deception: A Devastating Insider's Portrait of the Mossad,* by Victor Ostrovsky (the book, it transpired within a matter of months, is of dubious reliability), that alleged that Israeli intelligence had discovered *before* the fateful act that Syrian terrorists were planning to stage the attack that killed 241 U.S. Marines in Lebanon in 1983. Shamir, he wrote a few months later, is an "unreconstructed thug." There are more illuminating ways to communicate what one wants to communicate about Shamir, however negative. "The Israeli state does not recognize intermarriage between Jews and non-Jews as valid, which means that Israel's Jews as well as its Arabs are denied some of the rights we take for granted here." That isn't exactly correct. Israel, as a Jewish state, will not issue a license to a Jew to marry a non-Jew. But an intermarriage transacted abroad (e.g., in Cyprus or Rhodes) yields equal rights to the couple on their return to Israel. "Though Israel doesn't have a formal constitution, it does have what it calls its Basic Law, under which Jews are more equal than others. Israel's High Court has ruled that the Basic Law actually precludes equal rights for non-Jews. 'It is necessary,' the court says, 'to prevent a Jew or Arab who calls for equality of rights for Arabs from sitting in the Knesset or being elected to it.' And even if a Jewish majority passed a law extending full rights to non-Jews, such a law would be invalid." It is difficult to comment on this because although laws passed by the Knesset are binding, it is true that laws defying the Torah are unlikely to get passed. What results, in a Jewish state with secular interests, is a congeries of paradoxes, like that of the mixed marriage contracted abroad. Another is the right of return of the Jew—and his non-Jewish relatives. An estimated 30 per cent of the Russian immigrants are related to Jews, but not themselves Jewish. They will enjoy identical rights.

In another column, Sobran writes, "John Kifner of the *New York Times* sums up his [Kahane's] position shrewdly: 'Jewish philosophy, Rabbi Kahane contended, was never based on Western democratic principles, but on Jewish ritual law, which he said forbade close contact with non-Jews.'" Kahane was a fanatic, Sobran explained. "At the same time, he had enough empathy (he called it 'respect,' though that was stretching a point) for the Palestinians to understand that they would never be content to be semi-citizens of a Jewish state. In that sense [Kahane] was neither a fool nor a hater—just a keen-witted fanatic. His blunt conclusion formed the title of one of his books: *They Must Go*. He even hinted that violence against liberal Jews would be a 'mitzvah,' or good deed; they called him a Nazi, but in his own eyes he was being truer to authentic Judaism than they were."

It is simply unrealistic to conclude that Joe is here suggesting anything other than that Kahane may have the truer insight into authentic Jewish theology—which position might be defended by here and there a Jewish theologian, but as applied to contemporary Judaic practice is self-evidently irrelevant, even as the suggestion that the late Father Leonard Feeney of Boston (who preached the necessary damnation of unbelievers) was in fact the most authentic spokesman of the true Catholic faith is self-evidently false. Kahane's position was seen by the overwhelming majority of Jews as a narrow and extreme projection of Jewish law, and there is no serious movement to press his demand that the Israeli Arabs be expelled.

The Great Bifurcation

If we were searching out theological genes that sired current tensions within Judaeo-Christianity, it is obvious that the great bifurcation came with the advent of Jesus, who is called a prophet by Jews but also, in the nature of the situation as viewed by Jewish orthodoxy, an impostor; while the Christian venerates Jesus as the Incarnation. The Roman church, which is senior in respect of religious taxonomy in the Western world, does not regard Judaism merely as schismatic, like the Eastern Orthodox Church, nor even, like the Protestant denominations, as heretical. The Jews—never having been Christians—are removed one step further: on the negative side, they are "invincibly ignorant," refusing to acknowledge the truths of the Christian Gospel. On the positive side, they are the people of the First Covenant, presaging the Second. And if Jesus built his Church upon a Rock, that Rock sat solidly on the ground of Judaism. Joe Sobran is suggesting that there is something to be said for Rabbi Kahane's reading of the necessary derivative relationship between Christian and Jew. If he is right, then of course Kahane's anti-Christianity postulates a complementary anti-Judaism.

In April 1986 Joe's column read, "Although the great Jewish theologian Moses Maimonides insisted that it was as wrong to kill a gentile as a Jew, it seems strange that this should ever have been a matter of controversy, and Maimonides was in some quarters regarded as a heretic. The Yiddish word for gentile, 'goy,' is contemptuous; 'goyishkopf'—literally, 'gentile-headed'—means 'stupid.'" This is breakaway definitional polemicism, inasmuch as "goy" means, simply, "Gentile" and, to the extent that, historically, it has been used to denote those-who-are-not-of-the-true-faith, is no more invidious than any other interreligious sequestration. It is as fair to say that "goy" is inherently invidious as it is to say that "Jew" is invidious.*

Joe dwelled often on the American, Jonathan Pollard, who spied for Israel. He acknowledged that the government of Israel insisted that the

---

*A Jewish scholar advises me that "goy" can be and often is used disparagingly, as in, "a real goy." He points out that probably the incidence of "goy" being used disparagingly by Jews is about equal to the incidence of "Jew" being used disparagingly by Gentiles.

spying in America had been done outside its knowledge; Joe dismissed this denial as perfunctory and implausible, and belabored the Israeli government, denouncing it as a fickle friend of the United States.

Friendly nations do not spy on one another is the—problematical—premise here. I myself hope the United States has spies in every country whose policies are of vital concern to us, whatever the temperature of our fraternal diplomatic relations with one another. I hope we have a spy or two operating in Israel, given our intimate concern to know everything that can be known about Israel's strategy. It would be something entirely different if Israel had turned U.S. secrets over to the Soviet Union. Joe did not make that charge. Seymour Hersh subsequently did, relying in his book *The Samson Option* on testimony given by someone widely thought to be a confidence man.

Does Anyone Agree?

When I announced, with the backing of my colleagues, *National Review*'s dissociation from Joe Sobran's columns, the reactions were varied enough themselves to motivate an inquiry into the current understanding of anti-Semitism. Listen, at one end, to Richard Cohen. He wrote in his column for the *Washington Post*:

> Buckley, in an extraordinary move, has dissociated himself in the *National Review* from Sobran's writings but not—note—from Sobran himself. He remains one of the *Review*'s three senior editors.
>
> What Buckley does is important. As the founding editor of the nation's most influential conservative journal and as both the friend and ideological mentor of President Reagan, Buckley is a figure conservatives look to for cues. Anti-Semitism is infecting attitudes toward the Middle East, and Buckley is in a position to say what is and what is not permitted ... from his friend and colleague. His is a painful task. But one can fairly ask how the Joe Sobran–Bill Buckley relationship is, in essence, different from the one Jesse Jackson had with the Rev. Louis Farrakhan. Jackson initially went the Buckley route and dissociated himself from Farrakhan's statements. Finally, when others pointed out that those statements reflected the man, he severed the relationship entirely. [Comment: Jesse Jackson was running for President. The criteria that govern personal conduct are dominated by that consideration. Dwight Eisenhower deserted George Marshall in order to enhance his prospects of winning the White House. Editors are under stresses of a more reflective nature.]
>
> ... Buckley himself rejects particular Sobran writings, but embraces the whole man. But anti-Semitism can be deduced from the way a person conducts himself. In Sobran's case, the conduct in question is his writings, and those put his anti-Semitism beyond doubt. ...

As Buckley notes, American conservatism has come a long way since it was polluted by anti-Semitism—and some of the credit is his. But the continued presence of Sobran on the masthead of America's most influential conservative magazine is a step backward. Sobran is no martyr to the hair-trigger sensitivities of Jews but a victim of his own poison pen. Reconsider, Bill Buckley, before Sobran's ink stains your own cause.

Occupying the middle ground was, for example, Professor Paul Gottfried (himself Jewish), who wrote to *The New Republic* "... some neoconservatives reacted hysterically—even opportunistically—to Joe Sobran's observations about American Jews. But I do not believe that Sobran is blameless in this particular matter. His remarks on the Jewish persecution of Christians [not here reproduced] reflect a woeful ignorance of history, and his praise of the neo-Nazi *Instauration* was inexcusably offensive."

At the what's-going-on-here? end was, for instance, Manuel Tellechea of the *New York City Tribune,* who predicted that Sobran would resign from *National Review* rather than accept the rebuke of his colleagues. More, "If Buckley truly believes Joseph Sobran not to be an anti-Semite, he should dismiss as either malicious or misinformed *anyone* who would so slander him, Jew or gentile. It is a debt he owes to friendship and to justice." Mr. Tellechea has an explanation for my misbehavior. "Buckley is a national icon. In fact, not a few liberals have had a sort of crush on him for years. 'He is a fascist, of course, but what a wonderful writer.'"

Therein the explanation! "Buckley is [would be?] a man of iron not to have succumbed to such entreaties. But because he is so accustomed to adoration and so above the fray, he does not understand that the criticism he weathers so easily, when directed at one such as Sobran, who is not a national icon and not particularly lovable, can wreck a man's career and leave his reputation in tatters. He shouldn't recommend to Sobran that he ignore his enemies, nor should Buckley ignore them. And, of course, he shouldn't give Sobran's adversaries even an inch of rope with which to hang him. Buckley, after all, believes in Sobran's innocence, doesn't he?"

The instinctive feel of the majority of the eighty-odd readers of *National Review* who wrote in was to wonder whether I had knuckled under to trendy pressures. I replied (perforce) by form letter, immediately acknowledging that this was the device I was necessarily driven to. My letter included the following sentences:

> I have read your letters, many of them surpassingly sensitive and intelligent, with great care. The general positions I adopted ... reflect our considered judgment of the issues involved. Beyond reiterating this—we are bound, in the last analysis, to act with right reason, according to the dictates of conscience—there isn't anything I can usefully add. ...

I do hope that those of you most vexed will consider the possibility that you misread the editorial I wrote, and will do me the favor of rereading it.

A month or so later a letter from a rabbi. Daniel E. Lapin wrote from the Pacific Jewish Center in Venice, California:

> Mr. Buckley, I am not sure that I fully understand the fuss about Sobran. The writing of Richard Cohen et al. strikes me as disingenuous. Sobran's "Pensées" in *NR*, December 31, 1985, on the other hand, laid the foundations of a dozen sermons in my synagogue. As you may remember from our brief meeting when you spoke for Brandeis Bardin Institute in Los Angeles, my rabbinic credentials are adequate. . . . If there is any way I can be useful to you, Mr. Sobran, or *National Review*, I would be honored. Insofar as there is something called anti-Semitism (as opposed to anti-Godism), I just don't believe Mr. Sobran is one.

The range of opinion on *National Review* and Joe Sobran ran, thus, the gamut.

Partial Resolution

Four years later, in September 1990, after reading two pieces by him which I judged indefensible, I resolved wearily and sadly to dismiss Joe from the board of senior editors of *National Review*. I wrote out a personal letter:

> I read your column (9/20/90) last night, and this morning reread the piece you submitted to *National Review* ("Why *National Review* Is Wrong").
>
> I can only conclude that you can't stay on as a senior editor of *National Review*. You have made it plain that you are embarrassed by the positions we are taking [about the Iraq war and the need to move against Saddam Hussein by military force, positions motivated, Joe had said, primarily by the desire to help Israel]. I don't want to have to make plain how greatly embarrassed I am by the positions you are taking, but I am. Why don't you send in a letter of resignation as senior editor. Stay on as a contributor, if you wish. You know what I think of your talent, and I have to hope you have some idea of the sadness I feel about the turn of events.
>
> As ever affectionately . . .

I didn't send the letter. It was suddenly the season in which Pat Buchanan and Abe Rosenthal were locking horns on the subject of anti-Semitism and became the center of journalistic attention. I was persuaded by my colleagues that it would be a mistake to proceed against Joe on the eve of my resignation as editor-in-chief, distracting attention from *NR*'s thirty-fifth anniversary and its special edition, the subject of a thousand hours of labor.

Three months later—by which time Joe had become, for all intents and purposes, a member of the American pacifist movement—Joe agreed, most agreeably, to step down as senior editor, to occupy instead the position of critic-at-large, in which position he has no responsibility for editorial policy. And as such he writes for us, week after week, anthologizable copy about everything in the world west, south, north, and east of Tel Aviv.

The basic question—when does it become necessary formally to dissociate a journal from an editor's views that are not congruent—had been dealt with empirically. But not, to my satisfaction, the moral—sociological question that animates this inquiry:

What is anti-Semitism these days?

And, yes, what is anti-anti-Semitism?

2 · Pat Buchanan

Here is what Pat Buchanan actually said and did, or at least what he said and did that were the proximate causes of the explosion. On television (the McLaughlin program), he said: *"There are only two groups that are beating the drums for war in the Middle East—the Israeli Defense Ministry and its amen corner in the United States."*

Later in the program he was more explicit, his purpose obviously being to emphasize the singular interest the Israelis and their friends had in stopping Saddam Hussein. *"The Israelis want this war desperately because they want the United States to destroy the Iraqi war machine. They want us to finish them off. They don't care about our relations with the Arab world."*

At this point nothing had been said that was anti-Semitic, let alone arrantly so. Any threatened nation is concerned for its own interests, over against which others' interests are understandably subordinate. What had been done, however, was to pronounce a massive inaccuracy, namely that "only" two specified groups favored military action against Hussein.

Any government will "beat the drums" to arouse opposition to its enemy, and therefore the Israeli government, in doing so, was engaged in conventional national activity. So unless Mr. Buchanan was prepared to define the "amen corner" of Israel as comprising approximately 75 per cent of the American people—that was the number the polls then told us were supporting Administration policies—he was deluding himself, or his listeners, or both. On the other hand, if he had quoted the extent of the public's support, he would have been suggesting that the Israelis manipulate 75 per cent of American public support even for causes that are strategically anti-American ("They don't care about our relations with the Arab world"). Inevitably, when an intelligent person makes an assertion that is manifestly absurd, he arouses suspicions.

Why Did He Do It?

Why he did it, some people concluded, was that he wished to draw attention to the exorbitant influence of the pro-Israel Jewish American community on foreign policy. If in fact there is huge sentiment out there to resist Saddam Hussein by the use of U.S. military force, then surely—it is his tacit premise—that sentiment was generated not by rational thought about containing aggressors in areas critical to Western commerce, but by the lobbying power of Israel. The listener will then find himself wondering whether it is right that so few should govern the emotions of so many. Curiosity of that kind can lead to resentment; and resentment can lead to hostility, informed or uninformed, to those who exercise such inordinate influence on U.S. public policy.

But Pat was on a roll. Again on television, he came in with the wisecrack that Congress was "Israeli-occupied" territory. Urbane newswatchers can't have objected to this hyperbole as uniquely invidious, given that such excesses are so often the idiom of polemics. A generation ago the Majority Leader of the Senate, William Knowland, was dubbed somewhere by someone as "the Senator from Formosa." This was thought to be amusing (actually, it was), reflecting as it did the bellicose identification with a free Formosa (Taiwan) by Senator Knowland, a principal figure in a large public movement whose principal PAC was "The Committee of One Million against the Admission of Communist China to the United Nations." No historian would credit Israel with having less influence in Congress today than Formosa had in 1953.

Still, it was all beginning to add up. Even as those who taunted Senator Knowland during the Fifties did so intending to generate sentiment against the government of Chiang Kai-shek, so any reference to Congress as "Israeli-occupied" territory can be taken as encouraging resentment against the Israeli lobby and its backers. Breeding hostility, etc.

Buchanan did not at that point wade back into shallower water; on the contrary. Coincidentally with his reference to the amen corner, he pronounced the names of four important men who influence public policy, whom he identified with the hyperbellicose wing of the anti-Saddam forces. They were: A. M. Rosenthal, the columnist and former executive editor of the *New York Times;* Richard Perle, former assistant secretary of defense and a leader of the hawkish legions during the cold war; columnist Charles Krauthammer, an influential moral–political strategist, with Wilsonian internationalist inclinations; and Henry Kissinger. They have in common many things. But in the context of the polemical offensive by Buchanan, the most conspicuous of these is that they are all Jewish. This common denominator assaults the analytical mind in a way it wouldn't if the four strategists had been *uniquely* identifiable as advocates of a tough line against Saddam Hussein. But A. M. Rosenthal, columnist, was no more belligerent on the Hussein issue than James Jackson Kilpatrick, also a columnist; Richard Perle no more than Frank Gaffney, his former colleague; Charles Krauthammer no more than George Will; and Henry Kissinger no more than one of his successors as secretary of state, Alexander Haig. Four Christians.

The evidence that the Jewish factor was engrossing Buchanan mounted. And then whatever coincidence might in desperation have been pleaded for this aggregation of all-Jewish anti-Hussein activists, its usefulness expired when Pat Buchanan went on to write that if we went to war, the fighting would be done by "kids with names like McAllister, Murphy, Gonzales, and Leroy Brown." There is no way to read that sentence without concluding that Pat Buchanan was suggesting that American Jews manage to avoid personal military exposure even while advancing military policies they (uniquely?) engender.

I see no other explanation for it. Perhaps it was done impulsively. The iconoclastic daemon having a night out on the town? In that case it is a pity that, after Abe Rosenthal exploded and the quarrel between them became a national engagement, Buchanan told a reporter from *Time* magazine, "I don't retract a single word."

Rosenthal Strikes Back

What happened three weeks later—and the three-week interval became something of a side-issue, having to do with the organization of the Jewish lobby—was the column by A. M. Rosenthal. It was extreme in its conclusions, and the moment is appropriate in this essay to look at what I wrote about the controversy on September 17, 1990, three days after the Rosenthal column appeared. I will repeat here that much of the column as is relevant to this narrative:

> The hot talk . . . is of Abe Rosenthal's column in the *New York Times* (September 14) in which he, well, reads Pat Buchanan out of civilized society. What he says, flatly, is that Buchanan's statements about the U.S. intervention in Saudi Arabia, combined with other positions he has taken dating back to

his defense of President Reagan's visit to Bitburg, are the work of an anti-Semitic mind. He goes so far as to suggest that the kind of thing Mr. Buchanan says can lead to Auschwitz, and that he, Rosenthal, isn't going to let him get away with it, because he is guided by a famous moral injunction, delivered by Jesus on the Cross, on which Mr. Rosenthal improvises exactly to reverse its meaning, which becomes now, "Forgive them not, Father, for they know what they did."

. . . I write as a friend of both, though I have experienced A. M. Rosenthal, as it happens, ten times as frequently as Pat Buchanan, notwithstanding that Mr. Buchanan and I have occupied the same ideological foxhole since he became old enough to bear arms. I need to say this about the two gentlemen. About Mr. Rosenthal, that he has always walked about in rooms in which customized trip-wires wait confidently to ignite his footloose emotional gyrations: and when he comes upon them, the resulting explosion knows no conventional limits. I deem his attack on Pat Buchanan to be an example of: Rosenthal, gone ballistic.

And I deem Pat Buchanan to be insensitive to those fine lines that tend publicly to define racially or ethnically offensive analysis or rhetoric. This is best described by illustration. If Scholar A, spending a lifetime in psychometric anthropology, concludes that black Americans weigh in 15 points behind white Americans in conventional IQ tests, he runs a certain risk in publicizing his findings, though only the Know Nothings will denounce him as a racist for [doing so]. If, however, having done so he accepts an invitation to speak at a rally advocating an end to forced busing on the grounds that he is impelled by his findings to oppose the dilution of educational quality, sensitive moral calibrators are likely to suspect, even if they cannot successfully reason to that conclusion, that Scholar A is actively engaged in advocating invidious racial policies.

Every one of Pat Buchanan's positions touching on Israel, weighed discretely, [is defensible]—until his most recent one. It is unquestionably the case that Israel's political influence is out of proportion to Israel's strategic importance to the United States. It is certainly arguable that Mr. Reagan's decision to visit Bitburg was in the circumstances prudent. And it is conceivable that the defendant Demjanjuk, recently tried in Israel as a war criminal, is actually the wrong man. But these antecedent positions, joined now with Buchanan's statement, "There are only two groups that are beating the drums for war in the Middle East—the Israeli Defense Ministry and its amen corner in the United States," invite a cumulative judgment. One is that Buchanan reveals himself as an arrant anti-Semite—Rosenthal's verdict; the second (the overwhelming favorite), that Pat Buchanan is attracted to mischievous generalizations.

It is simply a fact that independent analysts, who are neither Jewish nor Israel-bonded, enthusiastically endorse Mr. Bush's policies. The same day that Rosenthal wrote, Buchanan also wrote—a column in which he recorded that "Among those cheering loudest the 'new international order' is the conservative *National Review,* our old friends and new critics, who dismiss us now as 'Bug Out, America' types, for resisting their call for air strikes and pre-emptive war against Iraq."

I concluded my column with a paragraph that can only be characterized, and perhaps excused, as a Moral Peroration. My uneasiness with the points it leaves unexplored prompted this further investigation. I concluded:

> The Buchanans need to understand the nature of sensibilities in an age that coexisted with Auschwitz. And the Rosenthals need to understand that clumsy forensic manners are less than a genocidal offense, and that when Christ pleaded for forgiveness for his executioners, He asked it on behalf of those who were blinded into doing the wrong thing. No one asked for that kind of forgiveness for the Nazis, and Pat Buchanan's trespasses are miles this side of the awful genocidal line in the sand.

What seemed like everybody then got into the act.

The Anti-Buchanan Case

Critics of Buchanan seemed eager to document that in laying special emphasis on the political motives of Mr. Bush's anti-Saddam policies, Buchanan was merely reiterating an ancient complaint against the power of the Israeli lobby. In recent years and months Buchanan seemed to have been attracted one after another to positions in which Jews had a special interest, almost always taking the contrary position. A summary of these was done by Joshua Muravchik, a scholar with the American Enterprise Institute. It was published in *Commentary* in January 1991, in an article entitled, "Patrick J. Buchanan and the Jews." His article was attacked vigorously and at substantial length in the letters column in an ensuing issue of *Commentary*, but Muravchik's subsequent defenses were mostly persuasive.

It is a lengthy article (about nine thousand words), 1) describing every position taken by Buchanan over the recent past that has attracted the attention of the anti-anti-Semites, and 2) analyzing the reasons Buchanan has given, when he has given any, for taking such positions. Muravchik closed his long essay by making a point that can't be ignored in an inquiry seeking to explore personal motivations. He cites Buchanan's complaint that " 'decent and honorable men, Left as well as Right, [have] had careers damaged and reputations smeared' by the accusation of anti-Semitism. Buchanan," Muravchik comments, "has not replied to my letters asking whom on the Left he had in mind, but in recent times public charges of anti-Semitism have been made in a sustained way against only two figures on the Left, Jesse Jackson and Gore Vidal. What can move Buchanan to such tenderness toward the likes of these two who, the Jewish question aside, represent everything he despises?"

Now Mr. Muravchik's point is in one way perplexing. If he is saying that Buchanan is dismayed by unfair attacks even on figures on the Left whom he dislikes or disapproves of, then he is paying Mr. Buchanan a compliment for deploring undeserved inferences even when at the expense of leftist victims, but clearly Muravchik was not intending to do so. If he is suggesting that the Right, rather than the Left, is more greatly disposed nowadays to anti-Semitic thought, I think he is wrong. Most probably, he is merely challenging Buchanan's bona fides.

In analyzing Buchanan's defenses, he brought up the singling out of four prominent Jewish geostrategists as distinctive in their support of George Bush's anti–Saddam Hussein program:

> Buchanan tried to argue that his litany of those seeking war in the Gulf consisted of Jewish names merely because his debate was with the "neoconservatives," many of whom are Jewish. But why is Buchanan spoiling for a fight with the neoconservatives? The alliance between them and traditional conservatives like him has been based largely on foreign policy, which he himself says is the most important of all issues. And although the collapse of Soviet power heralds a new era in foreign policy, Buchanan remains at one with many neoconservatives in believing that Communism—their common foe—is not yet finished. Is Buchanan attacking Jews, then, because they happen to be neoconservatives, or is he attacking neoconservatives because they happen to be Jews?

This is not an easy question for defenders of Pat Buchanan to handle, though he is hardly the only conservative who bitterly attacks neoconservatives without making it exactly clear why. And Muravchik is unanswerable on the particular point, namely that to the extent that one's interest is anti-Communist foreign policy, the neoconservatives have been indispensable allies. But on to the closing paragraph in Muravchik's attack:

> Both the *New York Post* editorialist and Jacob Weisberg in his article in *The New Republic* said that they did not want to get into a "semantic" squabble over "anti-Semitism," and indeed there may be no authoritative definition of the term. [Correct: there is not, there never can be: but attempts at periodic clarification are not a wasted effort.] But when a man falsely maintains that he is the victim of a "pre-planned orchestrated smear campaign" by the Anti-Defamation League [see below: 1) not pre-planned, 2) not self-evidently a smear; on the other hand, 3) very definitely orchestrated]; when he is hostile to Israel; when he embraces the PLO despite being at adamant odds with its political philosophy; when he implies that Jews are trying to drag America into war for the sake of Israel [alone]; when he sprinkles his columns with taunting remarks about things Jewish; when he

stirs the pot of intercommunal hostility; when he rallies to the defense of Nazi war criminals, not only those who protest their innocence but also those who confess their guilt; when he implies that the generally accepted interpretation of the Holocaust might be a serious exaggeration—when a man does all these things, surely it is reasonable to conclude that his actions make a fairly good match for [conventional anti-Semitism].

The Pro-Buchanan Case

The defenders of Pat Buchanan were in one respect unanimous: without any exception that I have seen, everyone who has known and worked with him dismisses the charge that in his personal behavior Buchanan has ever shown any animosity whatever to Jews. On this point, Muravchik commented, "They [defenders of Buchanan] do not understand that anti-Semitism comes in a variety of forms. One variant, what we might call country club prejudice, consists in an aversion to associating with Jews, but may entail no particular political content. On the other side, political anti-Semitism holds 'the Jews' culpable of miscreancy, but may entail no dislike for this or that individual Jew. The latter type is infinitely more dangerous."

Robert Novak, answering the vigorous anti-Buchanan article in *The American Spectator* by David Frum of the *Wall Street Journal*, put it this way: "[Frum's] is a wicked caricature that bears no resemblance to the Pat Buchanan I have known for over twenty years as a news source, a colleague, and a friend. Personally, he is a man of unfailing good manners and discretion who does not faintly resemble Frum's ruffian. Professionally, his self-discipline enabled him to perform with strict restraint in two hitches as a White House aide and with unvarying fairness as a moderator on CNN's *Capital Gang*. . . . Buchanan is no anti-Semite, as anybody who knows him well will avow."

Buchanan's defenders can be seen to be reasoning roughly as follows: a) Anti-Semitism is a disgraceful mindset. b) Pat Buchanan, given his exemplary character, has no disgraceful mindsets. Therefore, c) it has to be wrong to say of him that he is anti-Semitic.

This is to reason *a priori*, and there has seldom in modern controversy been a clearer case of a collision course between the two structures of logical thought. *A posteriori* reasoning would take what was said or written and reason to the mindset of the person who wrote those words, in this case excluding any possibility other than that they were motivated either a) by ignorance or b) by the desire to taunt or to express hostility. *Time* magazine's reviewer tended toward the second alternative—"What set them off," wrote William A. Henry III of Rosenthal et al., "was a typical Buchanan crack, which wrapped a core of fact in a coating of hyperbole." But Henry would go no further on the central question than to say that "for years Buchanan has appeared to go out of his way to rile Jewish sensitivities." David Frum, replying to Robert Novak, did so with some exasperation: "It is simply bizarre to suggest—as Robert Novak seems to—that it is unfair to judge a writer by his writings. Patrick Buchanan has put millions of words into print; if the essence of the man is to be found anywhere it is there, and not in his friends' polite comments about what an affable chap he is."

But if it is indeed anti-Semitism, or iconoclasm, is it obsessive, or merely passing misfancy? Novak had made a vulnerable point when he wrote that Buchanan has after all written millions of words that do not even touch on Jewish questions (the classic antecedent of this form of casuistry is the legendary Irishman being tried for murder who volunteers to bring in thirty people who did *not* see him commit the crime). As might have been expected, defenders of Buchanan made much of the excesses of Abe Rosenthal, Novak going so far as to blame him directly for the general onslaught ("Abe Rosenthal's infamous *New York Times* column triggered the campaign suddenly defaming Buchanan as anti-Semitic").

This charge—that Rosenthal triggered the general reaction—was, up to a point (one or two other critics had here and there gone after Buchanan on similar grounds), chronologically correct, but ultimately irrelevant. You can accuse someone of doing more than he actually did and still take credit for being the first to point out an iniquity. What troubled so many— perhaps most of the critical community who feel that they have an intellectual and moral stake in the questions posed—was the failure to resolve the relevant questions raised. This is clearly seen merely by examining the letters section of *Commentary* cited above (May 1991), after the attack by Muravchik, or of *The American Spectator* (September 1991), after the attack by David Frum. Although most of those who wrote in were violent partisans either of Buchanan or of his critics, what happened in those letters pages was not an example of thesis and antithesis producing resolution. Instead, one walked away from a reading of the collection with a heavy heart over the moral confusion: Just what are we dealing with here?

Was Buchanan a Corporate Target?

It came as something of a shock to the Buchanan camp when the *New York Post* (which prominently runs Buchanan's columns) defended Rosenthal. "When it comes to Jews as a group—not Israel, not U.S.–Israeli relations, not individual Jews—Buchanan betrays an all-too-familiar hostility. [Correction: It was not "all too familiar." That Buchanan had over the years taken positions opposed to those of organized Jewry surprised most people.] A. M. Rosenthal did not produce a 'contract hit.' [It wasn't strictly a "contract hit," but as we shall see, it transpired that he had received a docket of sorts on Buchanan.] He [Rosenthal] faced some painful facts."

The question whether Rosenthal's attack triggered the ensuing general attack is in any event irrelevant (except to the question of how organized are the anti-anti-Semitic forces). Rosenthal's having called attention to a transgression does not make him responsible for a transgression of his own except insofar as he went beyond whistle-blowing to make charges that were themselves indefensible. On the matter of why did Rosenthal blow the whistle, the Washington Times's Ralph Hallow asked the question most directly—Why had no other columnist or commentator gone after Mr. Buchanan as an anti-Semite? "[Rosenthal] responded that he has been receiving many calls from 'people in our business who said they agree with me and that what I did was courageous.' He said these same people told him they had been afraid to attack Mr. Buchanan because he is widely published, appears on television, is written about abroad, and has lots of friends who defend him. [This is not inherently believable. It isn't dangerous, so far as one can see, to attack someone as an anti-Semite if the case against him is at least plausible.] [Rosenthal concluded], 'I didn't attack him because of what he said about Israel or Iraq but because he put it in anti-Semitic language.'"

The question quickly—and logically—arose, and was widely asked: Just how long had this kind of thing been going on in Pat Buchanan's forum? Heritage, a weekly newspaper in Los Angeles, ran an editorial referring to Buchanan as the "glib-tongued anti-Semite who was denounced by New York Times writer A. M. Rosenthal, for his nastiness and ugliness."* Such language suggests that Buchanan's anti-Semitism had been as much a part of the forensic landscape as, say, Martin Peretz's philo-Semitism. The New Republic editorialized (September 15): "Buchanan-watchers, students of prejudice in America, and political teratologists have known of Buchanan's anti-Semitism for years." And added, pre-emptively, a defense against a point that would be raised widely in the days ahead by Buchanan's defenders: "No, he is not like Hitler. Hitler, however, cannot be allowed to set the standard. Lesser bigots cannot be protected from criticism by the magnitude of Hitler's achievements in bigotry."

The point is well taken. One need not, in order to qualify as an anti-Semite, defend the Holocaust or cry out for another one. David Harris,

---

*The succeeding sentence: "And when a William F. Buckley leaned back on his guru couch to defend Buchanan with his own excessive pompous smugness, one can only say: ach!"

the director of the American Jewish Committee's Office of Government and International Affairs, wrote that "Buchanan's venomous streak, which knows no bounds, cannot be ignored," which of course begs the question why it was for the most part ignored until Rosenthal struck. Jack Newfield, writing for the *New York Observer*, said that "Mr. Buchanan's pathological hostility to Jews has been obvious to Jews like myself for many years. I have written about it in *The Village Voice* and the *Daily News*." One can only assume that these attacks on Buchanan, Anti-Semite, hadn't been read by anybody who took them seriously. Newfield went on, "Pat Buchanan and Joe Sobran are way over the line when it comes to religious, racial, ethnic, and sexual bigotry. They are hatemongers."*

The New Republic's Fred Barnes tried to clarify the simple point: Is Buchanan, based on his writings, an anti-Semite? "If your definition is someone who is personally bigoted against Jews, doesn't want them in the country club, I don't think Pat is that. If your definition is someone who thinks Israel and its supporters are playing a bad role in the world, Pat may qualify."

The Special Role of Israel

Again and again the issue of attachment-to-Israel as the litmus test arises. Elie Wiesel said to the *Washington Post*, "Although I very rarely use the word 'anti-Semite,' I must say [Pat Buchanan] comes very close to fitting that category." Wiesel goes on to list the now-familiar compilation of Buchanan's presumptively anti-Jewish positions, and includes "a man who is constantly criticizing Israel."

Allan Brownfeld, a syndicated columnist who is himself Jewish, wrote on the question in the January 1991 *Chronicles*, reaching very different conclusions from the critics, some of them highly provocative. On the matter of Israel fixation he is emphatic:

> Today, anti-Semitism in America has been redefined as anything that opposes the politics and interests of the state of Israel. One cannot be critical of the Israeli prime minister, concerned about the question of the Palestinians, or dubious about the value of massive infusions of American aid to Israel without subjecting oneself to the possibility of being called "anti-Semitic."

*Just as Rosenthal had overdone it in the language he used in attacking Buchanan, Newfield now overdid it (it is rare, among those who write heatedly about racial prejudice, that whistle-blowers restrain their own prejudices). Thus Newfield, so to speak out of the blue: "George Will is a slightly more complex and ambiguous case. If he is not quite a bigot, then he certainly traffics in anti-black stereotypes of a particularly partisan and insulting kind. Mr. Will seems to plagiarize his metaphors from the unconscious of Roger Ailes. He is no Walter Lippmann. He is more like his former employer Jesse Helms." The least inaccuracy in these sentences is that George Will once worked for Jesse Helms.

Brownfeld cites the book *The New Anti-Semitism*, by Arnold Forster and Benjamin R. Epstein of the Anti-Defamation League, and says:

> The new definition includes "a callous indifference to Jewish concerns expressed by respectable institutions and persons . . . who would be shocked to think of themselves as anti-Semites." [Here is a classic example of circular reasoning: Henceforth, anyone who takes position A shall *eo ipso* be deemed an anti-Semite. X has just now taken position A. X is therefore now an anti-Semite.]
>
> Thus, the nature of the "new" anti-Semitism, according to Forster and Epstein, is not necessarily hostility to Jews as Jews or toward Judaism— which all men and women of good will deplore—but, instead, criticism of Israel and its policies.
>
> In a June 5, 1983, *Washington Post* article entitled "Anti-Semitism Has Changed," [the late] Nathan Perlmutter, then national chairman of the ADL, expanded upon this thesis. He noted that the search for peace in the Middle East is "littered with minefields that endanger Jewish interests" and declared that the "fevered language" used by the media in describing Israeli actions during the invasion of Lebanon illustrated "how decent yearnings for 'peace' in an alchemy of historical ignorance, and hyperbole, stir anti-Semitic imagery."
>
> One of those who [have] freely used the charge of anti-Semitism to silence critics of Israel is Norman Podhoretz, editor of *Commentary*. In an article entitled "J'Accuse" [*Commentary*, September 1982], he charged America's leading journalists, newspapers, and television networks with anti-Semitism because of their reporting of the war of Lebanon and their criticism of Israel's conduct. Among those so accused were Anthony Lewis of the *New York Times*, Nicholas von Hoffman, . . . Joseph Harsch of the *Christian Science Monitor*, Rowland Evans, Robert Novak, Richard Cohen, and Alfred Friendly of the *Washington Post*, and a host of others. Of the criticism of Israel by these journalists, many of whom were Jewish themselves, Podhoretz declared: "We are dealing here with an eruption of anti-Semitism."

The episode to which Brownfeld refers is well remembered by readers of *Commentary*. It was the general judgment of the concerned community (I was among the critics, devoting a column to the subject) that Podhoretz's fears and condemnations were exaggerated, but in that respect he was hardly exceptional—the Israeli military offensive aroused high passions. Mr. Podhoretz on this occasion classified as anti-Semitic anyone who ascribes to Jews characteristics uniquely Jewish or, correlatively, denies to Jews rights acknowledged in others. His particular point being that Israel's attack on Lebanon was justified by the conventional rights that inure to beleaguered countries, and that therefore to have singled Israel out for criticism, when others in similar circumstances would escape criticism, was anti-Semitic.

The point is logically sound, but even so doesn't answer the broader question whether anti-Semitism was the presumptive prime mover in those who criticized Israeli practices. Brownfeld is justified in his exploration. He goes on to search out Israeli anti-Semitism:

> Norman Podhoretz was also willing to attack Israeli critics of Israel's policy in Lebanon, and did so publicly at the March 1986 International Colloquium of Jewish Journalists. The Jerusalem meeting focused on whether Jewish journalists in general and Israeli journalists in particular have a special obligation of restraint in reporting controversial aspects of Israeli life. Writing in the *Jerusalem Post,* columnist Moshe Kohn reported: "The debate was led off by Norman Podhoretz ... He opened by laying down the 'axiom' that 'the preservation of the Jewish people involves above all else ensuring the survival of Israel.' From this, he said, follows a second axiom: 'It is in Diaspora Jewry's own self-interest to man the ramparts in the relentless ideological war being waged against Israel,' which, he said, 'I take to be a war against the Jewish people as a whole.' So 'the role of Jews who write in both the Jewish and general press is to defend Israel, and not to join in the attack on Israel.'"

According to Brownfeld, Podhoretz was grilled on the spot.

> Mr. Podhoretz admitted that Jews have a right to criticize. However, when asked if he could think of an Israeli action of which he might [I assume he meant, publicly] disapprove, he declared, "The only decision by Israel that I know I'd criticize publicly would be one to join a Communist alliance."

The point to ponder here isn't whether some of Israel's friends are uncritical to the point of losing their usefulness even to Israel. (*My country right or wrong, but right or wrong my country* is emotionally understandable when the fatherland is threatened, but less often sound advice for a patriot.) Our inquiry is into the organic composition of anti-Semitism. Having written in 1991 about a Podhoretz excess in 1982, Mr. Brownfeld would, one would assume, feel the responsibility to cite examples of Podhoretz's irrationality in leveling the charge of anti-Semitism with reference to the new criterion. But in his article for *Chronicles* he doesn't do this. Evidently he deems sufficient his citation of Norman Podhoretz's 1982 article. Israel's invasion of Lebanon and the deportment of its army posed complicated questions and in 1982 generated much criticism of Israel's government. We are better off ignoring that divisive episode to concentrate on the implications of the later Podhoretz speech as judged by his own conduct. Does he in fact proceed as if any critic of Israeli policy, Jewish or Gentile, is *eo ipso* anti-Semitic? Logically we begin by asking, How did he react to the Buchanan–Rosenthal exchange?

Podhoretz reacted by publishing the long piece by Muravchik, described above. Nowhere in that lengthy essay is any demand made of Buchanan (or of anyone else) that is manifestly irrational. That is to say, it is nowhere assumed that mere opposition to an Israeli policy constitutes anti-Semitism. Since Mr. Podhoretz, in the nine years since 1982, hasn't left a trail of imputations of anti-Semitism against everyone who criticizes Israeli policy, we should assume that Podhoretz's speech in Israel, coming to us third hand, contained qualifications, either made explicitly and not recorded or else left implicit, that Mr. Brownfeld either is not aware of or else is disinclined to quote.

Even so, the point survives: Is criticism of Israel's policies a symptom of anti-Semitism, active or latent? It is almost universally agreed that this isn't so, and it is hard to maintain otherwise, if only because of the heated opposition within Israel itself to many Israeli public policies. But it is less clear whether the formal, organized American Jewish lobby stops short of assailing as anti-Semitic those whose only offense is opposition to this or that policy of Israel's.

What about the Jewish Lobby?

It is relevant to inquire into the power of what one might just as well call the Jewish lobby. How much power does it have? If (*arguendo*) it were omnipotent, then it would be (should be) feared, if only for that reason: one doesn't want omnipotent lobbies arguing in behalf of anything, not even the Bill of Rights. Is it omnipotent? Nearly omnipotent? Dangerously potent?

It is almost everywhere implicit, and here and there explicit, that such lobbies are at work and, in the case of Pat Buchanan, that they have been at work hoping—well, hoping to silence him. To inquire whether they are so engaged is not to pass judgment on whether they are justified in being so engaged. There are those, J. S. Mill most prominent among them, who believe that so long as a single person clings to a belief, the question whether that belief might be correct should not be treated as closed. I think of that as the acme of epistemological pessimism, the seedling from which, among other things, that notion of academic freedom prospered which holds that all ideas should, in a famous phrase, "start out even in the race." (By that protocol, a college teacher should not indicate to a student reading the *Communist Manifesto* alongside the United States Constitution which of the two documents better harmonizes with democratic ideals.)

But forgetting for the moment those who believe that every point of view should be evenhandedly ventilated, the question to ask here is: In a civilized culture, should someone who is, in the opinion of the reasonable community, an anti-Semite be removed from public forums? This, obviously, not by the hand of the law, but by the exercise of a citizenry determined to discourage uncivilized and potentially dangerous thought. And if the answer to that question is, Indeed, such folk should *not* be given forums from which to preach their bigotries!—then who are the logical spokesmen for the public in urging their removal?

Where will the pressures originate? Not from legislatures, not while there is still a Bill of Rights. Whence, then?

Who? In response to pressures from whom? From the Israeli lobby? From watchdogs, like the Anti-Defamation League, that monitor racial slurs?

On whom should they put pressure? Editors and station managers and publishers? Book-sellers?

And what are the appropriate pressures, in the 1990s?

In 1945, superintending arrangements in West Germany, the victorious allies forthrightly and without apology forbade any pro-Nazi literature in the schools. As mentioned above in passing, we at *National Review* faced the problem in embryo in the Fifties. Ours was the nascent voice of responsible conservative thought. I had brought together men of immense learning and moral prestige, for instance John Dos Passos, Frank Meyer, Whittaker Chambers, Max Eastman, James Burnham. For a few months after leaving the CIA I had worked for *The American Mercury,* whose editor and publisher was William Bradford Huie, a bright and enterprising editor and novelist (*The Revolt of Mamie Stover*), one of whose causes became equality for Negroes, as they were then called. He lost control of the *Mercury,* and I left it. It was sold to Russell Maguire, a wealthy munitions maker who was, well, anti-Semitic. For two or three years he left the *Mercury,* untouched by his prejudices, in the hands of a Hearst lieutenant, but after a while the weeds began to creep up.

I faced the problem that a half-dozen respectable names from the conservative movement were still associated with the *Mercury,* as "consultants" or "contributing editors," and that some of those names appeared also on the masthead of *National Review.* After reading a particularly blatant issue of the *Mercury* (this was about 1958), I thought the time had come to act decisively, and accordingly addressed a note to the writers on the masthead of *National Review* and told them that those of them who were also on the masthead of the *Mercury* would need to choose from which masthead to retire. In almost all cases (there was only one exception), they stayed with us.*

Two or three years later, the *Mercury* was mortally stricken with advanced nativism. For a while, the wild General Edwin Walker, who had

---

*A few years later I took an identical position about mastheads, this time in respect of the John Birch Society. The Birch Society was never anti-Semitic, but it was a dangerous distraction to right reasoning and had to be exiled. *National Review* accomplished exactly that.

been dismissed from his command in Europe for verbal irresponsibility, was made its editor. General Walker was supremely illiterate, which under the circumstances was a blessing. Some will remember that Lee Harvey Oswald, practicing for his big day on Dealey Plaza, aimed his rifle at General Walker one night, firing through a windowpane. (On that occasion, ironically, he missed.)

How Does One Block Anti-Semitism?

Forty-five years after the death of Hitler, the penal code of Germany still forbids the *advocacy* of Nazi ideas, but not the distribution of Nazi literature, which presumably survives in Germany in the same sense that toxic cultures survive in laboratories. My understanding is that no serious observer of the German scene believes there is anything like a clear or remote danger of any serious rebirth of a Nazi movement, though there is concern, in my judgment primarily moral rather than political, over suppurations here and there of neo-Nazism. Probably (this is my guess, at any rate) the incidental wigwam of a Nazi witch doctor would be ignored by the German government, rather than being destroyed and its owner prosecuted. If so, this is defensible civic conduct, taken by responsible men and women who while aware of the hideousness of what happened yesterday—more accurately, the day before yesterday—are confident that there is no prospect of its happening again; or else that the threat of any such thing is so remote as to fail to justify the kind of proscriptive vigilance thought to be appropriate in 1945.

On the question whether an anti-Semite should be given a forum in respectable company, David Frum has highly developed opinions, which he ventilated in that *American Spectator* article (July 1991). About Pat Buchanan he summarizes: "His real message is inseparable from his sly Jew-baiting and his not-so-sly queer-bashing, from his old record as a segregationist and his current maunderings about immigrants and the Japanese. And it's not a message that can be accommodated in any conservatism—Big Government or Small—that seriously hopes to govern a great and diverse country; in fact, it's exactly the kind of message that William F. Buckley thought he had purged from American conservatism back in the 1950s and early 1960s, when he chased Gerald L. K. Smith and the John Birchers away from *National Review*."

Very well, then, if the objective is ostracism, how is this operation managed? Is it primarily the responsibility of the Jewish, or anti-anti-Semitic, lobby?

During the controversy, Buchanan had asked out loud, Why was it that Rosenthal waited three whole weeks before firing back at him for the remarks he made on the McLaughlin show? Rosenthal talked vaguely, as we have seen, about friends who had brought the Buchanan material to his attention. In fact, as the story developed, it was rather more formal than that. "Rosenthal based his attack upon Buchanan on material provided to him—and other journalists around the country—by the Anti-Defamation League of B'nai B'rith," Allan Brownfeld was able to document. "Abraham Foxman, National Director of the ADL, acknowledges that the ADL issued a statement critical of Pat Buchanan. 'I'm sure that Abe Rosenthal saw it,' Foxman says. 'It wasn't a secret. He then did what he did.'" (Foxman subsequently denied that his organization had "called a single editor to request removal of Buchanan's column, nor would we.")

Brownfeld went on: "The ADL is part of a larger coalition of groups, some of which have assumed for themselves the role of attempting to silence those advocating ideas with which these groups disagree. The house organ of the American Israel Public Affairs Committee (AIPAC), *Near East Report*, urged its readers to exert pressure on local newspapers around the country to replace Pat Buchanan's column with that of another conservative columnist, such as George Will. Even Harvard Professor Alan Dershowitz, ordinarily an outspoken advocate of the First Amendment, declared that Buchanan should be removed from the national media. 'CNN should take him off the air and major American newspapers should stop running him,' Dershowitz told the *Washington Jewish Week*."

Brownfeld tells us that on the other hand there was "widespread defense" of Buchanan. Now that can be thought to be good news abstractly, insofar as it is testimony to the liveliness of civil liberties and pluralism, but not-so-good news insofar as it suggests the toleration of bigotry or indifference to it. But an indifference to bigotry can't easily be thought to have motivated those specifically cited by Brownfeld, especially the "prominent Jewish Americans"—including Paul Gottfried, Leon Hadar, Ronald Hamowy, Sheldon Richman, Murray Rothbard, and Murray Sabrin—who were among the signers of a pro-Buchanan advertisement in the *New York Times* in October 1990. Inevitably it will be surmised by many Jewish critics of Buchanan that his "Jewish defenders" are perhaps professional apostates, on the order of Alfred Lilienthal, whose principal occupation over the years has been criticism of Israel. But that charge cannot be sustained against persons of this intellectual quality.

Where Israel Is Concerned . . .

It is the moment to note and ponder comments by Eric Alterman, a senior fellow of the World Policy Institute. Writing in *The Nation* (November 5, 1990), he took issue with Rosenthal—because he thought it wrong for him to assume that all American Jews were affronted by the criticisms made by Buchanan of our Middle East policy.

> To Rosenthal, Buchanan's indictment implicates all Jews, including, I imagine, my 11-month-old nephew. To anyone with the slightest degree of political sophistication, however, the quote [Buchanan's "amen corner"] implies "some Jews," or even "those few people, who happen to be Jewish, along with some non-Jews like Alfonse D'Amato." Interpreting criticism of particular Jews to embrace all Jews is itself a kind of anti-Semitism. Thus "the Jews," not Ivan Boesky or Dennis Levine, are behind the insider-trading scandal. "The Jews," not Karl Marx . . . , wrote the *Communist Manifesto*. "The Jews," not Abe Rosenthal, are responsible for the literary crimes that grace the *New York Times* op-ed page twice a week.

On this point Michael Kinsley of *The New Republic* was in agreement. Daniel Lazare quotes him in the *New York Observer* (October 1, 1990):

> Something that sounds like anti-Semitism may not be. Mr. Kinsley, for instance, pointed out that Mr. Rosenthal's column was devoid of evidence to back up his assertion that Israel's "amen corner in the United States" was an anti-Semitic codeword: "All the column said was, 'J'accuse—I have refrained from saying it, but I can refrain no longer. I hereby say it. There, I've said it.' That was the essence of the column. It didn't have either evidence or argument. I'm not saying there is no evidence or argument to be mustered, but he simply didn't do it."

Confronted with this objection, Rosenthal was simply impatient, as already cited: "I didn't attack him because of what he said about Israel or Iraq but because he put it in anti-Semitic language." Raising the question of how to avoid anti-Semitic formulations when criticizing Israeli policy.

The diversity of opinion on Mideast policy among learned Jews comes through briefly but forcefully in a fundraising letter from the editor of *Tikkun* ("A Bimonthly Jewish Critique of Politics, Culture, & Society"), which once described itself as a "left-wing *Commentary*." Michael Lerner ("Ph.D.") writes to his supporters,

> Iraqi aggression in Kuwait has further complicated the task of the Israeli peace movement—particularly given the foolish action of many Palestinians in supporting Saddam Hussein. My editorial in the September issue attempts to explain their support for Hussein in terms of the continuing frustration they've faced with an Israel that repeatedly asserts its unwillingness to negotiate land for peace. But while I think Palestinian support for Iraq does not provide good grounds to discount their struggle for national self-determination, I must say that personally I find it discouraging that many of them identify with such a destructive and vicious person as Saddam Hussein. I understand why so many Israelis are scared—both by Iraq and by Palestinian support for Saddam Hussein. And it certainly makes things much more difficult for us in the peace camp: we must oppose Saddam Hussein and yet not

allow Iraq to become the newest excuse for continuing to deny Palestinians the rights they deserve. In this process, we must also stress our solid commitment to Israeli security and survival.

That statement could have been signed by Joe Sobran or Pat Buchanan, but passes unnoticed written by a Jew, addressed to other Jews, in language studiedly sober.

Back to Eric Alterman in *The Nation*:

"Jewish pressure" is thrown around all the time in Washington and it is done so proudly. The American Israel Public Affairs Committee (Aipac), the "pro-Israel" lobby in Washington, has spent the past ten years purposefully building and enhancing its reputation for deploying its "Jewish pressure" on matters it deems to be of Jewish concern, from Egypt to El Salvador. In that regard, anyway, it has done a pretty fair job. Just what did Rosenthal think Aipac director Thomas Dine had in mind back in 1984 when he announced, after the defeat of Senator Charles Percy (who supported the establishment of a Palestinian entity), that "all the Jews in America, from coast to coast, gathered to oust Percy. And the American politicians—those who hold public positions now, and those who aspire—got the message"? Goyish pressure?

Alterman goes on, nudging up against a critical point everywhere acknowledged abstractly, but with which some anti-anti-Semites have practical difficulties.

The equation of anti-Semitism with opposition to Israel's government and with the "pressure" its supporters and operatives exert on the American political process demeans the lives of those who have suffered under true anti-Semitism—and there is no shortage of those—and silences legitimate debate on U.S. policy in the Middle East. A recent fundraising letter sent out by the American Jewish Congress and signed by its executive director, Henry Siegman, veered uncomfortably close to this territory as well. The letter accuses James Zogby, president of the Arab American Institute, of being a proponent of "the new anti-Semitism" and appears to link him with neo-Nazi David Duke, as well as with the proudly anti-Semitic Louis Farrakhan, on the basis of Zogby's campaign to limit the influence of pro-Israel PACs in American elections. The AJC's objection, according to the letter, is that Zogby insists that five U.S. senators who received a great deal of pro-Israel PAC money are "not operating in the interests of the people who elected them."

Is this action by AIPAC discriminatory in the objectionable sense? No, not really. Alterman cannot here be denied:

A pro-Israel PAC would have to be stupid to raise money for people whom it did not expect to behave in its interest. Aipac and its related PACs have been accused of a great many things, but stupidity—particularly in the raising and spending of campaign contributions—is not one of them.

Alterman is amused, or rather not amused, by AIPAC's gyrations on the matter of freedom of expression:

> Following on Rosenthal's column, Aipac sent an advisory to its 50,000 members, encouraging them to meet with newspaper editors in order to "ask them if they believe the Buchanans are presenting information their readers want." Aipac suggests that its members offer the names of Norman Podhoretz and other far-right-wing Shamir government cheerleaders as alternatives, or such "liberals" as (I kid you not) Alan Dershowitz, Charles Krauthammer, and one A. M. Rosenthal. "No one is saying the Buchanans should have no right to express their views." Who—Aipac? Of course not. But just the same, Aipac would like to see Buchanan silenced and replaced with pundits who are "fair-minded when it comes to the Middle East."
>
> Buchanan is perhaps being a bit paranoid when he suspects a "pre-planned, orchestrated smear campaign" designed to deprive him of his readership. But with Aipac and Rosenthal after him, need we remind ourselves that even paranoids have real enemies?

We are left here with an American Jew who opposes Israeli policies 1) calling attention to the anomaly that any non-Jew who also opposes those policies runs the risk of being called anti-Semitic; and 2) defending an "Israeli" line as defined by Israeli lobbies, while raising the question whether defiance of that line warrants the anti-Israel tag, in particular to the extent that "anti-Israel" evolves into "anti-Semitic." And we are left with the question of how to train the moral faculties to distinguish between those whose anti-Israel positions evolve (whether or not they know it) from anti-Semitic impulses, and those anti-Israelis unaffected by the Jewishness of the Israeli nation. I find it impossible to defend Pat Buchanan against the charge that what he did and said during the period under examination amounted to anti-Semitism, whatever it was that drove him to say and do it: most probably, an iconoclastic temperament.*

So then, if such anti-Semitic impulses exist, do they usually also overwhelm rational faculties? Become obsessive? We know of historical examples in which this has in fact happened. ("I had a letter yesterday from Peg," Murray Kempton told me years ago, driving back from Westbrook Pegler's funeral. "I knew he was sick. He wrote seven pages and didn't once mention David Ben Gurion.")

---

*Several weeks after these words were written, some cartoonists, and one or two columnists, reached out to link Pat Buchanan with David Duke, after Duke's gubernatorial race in Louisiana and Buchanan's projected entry into the presidential race. The linkage is morally irresponsible, as careful readers of this essay will acknowledge. Duke the sometime KKK wizard and Nazi enthusiast is as reasonably linked with Buchanan as Norman Thomas is with Stalin.

3 · *The Dartmouth Review*

On October 4, 1990, the Student Assembly of Dartmouth College held a rally. It was a huge affair, probably the most massive gathering of Dartmouth students, faculty, and administrators at any Dartmouth function since the Grateful Dead's appearance in the Seventies. Why?

The rally was brought forth under the banner, "Dartmouth United Against Hate." Twenty-five hundred people were there, according to the press. Speakers were James O. Freedman, the president of Dartmouth; two professors; and student leaders from the African-American Society, Dartmouth Hillel, Native Americans at Dartmouth, the International Students Association, and the Student Assembly.

What engendered this extraordinary convention was a single issue of *The Dartmouth Review* distributed six days earlier. The *Review* is a weekly publication, ten years old, sponsored by conservative dissenters among Dartmouth students. Ever since its inception, the *Review* has carried under its logo what it calls "The *Review* Credo," a quotation from Theodore Roosevelt—"*Far better it is to dare mighty things, to win great triumphs, even though checkered by failure, than to rank with those poor spirits who neither enjoy much nor suffer much, because they live in the gray twilight that knows neither victory nor defeat.*"

But in the October 3 issue, "The *Review* Credo" read: "Far better it is to dare mighty things, to win great triumphs. *Therefore, I believe today that I am acting in the sense of the Almighty Creator: By warding off the Jews, I am fighting for the Lord's work:* gray twilight that knows neither victory nor defeat." The lines sandwiched in between the two clauses by TR are from Adolf Hitler's *Mein Kampf*.

The Immediate Aftermath

Here is what was done by the editorial staff of *The Dartmouth Review* when the mutilation was spotted and in the days immediately after:

1. All issues of the *Review* not already distributed (it was three days before anybody saw the imposture) were destroyed.

2. An apology was printed and distributed throughout the campus.

3. The district attorney of the state of New Hampshire was asked to conduct an investigation of the editorial substitution, a felony under state law.

4. A request was made to the trustees of *The Dartmouth Review* to dispatch a member to conduct his own investigation.

5. The editor of the *Review* volunteered to take a polygraph test designed to inquire whether he had foreknowledge of the act of sabotage.

Concurrently, the Dartmouth administration:

1. Organized the anti-hate rally.

2. Conducted an interview with Fox Butterfield of the *New York Times*, insisting that the quote from Hitler had been published intentionálly and was characteristic of the editorial policies of the *Review*.

3. Drew attention to the appearance of the Hitler quote the day before Yom Kippur, a sacred day in the Jewish calendar.

4. Contracted to write an op-ed page piece for the *New York Times* (signed by Freedman) about the incident, and to publicize it wherever opportunity lay.

President Freedman was off to a give-no-quarter start. His address to the anti-hate congregation contained the following sentences. "For ten years *The Dartmouth Review* has consistently attacked blacks because they are black, women because they are women, homosexuals because they are homosexuals, and Jews because they are Jews. Now, in an act of moral cowardice that extends that reprehensible pattern, it relies on Hitler's *Mein Kampf* on the day of Yom Kippur. Appalling bigotry of this kind has no place at the College or in this country. . . . I am very angry."

The more sober community, looking in on Hanover, was understandably perplexed, and several commentators even spoke of the likelihood of sabotage. But Freedman ruled out the possibility. Asked by the *Wall Street Journal* how he would feel if it were in due course established that the Hitler quote was inserted by a saboteur, his reply was, "I just haven't thought about that." And to the *Boston Globe*, "It's hard to believe it was an accident."

The Investigation by the ADL

The Anti-Defamation League of B'nai B'rith, which is formally concerned with evidence of anti-Semitism, accepted the invitation by *The Dartmouth Review* to look into the incident. A Commission was established under the chairmanship of Richard D. Glovsky, an alumnus of Dartmouth, a former assistant United States attorney for the district of Massachusetts, where he was chief of the Civil Division from 1978 to 1980, and a principal in the Boston law firm of Glovsky & Associates. The ADL Commission issued its findings on January 8, 1991, in a substantial report.

The very first sentence in the report read, "On the day before Yom Kippur, the holiest day of the year for Jews throughout the world, the following quote from Adolf Hitler appeared on the masthead of *The Dartmouth Review*."

Question: Was it relevant to note that Yom Kippur was the following day? As it happened, saying so served at least the purpose of correcting the chronology of President Freedman, who at the Hate Rally had placed the *Review* publication not on the day before Yom Kippur, but on Yom Kippur. It would seem to this observer that, just to begin with, few Americans know when Yom Kippur falls, let alone what exactly it represents in Jewish theology. This ought not to be surprising, given the small size of the Jewish population in America (under 3 per cent), much of it secularist. A poll conducted in England in the spring of 1991 revealed that 34 per cent of Englishmen do not know what Easter Sunday is supposed to celebrate, and 39 per cent do not know what happened on Good Friday.*

But more important, the publication of the genocidal remark by Adolf Hitler would have been equally appalling any day of the year. To relate it to Yom Kippur seemed therefore an irrelevant, endogamous distraction. In the spring of 1991, when William Smith and his uncle Senator Edward Kennedy were drinking at 3 A.M., following which (it is alleged) young Smith raped a woman, it was noticed by only a very few people as seriously relevant to the event that the drinking had started on Good Friday and the (alleged) rape was committed on Holy Saturday. A rape one week later or one week earlier would have been equally scandalous.

Quite reasonably, the ADL set out to inquire whether there was a tradition of anti-Semitism in *The Dartmouth Review*. The examiners went back to the year 1982, when—to quote from the Commission's report—"The *Review* ran an item entitled 'Grin and Beirut,' which stated that with the erection of a ceremonial Jewish sukkah 'on the West Bank of College Hall' the 'Zionists have gone too far.' Shortly thereafter, the Jewish sukkah [a sukkah is a Jewish ceremonial shelter associated with the Sukkoth festival] on campus was clandestinely destroyed. The Commission found no evidence to link the sukkah destruction to the article."

That absolution by the ADL could not have been expected to satisfy everyone retroactively. "This was a despicable act of anti-Semitic vandalism perpetrated in a school that has—to put it mildly—a reputation for ignoring the sensitivities of the Jewish members of its community," Ronald Kiener, a visiting lecturer in the religion department, wrote in a letter to *The Dartmouth* (the regular student newspaper). And Rabbi Michael Paley, associate chaplain at the college, "while defending Dartmouth as a place no more difficult for Jews than other Ivy League schools," as the

---

*The validity of that poll has been questioned, but even if the figures are wrong, the point survives. For probably the majority, holidays that began as religious holy days are secular in meaning and observance.

Boston Globe reported his comments, "acknowledges, 'Dartmouth is a place that fosters homogeneity, and Jews are a minority ... there is a problem with Jews here [because] there is a problem with anyone who doesn't fit the Dartmouth image.'" Once again: The problems of a minority *qua* minority are not to be confused with the anti-Semitic virus we are seeking to isolate. And the statement by Rabbi Paley is about the Dartmouth scene, not about anti-Semitism within *The Dartmouth Review.*

The most fevered reaction came in a letter published by *The Dartmouth,* and one does well to note, with pain, the intensity of it. The letter was signed by 11 Jews who identified themselves as from "the Upper Valley, including Jewish students at Dartmouth":

> *The Dartmouth Review* published a satirical article characterizing this religious symbol [the sukkah] as a "settlement on the West Bank of College Hall" and as part of a Jewish extortion plot against Dartmouth. The appearance of such an article, amid signs of a rising tide of anti-Semitism here and abroad, and the linking of the sukkah to Israeli government policies in the West Bank which are opposed by many, if not most, Upper Valley Jews, reflects a lack of judgment and responsibility that would be astonishing were the editors of *The Review* ever known to have adhered to minimal journalistic standards.
>
> We condemn the destruction of the sukkah. We assert our right to live as Jews at Dartmouth and in the Upper Valley free from intimidation. We condemn the cheap attacks of *The Review* on Jews, blacks, women, gays, and any other group that its editors decide offer opportunities for pandering to prejudice.

The Question of Editorial License

One pauses here to consider the factor of student humor; in fact, of humor in general.

In 1982 the Israelis were indeed on the march in Lebanon, and the controversial settlements on the West Bank had begun. In reaction to the sukkah's construction (illegal, by Dartmouth regulations) the wisecrack was, prima facie, entirely innocent of racist or religious spite—that the "Zionists" had "gone too far" on "the West Bank of College Hall" is an amusing campus application of an international incident. ("Winthrop House Is a Distressed Area," was the banner with which Harvard students welcomed President-elect John F. Kennedy back to his undergraduate quarters, without profaning the West Virginian poverty that gave rise to the phrase.) The *Review*'s brief editorial note had gone on to say, in mock solemnity, "A spokesman for the Dartmouth Hillel has flatly refused to remove the ceremonial shack without guarantees from President McLaughlin for increased aid for the Judaic Studies Department, and a new Jewish dormitory on the banks of the Connecticut River. A buildup of Cadillacs is rumored along the outskirts of the city of West Lebanon, N.H." Good college-humor stuff, and anyway, the *Review*'s longtime championship of Israeli causes should have sobered up its 11 critics. One concludes that they were affected less by the few sentences that appeared in the *Review* than by the sharp public criticism of the Israeli military (indeed, much of it by Israelis) that upset Norman Podhoretz and caused him to write his essay "J'Accuse" at about the same time.

The *Boston Globe* had put this lead on the sukkah story when it happened: "It was a chilly, dark night, with little light from a late-rising moon, when two, maybe three tipsy vandals tore down the makeshift shelter." The effort, halfhearted, to put an anti-Semitic construction on the event did not catch fire with the *Globe*'s reporter. Rabbi Paley was quoted: "Anti-Semitism comes in a lot of different flavors. . . . The destruction was probably done by someone drunk and out of control—but if it had been a [Christmas] manger scene in the middle of the Green, it would not have been a target." That may be true; but even if it were, the incident would not have added up to anti-Semitism. The Christmas manger is universally recognized as a religious symbol, not to be trifled with except by the Supreme Court; not so the sukkah. Insularity, not prejudice, would be implicated here. The newspaper story went on to report that the jape about the Zionists going too far had been "intended to be witty, . . . and was written by Jews."

After looking at the sukkah incident in search of racism, the ADL Commission moved on to the destruction of the anti-apartheid shanties in January 1986. This act was done by *Review* staffers not a bit covertly—on the contrary, perhaps even with a touch of ostentation—on the grounds that by removing the shanties they were enforcing regulations official Dartmouth, by reason of ideological funk, was itself neglecting. The shanty wreckers were severely punished, some of them even suspended from college for several terms.

It was alleged at the time by some of their critics that the student editors were activated by racist (anti-anti-apartheid) motives. Attention was given once again to coincidental holy days: The anti-*Review* chorus pronounced the destruction of the shanties as especially blasphemous in that the deed was done on the birthday of Dr. Martin Luther King. This charge was inconvenienced by an indigestible datum: Dr. King's birthday is on January 15, and the shanties were destroyed on January 21. The ADL Commission pointed out, however, that in 1986 Dr. King's birthday was officially celebrated on January 20, which point helped the sacrilege-seekers a little, though leaving unanswered and unanswerable the question: If the whole idea was to strike a blow against those who were striking a blow against apartheid and to magnify this anti-black effrontery by doing it on the birthday of Martin Luther King, why not tear down the shanties on the birthday of Martin Luther King, rather than six days after his actual birthday? Or tear them down on the day of his official birthday celebration, not one day after? On top of that problem, the racist-bent critics had the problem of coping with the sustained editorial protests against the (illegal) shanties, denounced and resented as violations of the zoning regulations of Dartmouth College, which prohibit structures on the Green whether designed to protest apartheid or affirm Coca-Cola. The *Review* had engaged in criticism of the shanty infractions ever since they went up, and that was two months (and three days?) before the birthday of Martin Luther King.

The major attraction, in the search for anti-Semitism in the history of *The Dartmouth Review*, was one article. To quote the Commission:

> In its October 19, 1988, issue, *The Review* published an article entitled "Ein Reich, Ein Volk, Ein Freedmann." The author of the article was James Garrett, who *The Review* represented to be "a survivor" [i.e., of Hitler's Germany]. The article compared President Freedman, who is Jewish, to Adolf Hitler. It referred to President Freedman as "Der Freedmann," cited his only book as *Mein Krise und Administrationen*, said Mr. Freedman's speeches "could whip up professors into frenzies of hysterical joy," and . . . claimed that President Freedman converted the Campus Police to a private army "absolutely subject to [Freedman's] will, the legendarily brutal SS." One week later *The Review* depicted President Freedman in a cartoon as Adolf Hitler.

The article in question was in dubious taste, but its appearance does little more than remind us that sometimes sophomores do sophomoric things. It is not plausible that young Mr. Garrett was undertaking to trivialize the Holocaust by his caricature of the college president as Adolf Hitler. It had been popular, especially during the Sixties, to refer to policemen as "pigs," or indeed as "Nazis." The derogation was never (in my judgment) funny, but it wasn't widely interpreted as an indication of latent insensitivity in the Woodstock Generation to Auschwitz or, for that matter, to policemen suffering from identity crises. As to the personal record of the author of the article, Garrett had, earlier in the year, written a piece denouncing Dartmouth's recognition and funding of a pro-PLO student organization, the Committee for Palestinian Rights. During the debate that followed the Hitler article, Garrett and his fellow editors contrasted their own record on Israel and the Jews with that of certain other members of the Dartmouth community, in particular those who had been responsible for inviting Professor Angela Davis, the black Communist official once mixed up with the Black Panthers, to Dartmouth to give a lecture celebrating the anniversary of coeducation. "Ironically," the *Review* said in its own defense, "those who stood and cheered after Davis's meandering diatribe against men, whites, Jews, and anyone else she could think of" were now criticizing the *Review*. "Professor Arthur Hertzberg, a member of Dartmouth's current cabal of moralists, calls the *Review*'s editor a 'pre-fascist thug ... [a] dog' in virtually the same breath with which he deplored Garrett's comparison of Freedman to Hitler. ... Other professors and administrators who signed on to this ill-conceived hate campaign have already shown us that their intellectual integrity is nonexistent."

Moslems and Penguins

The ADL, as already suggested, did not confine its investigation to past acts of the *Review* that bore directly on the Jewish question. A general curiosity governed in respect of sensitivity to the feelings of minorities, and the Commission noted that "in the summer of 1990, one issue of the *Review* compared the deaths of 1,400 Moslems in Mecca with the deaths of 7,000 penguins. After receiving objections, it apologized in a subsequent issue to the 'penguins.' In yet another issue, it apologized for the initial analogy." ("Apology. In our Summer Issue and September 19 issue, we made several remarks that were quite upsetting to Arab students. These remarks went over the line of good taste, and we apologize to Arab Dartmouth students and the Community at large.")

We have here an example of the problems a serious, partisan journal has when it gives way to *National Lampoon* humor, which is always going to happen. Young editors, so to speak after two beers, decide it would be hilarious to compare the death of penguins to that of Moslems. They are upbraided for doing so, and after three beers and much hooting they decide to apologize—to the penguins ... The next morning, the hangover brings forth a prim note of contrition.

It makes sense to examine episodes of that sort with reference to the ambient culture and to local and institutional traditions. It was, after all, the quarrel between those sons of Dartmouth who wanted to hang on to the Indian as the traditional college symbol and those who, aspiring to political correctness, wished to replace it that gave birth to the special tensions associated with Dartmouth College. The editor's page in *The American Spectator* overflows with tall-tale American humor, and R. Emmett Tyrrell would be entirely disoriented if he thought it necessary to apologize every time he got Moslems and penguins mixed up. *Private Eye* and the *National Lampoon* would of course go out of existence if so constrained. But ... *quod licet Jovi, non licet bovi: The Dartmouth Review* has occasionally to exercise restraint in order to assert its vaunted essential seriousness. *The American Spectator* manages this by the solid line drawn between Mr. Tyrrell's opening column and the balance of the issue. Such editorial contrivances can be useful.

It has not been officially established who inserted the Hitler quote in the *Review*'s logo. The ADL Commission asserted that "a staffer" was responsible, and the Review's management no longer challenges that probability. Close students of the case have a reasoned idea who it was. If they have the right man, his motives for the mischievous act were unpleasant but were absolutely unrelated to anti-Semitism, given that his acquaintances record not a single episode, written or spoken, that suggests that he suffers from this infirmity. Of the three young editors who had regular access to the relevant computer, two agreed to take polygraph tests, did so, and passed. The third declined.

The Dartmouth Case Goes National

The Hitler-quote incident became national news. Some eighty U.S. congressmen signed a petition condemning the *Review*, which is more congressmen than condemned Kristallnacht in 1938. The Dartmouth administration fought lustily to pin anti-Semitism on the *Review* staff, but the counterattack grew. Official Dartmouth had allies, but they tended to sound formalistic ("We don't like *The Dartmouth Review* and therefore choose to believe that its editors are pro-Hitler") rather than analytical ("Why on earth would *The Dartmouth Review*'s editors *be* for Hitler?"). Cecil Johnson, a black columnist for the *Fort Worth Star-Telegram*, wrote, "Evidence is surfacing that most of those supposedly persecuted student publications, which delight in minority-, gay-, and feminist-bashing and often lapse into gross anti-Semitism, are part of a network that is supported by wealthy and influential conservative individuals and foundations with suspect motives. . . . Perhaps there was sabotage. Still, based upon the past excesses of *Review* staff both in and out of print, there is no doubt that they were capable of such an affront." Mr. Johnson gave voice to what many others were undoubtedly saying to themselves, namely, It doesn't appear that the Hitler thing was done intentionally, which is rather a pity, given that an auto-da-fé by *The Dartmouth Review* is overdue.

The editor, Kevin Pritchett, was difficult to cope with. A local paper (the *Barre Times Argus*) interviewed him and ran the story under the headline, "Is He Villain or Victim?" The interviewer concluded, "Pritchett swears he still has no idea who replaced the magazine's traditional credo . . . 'I mean, Jesus, it's so stupid,' Pritchett says. 'Let's say that I'm the evil anti-Semitic person that did this. It would be like shooting myself in the head. It's something that's unthinkable.'" Richard Cohen, the liberal op-ed columnist for the *Washington Post*, echoed Cecil Johnson's frustration. He wrote with self-evident frustration that the "right-wing brats at the loathsome *Dartmouth Review* may be getting a raw deal."

Pursuant to my practice as above, I quote my own comments on the case as of October 5, 1990.

> I was practicing my scales in North Carolina a couple of days ago, called in to my office, and received word that AP, the *Boston Globe*, the *New York Times*, the *Washington Post*, ABC, CBS, and NBC wished to talk to me.* It flashed through my mind that my wife had defected to the Khmer Rouge, or that my magazine had in my temporary absence come out for Teddy Kennedy for President. No no, I was reassured, it was the Dartmouth situation they all wanted to talk to me about. What was the Dartmouth situation?
>
> As everybody now knows, the latest issue of *The Dartmouth Review* appeared not with the traditional logo from Theodore Roosevelt giving "The *Review* Credo," but with a supplanted stretch of text that no one happened to notice for three whole days. (How often do you pause to read, "All the News That's Fit to Print" when you pick up the *New York Times*?) [The column went on to describe what happened, and the reactions of the editor and of the college administration.] . . .
>
> You would not think that that episode would become a national story, but wait.
>
> Official Dartmouth . . . decided to explode. There is nothing Dartmouth President James Freedman is better at doing than calling the attention of the whole world to the putative delinquencies of his own college. After all, *The Dartmouth Review* is made up of Dartmouth students, it has been around for ten years, its graduates have distinguished themselves in various lines of activity, and it is wonderfully popular with an alumni body much of which reels with embarrassment at Dartmouth's dogged, humorless liberal trendiness.
>
> Now the question is reasonably asked: Is it possible that the editor-in-chief of *The Dartmouth Review* himself injected those lines from Hitler, was frightened by what he had done, and pretended it was the work of someone else? Well, that is a hypothesis worth a moment's attention. It does struggle, however, against the odds.

---

*I should here record that *The Dartmouth Review*, from the first issue on, has included in one of its many tiers on the masthead, "Special Thanks to William F. Buckley, Jr." I have never been told exactly why this practice originated, or at whose prompting. I have never been consulted by the editors about policy; I would as soon the *Review* ended the homage, but I continue to feel it would be ungrateful, even snotty, to say so. I say so now only under duress, in a document that requires me to specify my exact relationship to the *Review*. No doubt the appearance of my name, year after year, was one reason why the news media descended on me. The same masthead lists "The *Review* Advisory Board—Patrick Buchanan, James Cleveland, George Gilder, Guy Hawtin, Mildred Fay Jefferson, Russell Kirk, William Rusher, R. Emmett Tyrrell, James Whelan, Walter Williams." The ADL Commission reports that none of the Advisory Board has ever been consulted by the *Review*'s editors about policy.

Kevin Pritchett is a black student, rather sensitive to race prejudice. For three summers he has worked at the *Wall Street Journal*, distinguishing himself as an intern. Nobody has ever heard him utter an anti-Semitic word. Nor, for that matter, has the Review, which revels in controversy, ever been charged with anti-Semitism. It is, instead, charged with sexism, homophobia, and (non-anti-Semitic) racism, the latter primarily because of its defiant defense of a continuation of the use of the Indian symbol, plus one column using black doggerel to make fun of extremes of affirmative action. Homophobia is of course defined as a belief that homosexuality is aberrational; and sexism means you didn't come out for a woman for President, or for coeducational fraternities.

But so anxious was President Freedman to give the impression that the Hitler quote was the collective responsibility of all the editors of the *Review* that he called an anti-hate rally, in which a thousand or so Dartmouth students convened to prove that they hated hate more than anybody since St. Matthew.

But the hate-haters are going to have to practice a little, as witness the treatment of one writer for *The Dartmouth Review*. Outside his dormitory, students gathered to chant "Sieg Heil!" And outside his door a large swastika was placed, decorated with the phrase, "Nazi Pig."

Andrew Baer, '93, was not amused. Perhaps because, as he put it in a public statement: "I am a staff writer for *The Dartmouth Review* and a descendant of Holocaust survivors. More than thirty members of my family perished in ways so horrible that they defy description. They died for one reason and one reason alone, because they were Jewish."*

In his op-ed piece for the *New York Times*, President Freedman continued his comprehensive charges against the *Review*, repeating the charge: "For the past ten years *The Dartmouth Review* ... has attracted national attention with its brazen attacks on blacks, women, homosexuals, native Americans, and Jews." Two months later, President Freedman was required, by his prejudgment, to ignore the finding of a human-rights official. Here is the Associated Press account of December 31, 1990:

No Bias Seen in "Review"
By The Associated Press
MANCHESTER—The head of New Hampshire's Human Rights Commission is wondering "what all the fuss was about" regarding criticism of *The Dartmouth Review*.

---

*The column concluded, "It is an old temptation to fool just a little bit with the authorized text. Thus the *London Times*' early edition reported that the Queen, on returning from her coronation, 'paused at Westminster Bridge and peed over the City of London.' The *New York Times* never caught the hacker who would certainly have lost his job for inserting the single comma in the headline on the social page, 'Jacqueline Screws, / Becomes Affianced.'

"Mr. Pritchett thinks he knows who the malefactor is. If he will just identify himself, he is guaranteed to receive an honorary degree from President Freedman."

Barry Palmer of Nashua, a copy editor for the *Union Leader* of Manchester, said he read two years of issues of the *Review* and found no evidence of discrimination against blacks, women, homosexuals, or Jews.

Palmer, the commission chairman, said he conducted the study as an individual, not on behalf of the commission, after continued criticism of the paper by Dartmouth College President James Freedman, who said the paper consistently attacks those groups.

Criticizing blacks, women, homosexuals, or Jews is not prejudice as long as the criticism is based on performance, and not sexual or racial status, Palmer said.

Political profiteering from the episode was rank. In a later column I gave an example:

Alan Lupo, a correspondent for the *Boston Globe*, writes about John MacGovern, who is running hard and successfully [for Congress] against the incumbent head of the Democratic Party of Massachusetts. MacGovern was one of the founders of *The Dartmouth Review* and refuses to disavow it for the best of reasons, namely that other than occasional sophomoric excesses, the paper—which has had three women editors, Jewish editors, Third World editors, and has been consistently pro-Israel in foreign affairs—is none of the things popularly suggested. Lupo reveals that MacGovern's father was a Jew-hating Feeneyite. . . . That's true. And he died when MacGovern was four years old. Lupo concludes, "MacGovern may not have a bigoted bone in his body, but his history and associations raise serious questions about his judgment and his qualifications for Congress."

Meanwhile his opponent, the incumbent Atkins, has a radio ad. "'By warding off the Jews, I am doing the Lord's work.' Adolf Hitler wrote those words back in 1924, words of hate and intolerance. But those words are back to haunt us. *The Dartmouth Review* printed those words on its masthead on Yom Kippur, and John MacGovern, candidate for Congress and founder of the *Review*, refuses to separate himself from those words of hate."

The Israel Connection

In the sections on Joe Sobran and Pat Buchanan we examined the question of a nexus between anti-Semitism and opposition to the policies of Israel. We have looked at statements that suggest that hostility to Israel 1) has zero connection with anti-Semitism, 2) warns of the possibility of latent anti-Semitism, and (the most extreme) 3) is tantamount to anti-Semitism. Believing as I do that opposition to Israel ought not to be thought of as presumptive anti-Semitism, I think it right to probe the contrapositive assumption, namely that friendship toward Israel exonerates one from any suspicion of anti-Semitism.

I think this is as a practical matter true, though not conclusively so. It is difficult to imagine someone who is anti-Semitic and pro-Israel. But such could exist, e.g., the (hypothetical) man who wishes Zionism to flower so that Jews in the rest of the world would be attracted to emigrate; so to speak, inaugurating an anti-diasporization.

In the Dartmouth case, the *Review's* editors and their friends made much, in their defense, of pro-Israel positions adopted by the journal over the years. In writing to the Anti-Defamation League urging it to undertake an investigation, *Dartmouth Review* trustee Dinesh D'Souza included in his letter the sentence, "Indeed, over the past ten years, the *Review* has steadfastly editorialized in favor of Israel—an increasingly rare position on college campuses." And added, "The newspaper has always had Jewish editors and staffers. These facts are hardly consistent with a pro-Hitler editorial policy." The journalist and novelist Sidney Zion was up front on the question: "*The Dartmouth Review* has strongly supported Israel for ten years. Anyone who says it is anti-Semitic is meshugga." In a statement written in its own defense, the *Review* appended a page headlined, "The *Review* Is Pro-Semitic and Pro-Israeli." It listed fourteen stories and editorials published in the preceding five years friendly to Israel and opposed to anti-Semitism, including, for example, articles under the headings, "Is the Romance Over? American Jews and the Left" (December 11, 1985, by Steve Kaplitt), and "Can the PLO Play a Part in Peace?" [No.] (May 30, 1990, by Allison Hoffman). The *Review* also drew attention to the student journal *Stet,* college-supported (unlike the *Review*) and Marxist, which is a tirade against Israel, assigning all the blame for the Arab–Israeli conflict to "Jewish aggression." The single issue of *Stet* I have examined would justify not the conclusion that its editors were anti-Semitic, but the suspicion that their passionate pro-Palestinianism might lead them, or has led them, in that direction. In any event, those who believe that anti-Semitism and pro-Israelism can't fit into the same editorial mindset had grounds on which to step forward to reject official Dartmouth's charge against the editors of *The Dartmouth Review.*

Mr. Butterfield's Anxiety

Among the dismaying results of facile and opportunistic charges of anti-Semitism is: pride-stoking. Pride can resist at almost any cost the call to—apologize. People are regularly wedded to positions they took even impulsively. A major victim of the episode was Fox Butterfield of the *New York Times.* I wrote him a personal letter on October 7. He replied with a telephone call when I was out of my office. Two subsequent attempts to reach him were unsuccessful. Three weeks later I gave up on him and published in my column the private letter I had written to him.

"Dear Fox, ... You know how highly I rate your work." (The reference is to his classic book on Mao's China, *China: Alive in the Bitter Sea*.) "For that reason I was especially alarmed by the lead sentence in this morning's *New York Times* piece on *The Dartmouth Review*, to wit, 'For a decade, many students and professors at Dartmouth College have watched with quiet dismay—and occasional anger—as a handful of writers at a conservative weekly shaped a public perception of Dartmouth as hostile toward blacks, women, and Jews.'

"I take the liberty," I went on, "of enclosing [my] column on the [*Dartmouth Review*] published today ... I record in it that there has never [heretofore] been a charge of anti-Semitism made against the *Review*. Racking my mind since reading your piece, I do recall something at the expense of President Freedman that used Third Reich formalisms of some kind or another, but it was clearly miscast drollery rather than anti-Semitism. I see only three or four issues of the *Review* every year. But I am highly sensitive to anti-Semitism and yours is the very first article I have ever seen in which it is matter-of-factly set down that the *Review* has that reputation. I am quite sure that you are wrong. If I am wrong, I do wish you would let me know of it, and I will, I assure you, take strenuous and public measures to disengage."

He did reply, by letter. He recited the story of the sukkah and the *Review*'s note that "the Zionists have gone too far." "The incident," he wrote, "rightly or wrongly, was blamed on the editors of the *Review*, and thus began a sense that the *Review* was anti-Semitic." As we have seen, the destruction of the sukkah was not blamed on the *Review* in responsible quarters, and the ADL Commission's report specifically exonerated the *Review*.

Butterfield went on to cite the "Ein Reich, Ein Volk, Ein Freedmann" story, examined above, which he said was viewed by some as anti-Semitic, and he added: "It is against this background that the latest flap occurred. . . . Honest men can differ over the meaning of these incidents. Perhaps they do only amount to miscast drollery. But having talked to the rabbi at Dartmouth and having listened to a number of Jewish undergraduates, I feel safe in saying that they believe the *Review* has anti-Semitic tendencies."

This is not responsible commentary for a *New York Times* reporter who began an important story, "For a decade, many students and professors at Dartmouth College have watched with quiet dismay . . . as a handful of writers at a conservative weekly shaped a public perception of Dartmouth as hostile toward blacks, women, and Jews." Two ambiguous incidents over a period of ten years, punctuated by regular pro-Israel editorial positions and the election of Jewish editors and staffers. Applying such criteria in search of anti-Semitism, Mr. Butterfield, I do not doubt, could accuse any journal in the United States of "shaping" a "perception" of anti-Semitism, though perhaps he would not succeed in documenting the ambient "quiet dismay."

The Toxic Waste

There is one guaranteed way to encourage anti-Semitism, and that is to discover it with thunderous indignation in the conduct or utterances of people you disagree with on matters that have nothing whatever to do with Jews or even with Israel. *The Dartmouth Review* isn't about Jews or about Israel, but it is loathed by the Dartmouth administration, which therefore calls it anti-Semitic. *The Nation* magazine can call *The Dartmouth Review* a "hate sheet" and nobody much cares, because (as we shall see below) people who aren't votaries don't expect reasonable editorial conduct from *The Nation*. But the immunities of those who huddle in the fever swamps do not extend to such as the president and administration of Dartmouth College or to important correspondents of the *New York Times*. The fallout of anti-anti-Semitology, moreover, while difficult to quantify, is nevertheless legitimately resented. One gentleman (a neighbor, his stationery reveals) buys the Freedman line and closes a letter to me, "The use of your name helps to give *The Dartmouth Review* credibility that it hasn't earned and doesn't deserve. Isn't it time to dissociate yourself by asking the *Review* to express its 'special thanks' to someone else?"

Another letter, this one from "parents of two sons who are graduates of Dartmouth College": "Most ominous and upsetting to us is the reported fact that several nationally prominent conservatives are supporting this magazine . . . Your name appears among them. . . . We consider you an intelligent conservative with no anti-Semitic or other racist views. Therefore it surprises and disappoints us that . . . you have not up until now come out with a repudiation of its activities." And from Humphrey Tonkin, president of the University of Hartford: "The article by James Freedman in today's *New York Times* only confirms what we already know* from several years of news reports. Don't you think it is time you publicly disassociated yourself from *The Dartmouth Review*?"†

---

*"It is not only what he doesn't know, but what he does know that isn't so." Freud—on Havelock Ellis, was it?

†R. Emmett Tyrrell of *The American Spectator* received such a letter, demanding that he withdraw as a supporter of *The Dartmouth Review*. His answer: "I have now read your letter twice: once while under the influence of a nigh unto invincible influenza and immediately after liberation. Frankly it reads best when accompanied by flu. I have decided to withdraw my association with *The Dartmouth Review* when all right-thinking profs withdraw their association with Dartmouth. The *Review* at least has the excuse of answering to a comic afflatus."

Some letters were intellectually vulgar beyond hope ("Would you knowingly support a publication that quotes Adolf Hitler in its credo?"). Others give the sense of enjoying an opportunity to intimidate. Gerald E. Kochansky, "Ph.D.," sends copies of his letter to Freedman, to the board of trustees of Dartmouth, to the board of directors of Hopkins Institute, and to the editors of *The Dartmouth Review*, the *Daily Dartmouth*, the *Boston Globe*, and the *New York Times*. The operative sentence of his letter is, "If you continue to support *The Dartmouth Review*, any reasonable observer will conclude that your failure to withdraw your financial support [I have never financially supported the *Review*] or to repudiate the publication demonstrates your own bigotry or your tolerance of bigoted attitudes and behavior." But then anyone who has a mailbox is an easy target of bigotry.

4 · *The Nation*

If the survival of Joe Sobran as a columnist, Pat Buchanan as a media conglomerate, and *The Dartmouth Review* as a thriving college journal is a setback for organized anti-anti-Semitology, it is probably the case that the great reversal began in 1986 with an article by Gore Vidal in *The Nation*. Here Vidal was genuinely and intentionally and derisively anti-Semitic by whatever definition of the term. There is this qualification: namely that he spoke from the Left, which, because it enjoys a certain immunity, watches its language less closely than the Right. It is an immunity that goes with the avant-garde, with iconoclasm. Moreover, in recent years—in particular since the Vietnam War—the Left has tended to identify itself with the anti-military establishment, and Israel gives the impression of being something of a garrison state and is—if only for that reason—an object of inertial disparagement and ridicule.

For Gore Vidal, who is attracted to impiety, Israel and its devout supporters are natural targets. The surprise came not so much when he attacked them as when, so to speak without giving it much thought, the editor of *The Nation*, himself Jewish, published the attack without comment.

The eyebrow-raising aftermath had practically nothing to do with what Vidal said (nobody much cared), but a great deal to do with his having got away with saying it in *The Nation*. Norman Podhoretz devoted the lead essay in *Commentary* (November 1986) to a long article he called

"The Hate That Dare Not Speak Its Name." He wrote about the failure of the Vidal piece to mobilize the community generally associated with interracial hygiene. As with his earlier essay ("J'Accuse"), Podhoretz failed to rouse the troops. We will explore alternative explanations why, the most plausible of them that anti-anti-Semitism is alarmingly frail as it walks into senior citizenship, forty years after the Holocaust.

The Vidal Piece

The two-page piece by Vidal was entitled "The Empire Lovers Strike Back." Ostensibly the essay was animated by Vidal's concern to strengthen a point previously made by him, namely that the white races of the world needed to band together to meet the economic challenge of the yellow races by calling off the silly cold war that divided us and the Soviet Union, with which we should be allied (this was three years before the liberation of Eastern Europe).

What Vidal was clearly most looking forward to was an opportunity to disparage Norman Podhoretz and his wife, Midge Decter. He went through a Lenny Bruce routine at their expense but then appeared to get very serious. He said that Podhoretz had moved right in the political spectrum in recent years. And he, Gore Vidal, knew why.

Well, why? Here is why.

> The reason for that is simple. In order to get Treasury money for Israel (last year $3 billion), pro-Israel lobbyists must see to it that America's "the Russians are coming" squads are in place so that they can continue to frighten the American people into spending enormous sums for "defense," which also means the support of Israel in its never-ending wars against just about everyone. To make sure that nearly a third of the federal budget goes to the Pentagon and Israel, it is necessary for the pro-Israel lobbyists to make common cause with our lunatic right. Hence, the virulent propaganda.

This is historical exegesis in the special style of Vidal and is interesting only in respect of the search for the shape, forms, and locus of anti-Semitism. Having said that Podhoretz's geopolitical views are anchored to the question, What is needed to continue to send $3 billion to Israel?, Vidal went on to write that Podhoretz is not really an assimilated American. "Rather, his first loyalty would always be to Israel. Yet he and Midge stay on among us, in order to make propaganda and raise money for Israel—a country they don't seem eager to live in. Jewish joke, circa 1900: A Zionist is someone who wants to ship other people off to Palestine."

You see, Vidal explains, Midge Decter has no historical sense of the wrong of American imperialism. This is so "because in the Middle East another predatory people is busy stealing other people's land in the name of an alien theocracy. She is a propagandist for these predators (paid for?) [*sic*], and that is what all this nonsense is about."

Vidal is hardly, in this screening, a mere insinuator:

> Since spades may not be called spades in freedom's land, let me spell it all out. In order to get military and economic support for Israel, a small number of American Jews, who should know better, have made common cause with every sort of reactionary and anti-Semitic group in the United States, from the corridors of the Pentagon to the TV studios of the evangelical Jesus-Christers. [I am genuinely at a loss as to what Vidal means here. That some American Jews collaborate with Christian fundamentalists who regard Israel as a chosen land? How?] To show that their hearts are in the far-right place, they call themselves neoconservatives, and attack the likes of . . . me, all in the interest of supporting the likes of Sharon and Israel as opposed to the Peace Now Israelis whom they disdain. There is real madness here; mischief too.

Vidal quotes Miss Decter: "Well, one thing is clear in all this muddle. Mr. Vidal does not like his country." Vidal replies, "Poor Midge. Of course I like my country. After all, I'm its current biographer. But now that we're really leveling with each other, I've got to tell you I don't much like your country, which is Israel."

At this point, as tends to happen to Vidal, he goes a little banshee. It is instructive to record his performance:

> Although there is nothing wrong with being a lobbyist for a foreign power, one is supposed to register with the Justice Department. Also, I should think that tact would require a certain forbearance when it comes to the politics of the host country. But tact is unknown to the Podhoretzes. Joyously they revel in the politics of hate, with plangent attacks on blacks and/or fags and/or liberals, trying, always, to outdo those moral majoritarians who will, as Armageddon draws near, either convert all the Jews, just as the Good Book says, or kill them.

In that last sentence, there is the sense of neuroses approaching typhonic speed in the mind, the sense of the rush of the daemon taking over the controls as Vidal becomes Captain Queeg tripping into the high delirium it was his original purpose to conceal.

Podhoretz Makes His Move

What actually to do about such a performance? To ignore it would seem to make primary sense, and one supposes this would have been done if the screed had appeared in *Screw* magazine, where Vidal has in the past left some of his deposits. But for all that *The Nation* is eccentric-left, it is here and there read by bright people, and the issue in which Vidal's piece was published was the magazine's 120th-anniversary issue.

Podhoretz decided to ignore what the article said, but not to ignore its appearance.

So what he did was write a letter and address it to each of "twenty-nine friends and supporters of *The Nation* whose names were selected both from the magazine's masthead and from the congratulatory messages which had appeared in the anniversary issue."*

As Podhoretz explained in an essay written several months later, Vidal's article "impressed me and many other people as the most blatantly anti-Semitic outburst to have appeared in a respectable American periodical since World War II. *The Nation* is a left-wing (or, some would say, a liberal) magazine run by an editor, Victor Navasky, who is himself Jewish. Yet one reader (who happened not to be Jewish) wrote in a personal letter to Navasky [copy to Podhoretz] that he could not recall encountering 'that kind of naked anti-Semitism' even in papers of the lunatic-fringe Right which specialize in attacks on Jews; to find its like one had to go back to the *Völkische Beobachter*. Nor was he the only reader to be reminded of the Nazi gutter press. 'I thought I was back in the Thirties reading *Der Stürmer*,' wrote another."

Podhoretz's lengthy essay cited historical stereotypes of the alien Jew, some exactly reproduced in Vidal's piece. He examined the possibility that Vidal was nursing personal grievances (not many Jewish critics have taken him seriously as America's "biographer," but then not many non-Jewish critics have either). And Podhoretz made ample room for the dislike by many Americans of positions associated with him and with his wife, and therefore of their derivative dislike of him (it is only human to move from the dislike of a position to a dislike of the position's sponsors). "What I most hoped for," Podhoretz wrote, "was not that others would spring to my defense, but that a protest would be mounted by people sympathetic to *The Nation*'s left-wing political position who would say that while they detested everything Norman Podhoretz, Midge Decter, and all the other neoconservatives stood for, and while nothing made them happier than seeing neoconservatives raked over the coals, they were

---

*They were: Floyd Abrams, Bella Abzug, Leonard Bernstein, Norman Birnbaum, Bill Bradley, Arthur L. Carter, Ramsey Clark, Arthur C. Danto, Osborn Elliott, Richard Falk, Frances Fitzgerald, Fred Friendly, Seymour Hersh, Arthur Hertzberg, Charlayne Hunter-Gault, Peter Jennings, Edward Kennedy, Edward Koch, Elinor Langer, Eugene McCarthy, Sidney Morgenbesser, Aryeh Neier, Robert Silvers, Paul Simon, Gloria Steinem, Rose Styron, Mike Wallace, Tom Wicker, Roger Wilkins.

outraged by the reintroduction of anti-Semitism into American political discourse in general and their own political community in particular."

The result of the twenty-nine letters that went out from *Commentary* (signed by Marion Magid, the magazine's managing editor), was a total of eight responses. Of the eight, only five* "said they saw anything wrong with the article or with *The Nation*'s decision to publish it." Two (Norman Birnbaum, Tom Wicker) attacked the *Commentary* letter, "either saying nothing about Vidal at all (Birnbaum) or explicitly denying that his article was anti-Semitic (Wicker). The third, the journalist Roger Wilkins, writing to *The Nation* for publication, called Vidal's piece 'splendid.' By contrast, Wilkins said, the attacks on it as anti-Semitic were 'ugly mumblings,' a species of McCarthyism, and a threat to the First Amendment."

Podhoretz then re-examined the standard objection: "Striking a note that would be heard over and over again from defenders of Vidal, Wilkins declared: 'Scoundrels have many last refuges. One is to attack as anti-Semitic any criticism of the policies of any given government of Israel or of any supporters of Israel, no matter how frothing those supporters may be.' . . .

"To put the same idea another way," Podhoretz commented, "it is permissible to make anti-Semitic statements, but it is impermissible to call such statements anti-Semitic."

Anti-Israel Equals Anti-Semitic?

It was a melancholy day at *Commentary*, and indeed for the anti-anti-Semitic community. Podhoretz had been generous in making allowances,† but he did not disguise his dismay.

> . . . one glaring and ugly fact remained: a large number of prominent liberals and leftists who had publicly associated themselves in one way or another with *The Nation*, and whose names had appeared in one capacity or another in the very issue containing so blatantly anti-Semitic an article, had not been sufficiently outraged to register disapproval or to express a protest. Nor did many others on the Left respond by . . . describing Vidal's article as a foul anti-Semitic outburst and expressing dismay or disgust at the fact that a

---

*Floyd Abrams, Richard Falk, Rabbi Arthur Hertzberg, Sidney Morgenbesser, Aryeh Neier.

†"It may be that the politicians among them (Mayor Koch, Senator Bradley, Senator Kennedy) were never shown the letter by whoever handles their mail. This may also have been the case with the media personalities (Peter Jennings of ABC, Mike Wallace of CBS, Charlayne Hunter-Gault of PBS) or with a busy celebrity like Leonard Bernstein."

magazine professedly devoted to liberal ideals should have given house room to such an article.

Podhoretz quoted some commentators on the subject, and gave special room to Edwin M. Yoder, Jr., the highly literate columnist and editor, associated with the moderate Right. Podhoretz was greatly surprised by Yoder, who dismissed the Vidal essay as innocent of any true bias. It was, Yoder insisted, only "mischievous and cutting . . . in Vidal's best polemical manner."

Podhoretz wrote that Yoder "also counterattacked with the accusation that I, like many (most?) American Jews, have tried to silence any and all criticism of Israel by denouncing such criticism as anti-Semitic, even while pretending otherwise." Yoder had written: "Podhoretz graciously concedes that 'it is possible to criticize Israel without being anti-Semitic.' Thanks, we needed that. But has Podhoretz noticed that if one is critical of an Israeli policy one may be accused of attacking Israel's legitimacy? And, just beyond that, of being a crypto anti-Semite? It was that very logic that drove Podhoretz to mistake Vidal's hard-edged teasing for anti-Semitism."

Podhoretz, who is a skilled verbal pathologist, works hard and successfully to surface the relevant distinction. He did this most usefully here by quoting at some length from the history of his differences with *International Herald-Tribune* columnist William Pfaff, who had delivered (Podhoretz's description) "a lecture on how 'reasonable people' should conduct themselves in discussing the subject of Israel." But, Podhoretz comments, "his main concern . . . was clearly to establish the right of 'an American to criticize or oppose the policies of the state of Israel . . . without an anti-Semitic motivation being imputed.'

"Once again, then, the issue was shifted from the appearance of an anti-Semitic article in a respectable left-wing magazine to the alleged efforts by people like me to silence any and all criticism of Israel."

On this point Pfaff let it be known that he knew, he knew what would be the probable rejoinder. Podhoretz quotes him:

"I have . . . been myself denounced by Mr. Podhoretz as anti-Semitic because of things I wrote about Israel's conduct during the siege of Beirut in 1982," he told his readers. What he did not tell them was that in one of these "things" he had begun by asserting that in Israel's conduct "Hitler's work goes on," and he had concluded by predicting that Hitler might soon "find rest in Hell" through "the knowledge that the Jews themselves, in Israel, have finally accepted his own way of looking at things." In my article "J'Accuse," I did indeed denounce these words (*not* Pfaff himself) as anti-Semitic.

The engaging point here made has, of course, its complement at the other end of polemical exchanges on the question. Just as it is, at the very least, bizarre to compare the activity of the Israeli army in Lebanon in 1982 to that of the Nazi military anywhere—on the grounds, really, that any analogies between non-totalitarian military and such military as did the work of the Nazis and the Communists are misfits—it is also wrong for such as Abe Rosenthal to invoke Auschwitz when criticizing such things as were done by Pat Buchanan. Another way to put it is that comparisons between the conduct of the Israeli military and that of the legions of Adolf Hitler arouse, and should do so, visions of extermination-camp warfare, and the writer should not intend this unless—how to put it?—he *really intends* it, which is improbable. The comparisons are historically, morally, and forensically unseemly: both the comparison of Israeli military behavior to Nazi military behavior, and the escalation of an anti-Semitic wisecrack like Buchanan's into extermination-camp offensiveness.

Podhoretz continued:

> Since Pfaff (like Yoder a decent man who is intelligent enough to know better) remains convinced that comparing Israel to Nazi Germany represents a "reasonable" application to the Jewish state "of the same moral and political judgments as one applies to the conduct of other states," it is no wonder that all he can see in Vidal is an innocent "critic" of Israel like himself. What he does not see is that it is *he*, and Yoder and Wilkins and Wicker, who erase the line between legitimate criticism of Israel and anti-Semitism by their unwillingness or inability to distinguish between the former and a clear case of the latter like the Vidal article (or like his own comparisons of Israel with Nazi Germany).

This is solemn and responsible criticism, and it informs us, in our search for anti-Semitism, of the mischief done by hyperbole when it reaches out to the dark and highly exclusive corners inhabited by anti-Semitism of the Hitlerian kind. At the same time, it imposes disciplines on the anti-anti-Semites. An anti-Semitic crack like Buchanan's isn't of the kind that threatens the discrete territory of Auschwitz. In the post-Hitler world, the flight path of workaday anti-Semitism isn't genocidal. Restraint is enjoined rather by civility and reverence than by any sense of clear and present danger. To call somebody a "whore" in Hollywood exposes her to a different order of discomfort from calling somebody a whore in seventeenth-century Salem.

Yet the discontinuity is rhetorically difficult to handle. We have heard people distinguish between "country club" anti-Semitism and naked anti-Israelism and genocidal indifference. The pain comes from the historical knowledge that prejudice of the first kind can metastasize—and has done so, to be sure by mutation—into Auschwitz. The struggle would appear to be to re-legitimize the first kind of prejudice, as one of the evil fruits of free speech and association, while confining its moral offensiveness within reason. The area in which this fight is being waged centers not on country-club admissions, but on Israel. The conviction among some Americans, such as Yoder and Pfaff, is that U.S. policy is manipulated by Jewish Americans who are hell-bent on serving Israeli interests and are prepared to use the weapon of alleged anti-Semitism to immobilize their opponents. The other position is that there resides, in some people's criticisms of Israel, an animus; that that animus is traceable to anti-Semitic dispositions; and that these dispositions need hosing down by moral exposure, for fear that that great fever might be rekindled which once gave us the Holocaust.

The Reaction in "The Nation"

This essay is heavy with quotations from 1) offenders against interreligious comity, 2) defenders of same, 3) anti-anti-Semitologists, 4) analysts of the phenomenon, 5) persons who are confused by the question and tormented by it, 6) defenders of a code of honor in respect of questions having to do with anti-Semitism, and 7) opportunists, apologists, exhibitionists, and provocateurs, who seek to explore the modes by which the question of anti-Semitism is discussed. The classic preface to Fowler's paragraphs on the split infinitive comes to mind: "The English-speaking world may be divided into 1) those who neither know nor care what a split infinitive is; 2) those who do not know, but care very much; 3) those who know and condemn; 4) those who know and approve; and 5) those who know and distinguish." It is nevertheless useful, I think, to quote comprehensively from those who engage themselves in the quarrel, with one eye on their modus operandi, and the mind inquisitive as to their motives, especially to the extent that these are either unstated or presumptively disguised.

The issues of The Nation (April 26 and May 3, 1986) that devoted their Letters columns to discussing the Vidal piece are in this respect instructive.

One issue led off with a brief letter from First Amendment fundamentalist Floyd Abrams. Abrams deplored the Vidal essay and "the vulgarity to which Vidal is now reduced in his writing," regretting that The Nation would permit its anniversary issue "to be thus soiled." His objection, and the language in which it was phrased, suggested a chemical personal repugnance to what Abrams views as vulgar anti-Semitism. To this objection Vidal (whom the editor had invited to answer critical letters as they appeared) gave a flippant reply: "Simply because, as a lawyer, Floyd

Abrams lost *The Nation*'s First Amendment case to a bad novelist named Gerald Ford is no reason not to remain friends."*

Paul Weyrich, the conservative leader, president of the Free Congress Research and Education Foundation, wrote that, "thankfully, Vidal's vitriolic attacks are so patently unfair and wrongheaded that few except the most rabidly anti-Semitic and ultra-leftist will agree with them. . . . Podhoretz and Decter certainly don't have to prove their loyalty to the United States or explain their support for Israel, one of the few liberal democracies in the world"—a response that sought to defend not only Podhoretz and Decter, but Israel. To this Vidal commented, "Is it possible to have 'one of the few liberal democracies in the world' and exclude from citizenship more than 700,000 Arabs?" The answer to this is, simply, Yes: unless one is willing to rule out the legitimacy of a Jewish nation-state. Which is Israel's *raison d'être*. And the generality that citizenship is denied to Arabs does not distinguish between those Arabs who live in Israel proper and those who live in the captured territories. The former, as we have seen, have citizenship rights, including the vote, although it is true that civil disabilities attach to those of them who decline to serve in the military.

But on the question faced by those Israelis who fear demographic subjugation, there is the point to be made that if, ultimately, a vote were given to every Arab, the state the Israelis created, by means fair and foul, would evolve into another Moslem state. If the point is that a state cannot be designated as a "liberal democracy" if certain residents within that state are denied full citizenship, then the whole question arises of a state's authority over immigration laws, and corollary questions having to do with the effects of cultural factors on immigration laws. The Oriental-exclusion acts at the turn of the century were especially objectionable instituted by a country that prided itself on its melting-pot mission. But the society that passed those laws did not cease to qualify, on account of its sponsorship of them, as a liberal democracy even though it hadn't yet got around to giving the vote to seventh-generation Bostonian women.

In answer to Micah Morrison (deputy director, Committee for the Free World), protesting the charge of mixed loyalty, Vidal asks, "Question: What happens if the national interest of Israel is exactly opposite that of the United States? Under which flag does the Israeli-American serve?" To raise the question is to suggest that it is a question a Jewish American might one day need to ask himself. The implied premise is that if so drastic a divergence of interests should happen, the Israelis would clearly be wrong. To begin with, this is unsophisticated. Israel is peopled by refugees, and there is a hypothetical

---

*Floyd Abrams defended *The Nation* unsuccessfully when it prepublished without permission excerpts from President Ford's memoirs.

possibility that the future will see refugees from Israel. But then that also is so of the United States. Americans might some day leave America for the same reasons, *mutatis mutandis*, that impelled people in the seventeenth century to come to America.

A second objection is that the question sets up quandaries too surrealistic for the addressee to imagine. If an American citizen is also loyal to another country (protective toward it would more exactly describe what we are talking about), it should be assumed that this is so because that country inspires attachment, tracing to common ancestry, common religion, whatever. If that country and the citizen's incumbent country were now divided by irreconcilable differences, feelings toward the alien country would presumably evanesce: after all, American Jews choose to live in America, not in Israel. A Catholic would be hard put to answer an analogous question, since he would assume that if the Vatican were overtaken by anti-Christian elements, it would cease to be an institution to which the American Catholic felt any loyalty.

To Irving M. Levine of the American Jewish Committee, who cites proudly the hard-liberal credentials of the AJC and pauses to give *Commentary* what sounds like stepfatherly advice, Vidal replies that "the Podhoretzes are doing more to arouse the essential anti-Semitism of the American people than anyone since Father Coughlin." The planted axiom here is that the American people are essentially anti-Semitic. The postwar record of American behavior—toward Israel, toward racial discrimination, toward ecumenism—demolishes that assumption. It leaves open the one question: whether an unblinking endorsement by the preponderant majority of Jewish Americans of Israeli policies offensive to standards by which Americans judge other people, other nations, might revive an anti-Semitism that isn't exactly dead. That question raises the higher question of co-responsibility. We could, and did, become very anti-German while Hitler was in power, but a very few years after Hitler was dead, anti-German sentiment in America was pretty well gone. It might be said that this was so because there are natural affinities at work to unite a typical American and a typical German.

In the case of Japan, we became convincingly anti-Japanese in the days of Tojo, but after we hanged him we were benevolent toward the Japanese. There is, today, a rising anti-Japanese sentiment, but this has to do with economic damage attributable to Japanese prowess in the marketplace. Because the Japanese is distinctive in appearance, it is easier to personalize that prejudice.

In respect of the Jew it is different. If America turned against Jews because they were thought slavish defenders of intolerable policies, we would confront, in pursuit of anti-Semitism, more readily identifiable figures, in some cases, than the German-American; less readily identifiable, in every case, than the Japanese-American. Some American Jews have distinguishable physical features, and they do not, after all, attend Christian churches. Whether they are otherwise identifiable as Jews has to do with the questions introduced above concerning "group characteristics." Thirty years ago Israeli parents were complaining that their young children, finding themselves in a society in which anti-Semitic discrimination was inconceivable, were relaxing traditional standards, greatly needed elsewhere in order to excel. This would suggest that as acculturation proceeds, the American Jew will not be as distinguishable as he once was. The group characteristics of which Charles Seymour spoke are progressively impalpable. On the other hand, observers can confidently document that whatever the experience of young Israelis, there aren't yet any indications that Jewish affinity for intellectual distinction or for the arts is dissipating at a noticeable rate of speed.

To the editor of the *China Daily News*, Evans Chan, who wrote to *The Nation* to protest Vidal's Yellow Peril business, Vidal commented that, after all, the yellow races were doing no more to us than we have done to them in the past, and we have only to take the obvious countermeasures. "I propose that the United States and the Soviet Union—two economic wrecks, thanks to the arms race—as the two great powers of the Northern Hemisphere, unite in order to compete, *economically,* with the Asiatic world." Mr. Vidal's notion of the critical contribution that the Soviet Union is in a position to make to the economic ascendancy of the West will no doubt inspire reformers in what is left of the Soviet economy.

Rabbi Arthur Hertzberg regretted that Vidal "veers off into a diatribe against both Jews and Arabs, suggesting that he would not weep very much if they got out of America's hair, even if that meant that they would 'blow one another up, or whatever.' This is the screaming rhetoric of American nativism, in the accents of patrician highhandedness and self-righteousness. Gore Vidal has clearly been reading too much of Henry Adams." Vidal: "This was my 'screaming rhetoric': 'The time has come for the United States to stop all aid not only to Israel but to Jordan, Egypt, and the rest of the Arab world. The Middle Easterners would then be obliged to make peace, or blow one another up, or whatever.' The good rabbi, eager to add his eloquent voice to the chorus of hate, carefully left out 'to make peace,' the whole point to my suggestion. Luckily, I am used to being lied about." Anyone who lies about Mr. Vidal is doing him a kindness.

And What of Zionism?

Let us concede that some critics of Israel *are* in fact anti-Semitic. An illuminating way to put it is this: Suppose that Israel were, in a vague kind of way, an entirely model society, insulated from border wars or ethnic strife, vaguely liberal, progressive, something on the order of, oh,

Sweden. Resolute anti-Semites would then need to look for grounds other than the policies of the Israeli government in order to exercise their prejudice.

Would they merely refocus their energies on keeping the American Jew out of the country club? Or would they need greater scope to exercise their animus?

It is hard to say. Daniel Patrick Moynihan, when blasting the United Nations General Assembly in 1975 for its resolution "Zionism is a form of racism . . . ," reminds us that in the late nineteenth century, anti-Semitism was frustrated by the ambient secularism. So long as anti-Semitic energies could be directed at Jewish theological practices, anti-Semites could appease their appetites. But as religion began to matter less and less, differences in religious practice mattered correspondingly less and less; so that, for instance, the ancient wars between Catholics and Protestants became formalistic, except in those areas where Catholics and Protestants 1) occupied different territories, 2) came from different racial stock, and 3) yearned—or did not yearn—for national independence. This situation is unique to Ireland, where hostilities continue to this day, making possible the old saw about the visitor who is perplexed by the endless religious antagonism and blurts out, "But aren't there any *atheists* in Ireland?" "Yes," his guide concedes, "but there are *Catholic* atheists and *Protestant* atheists."

Moynihan places the evolution of ethnic anti-Semitism in the two or three decades before the turn of the century, his purpose here being to illustrate to his fellow delegates at the United Nations how terribly wrongheaded they were in imputing racism to Zionism.

The good guys in the General Assembly did not have all that easy a terminological time of it up against their tormentors who insisted on the Zionist–racist linkage, and this was owing to a technicality. Ambassador Abdallah al-Sayegh of Kuwait (and others) noted that Article 1 of the UN's Declaration on the Elimination of All Forms of Racial Discrimination included under the term "racial discrimination" any "distinction, exclusion, restriction, or preference based on . . . national or ethnic origin." Zionism, he charged, is a "concrete political ideology" manifested in "concrete practices which have the effect of excluding some people on the basis of their being non-Jews and including others on the basis of their being Jews—Jewishness being defined officially as an ethnic and not strictly religious definition."

Now this is in part true. Abe's mother, Rebecca, is Jewish. According to Jewish law, Abe is Jewish—unless he renounces Judaism and embraces Christianity. Absent such a renunciation, he has the right to instant citizenship in Israel (The Law of Return). That right extends equally to anyone, of whatever religious or ethnic background, who formally converts to Orthodox Judaism.

If Abe is indifferent to his religion but doesn't convert to Christianity, all he needs to do, should he desire full citizenship in Israel, is to adduce his mother's religion. This option is not available to non-Jews. Given that Abe's relation to his mother is biological and derivatively ethnic, his claim to Israeli citizenship can be held to trade on ethnic discrimination. And that puts Israel in violation of Article 1 of the UN's Declaration on the Elimination of All Forms of Racial Discrimination.

But to pursue this line of argument has the effect of disallowing Zionism as a legitimate sponsor of a Jewish homeland, and dumps us all into a discussion on the face of it unprofitable, inasmuch as any resolution that says that Jews cannot sponsor a homeland for other Jews, defined according to their own laws, is hardly worth having. Moreover, those who choose to rail against Judaism's sponsorship, under its laws, of a kind of apartheid should ask themselves rigorously whether it is the law they are objecting to, or its sponsorship by Jews. Those who have been protractedly upset by Israel's West Bank policies (which policies, unlike Judaic law, do not have the immunities that attach to religious traditions millennia old) and were indifferent to apartheid in South Africa betray either selective indignation or else indifference to human rights in sub-Saharan Africa, which makes them vulnerable as moralists.

The spirited and eloquent defense of Israel by Mr. Moynihan began with some syllogistic play. He reminded his fellow delegates that whereas in the UN there is always talk of "racial discrimination," there had up until that day (November 10, 1975) been hardly any talk of "racism." Moynihan singled out the

> one occasion that we have been able to find on which we know it to have been discussed ... the 1,644th meeting of the Third Committee on 16 December 1968 ... On that occasion—to give some feeling for the intellectual precision with which the matter was being treated—the question arose as to what should be the relative positioning of the terms "racism" and "Nazism" in a number of preambular paragraphs. The distinguished representative of Tunisia argued that "racism" should go first because, he said, Nazism was a form of racism. Not so, said the no less distinguished representative of the USSR, for, he explained, Nazism contained all the main elements of racism within its ambit and should be mentioned first. That is to say that racism was merely a form of Nazism. ...

> One cannot but ponder the situation we have made for ourselves in the context of the Soviet statement on that not-so-distant occasion. If, as the distinguished representative declared, racism is a form of Nazism, and if, as this resolution declares, Zionism is a form of racism, then we have step by

step taken ourselves to the point of proclaiming—the United Nations is solemnly proclaiming—that Zionism is a form of Nazism.

That semantical *jeu de mots* was very nice.

Professor Moynihan then delivered a paragraph on the history of the dreaded word:

> The word "racism" is a creation of the English language, and relatively new to it. It is not, for instance, to be found in the *Oxford English Dictionary.* [The first and, at the time Moynihan spoke, only edition.] The term derives from relatively new doctrines, all of them discredited [I am not sure that this is so, if somatological and psychometric criteria are weighed], concerning the human population of the world, to the effect that there are significant biological differences among clearly identifiable groups, and that those differences establish, in effect, different levels of humanity. Racism, as defined by Webster's Third *New International Dictionary,* is "the assumption that . . . traits and capacities are determined by biological race and that races differ decisively from one another." It further involves "a belief in the inherent superiority of a particular race and its right to domination over others."

Moynihan then moved in for the kill, but he gave the delegates a little historical foreplay:

> That meaning [the superiority of one race over another] . . . has always been altogether alien to the political and religious movement known as Zionism. As a strictly political movement, Zionism was established only in 1897, although there is a clearly legitimate sense in which its origins are indeed ancient. For example, many branches of Christianity have always held that from the standpoint of the Biblical prophets, Israel would be reborn one day. But the modern Zionist movement arose in Europe in the context of a general upsurge of national consciousness and aspiration that overtook most other peoples of Central and Eastern Europe after 1848 and that in time spread to all of Africa and Asia. It was to those persons of the Jewish religion a Jewish form of what today is called a national liberation movement. Probably a majority of those persons who became active Zionists and sought to emigrate to Palestine were born within the confines of Czarist Russia. . . .
>
> Now it was the singular nature—if I am not mistaken it was the unique nature—of that national liberation movement that, in contrast with the movements that preceded it, those of that time, and those that have come since, it defined its members not in terms of birth but of belief. That is to say, it was not a movement of the Irish to free Ireland or of the Polish to free Poland; not a movement of Algerians to free Algeria or of Indians to free India.
>
> It was not a movement of persons connected by historical membership in a genetic pool of the kind that enables us to speak loosely but not meaninglessly of, say, the Chinese people, nor yet of diverse groups occupying the same territory, which enables us to speak of the American people with no greater indignity to truth. To the contrary, Zionists defined themselves merely

as Jews, and declared to be Jewish anyone born of a Jewish mother or—and this is the absolutely crucial fact—anyone who converted to Judaism. . . .

The State of Israel, which in time was created by the Zionist movement, has been extraordinary for nothing so much as the range of . . . "racial stocks" from which it has drawn its citizenry. There are black Jews, brown Jews, white Jews, Jews from the Orient and Jews from the West. Most such persons could be said to have been "born" Jews, just as most Presbyterians and most Hindus are "born" to their faith, but there are many Jews who are converts. And with a consistency in the matter which surely attests to the importance of this issue to that religious and political culture, Israeli courts have held that a Jew who converts to another religion is no longer a Jew. In the meantime the population of Israel also includes large numbers of non-Jews, among them Arabs of both the Muslim and Christian religions and Christians of other national origins. Many of those persons are citizens of Israel, and those who are not can become citizens by legal procedures very much like those that obtain in a typical nation of Western Europe.

There are problems here, of course, tracing to the policies already described. The son of a Christian is in no legal sense "a Christian." That is not true of the son of a Jew, who, under the laws of Israel, is "a Jew," entitled to instant citizenship. On the other hand, no state has ever been established as a "homeland" for Christians. If such a nation had been founded, surely the probability is that the son of the Christian mother would be presumed Christian, and therefore entitled to the special treatment which it was the purpose of the Christian state to serve.

But the United Nations General Assembly was unmoved, and passed the Zionism-is-racism resolution by a vote of 72 to 35.

A Modest Proposal

On the question that irritates many Americans (myself included, from time to time), of U.S. Government servitude to Israeli foreign policy, I wrote twenty years ago something in the nature of a fantasy, though it was presented (in two syndicated columns) as a mock-serious Modest Proposal (my colleague James Burnham termed it a "metaphysical joke"). What set me off was candidate George McGovern, who had just received the Democratic nomination in Miami and had immediately made pledges to Israel of a kind that were out of season, given his sturdily anti-Vietnam campaign and its overtones of isolationism.

I recalled that when, in 1967, Israel had been threatened and the Six Day War exploded, prominent American liberals had paused in their clamor to get us out of the Southeast Asian imbroglio long enough to produce a highly publicized declaration for getting us *into* the Mideast imbroglio, causing Professor John Roche of Brandeis to remark wryly that their manifesto should have been labeled "Doves for War." They got quite sore at Professor Roche—sometime president of Americans for Democratic Action, and later an aide to President Lyndon Johnson—who was as resolutely pro South Vietnamese independence as he has always been for Israeli independence.

What it came down to in Democratic politics was simple: Where Israel was concerned, the encroaching demands for a reticent American international profile did not apply. I remember confronting John Kenneth Galbraith on the point in one of our daily television exchanges at the Democratic Convention in Miami. What he said, simply and honestly, was, "I confess I have a special affection for Israel."

"Indeed a lot of us do," I wrote. "Not only for reasons of compassion that reach into history, ancient and horribly contemporary. But because there is so much in the behavior of the leaders of the modern state of Israel that we need to learn from. . . . If General Dayan had managed our war agains Hanoi, that too would have been a six-day war."

McGovern, I wrote, "likes to point to Israeli democracy as his justification [for endorsing Israel], but this of course is disingenuous. After all, he is also quoted as desiring to recognize the 'legitimate' government of China, which can hardly be justified by his attraction to democratic government. Meanwhile Mr. McGovern angrily disparages the government of South Vietnam.

"The problem is to reason from the legitimacy of Mao Tse-tung's government on over to the illegitimacy of President Thieu's. Never mind. Better to be straightforward like Galbraith, and say simply that Israel occupies a 'special' place in the American heart.

"While you are at it, be even more straightforward than Galbraith. Recognize that on top of that special affection, a U.S. pledge to Israeli independence is for the time being necessary for anyone who aspires to be President, for the simple reason that the strategically situated Jewish community is for the most part very generous in backing political causes and very insistent on the matter of Israeli independence."

But, I warned, "what holds for Saigon today [this was July 1972] holds *mutatis mutandis* for Tel Aviv tomorrow. . . . The contradiction cannot hope to survive indefinitely. The Jewish community in Israel, and indeed in the United States, cannot reasonably suppose that an American public finally persuaded by George McGovern that we should consider the cold war ended will fail to act on the consequences of that assumption."

So, I concluded, elaborating a fancy that gave prominence to two elusively important considerations, there was a logical next step for those who feel that our relationship to Israel is something truly unique that should be shielded from the vagaries of public passion. "As things stand, we suffer most of the disadvantages, and enjoy none of the advantages, of separate nationhood. Why should we not propose to Israel annexation, as the 51st American state?"*

Israel as a Point of Light

The state of Israel raises additional questions, one of them caught in an exchange precipitated by Norman Podhoretz's accusations leveled in 1982 (in the essay "J'Accuse") against critics of Israel during the march into Lebanon. As we have noted, Podhoretz in that piece expanded on the conventional definition. An anti-Semite, he wrote, is someone who labels certain vices and failings as specifically Jewish, or, correlatively, denies to Jews rights unchallengeably accorded to others. Anthony Lewis had written about Israel's desire to "exterminate Palestinian nationalism" in preparation for the annexation of the West Bank. Lewis wrote to tell me that he was aware of the charge of a double standard as applied to Israel, but that he did not think it anti-Semitic to work a particular distinction. "Yes," Lewis wrote, "there is a double standard [in judging Israel]. From its birth, Israel asked to be judged as a light among the nations." This is effective self-retrieval, but the effect is not long-lasting. It is hard to find a nation that, at the moment of its emergence, does not crown itself as something of a city on a hill.

Israel is a modern state, beleaguered from the first day of its existence, opportunistic in its struggles to survive (as most countries tend to be), and it confronts, unresolved, questions about its future that deeply divide

---

*For the sake of the exercise, I carried on for a bit:

"What would we have to lose?

"If we are in any case committed to Israeli survival, as most political parties insist we are, pending that change in public attitude we speak of, then we would go to war in any case if Israel's sovereignty were threatened.

"Israel is geographically remote? It isn't any further from Washington than Alaska and Hawaii. . . .

"A language barrier? Ask Switzerland how insupportable that is. Anyway, Senator Robert Kennedy insisted, and won his point, that Spanish-speaking New Yorkers should be permitted to vote. Why not Hebrew-speaking Americans?

"If Israel's foreign policy were written in Washington, the Arab countries' fear of Israeli expansionism would end. We could begin by giving back to Egypt, and to Jordan, most of the territories conquered during the 1967 war, and retained by Israel, as Israeli officials have repeatedly assured us, for reasons of military defense only. If Israel becomes a part of the United States, there is no further question of attacking the State of Israel—as well attack the city of Chicago.

"The net result would be the introduction of a genuine state of serenity to the Arab region. . . .

"Would Israel object? Some Israelis unquestionably would, though not all by any means, provided we affirmed our dedication to states' rights, and pledged a constitutional amendment to modify the harsh restrictions against the public practice of religion improvised by the Warren Court. [Etc.]"

its own people. One-half of those Israelis who favor the occupation of the West Bank do so because they feel the pull of Biblical irredentism. But one-half do so only because they believe the occupation necessary for reasons of national defense. And (about) one-half of the country opposes occupying the West Bank, 85 per cent of whose residents are Arabs. The United States finds itself caught up in the internal quarrels of its stepchild, which didn't make it as our 51st state, depriving me of any chance of going down in history as a goy prophet.

In summary, during its history Israel has put forward four arguments in support of its special claims on the support of the West, and of America in particular. The first of these is, in effect, reparations for the Holocaust. The second, Israel's fidelity to the West during the cold war. The third, its democratic singularity in a virulently anti-democratic part of the world. And the fourth, and by far the most muted, Judaism's covenantal entanglement with Christianity, from which derives the religio-moral obligation of Christians to ensure the survival of the Jews. The first of these claims declines over time, as time distances us from the Holocaust. The second evanesces with the end of the cold war. The third is of diminishing strength, as that portion of America's pro-democratic fervor that was animated by cold-war alliances diminishes.

We are left with the fourth claim, which, however, makes the more secularized Jewish community, in combination with the hyper-Orthodox, uncomfortable. The result of all of this is a continuing effort to invigorate the first claim, but probably against the competing tug in America toward policies oriented not only to post-Nazi, but to post-Holocaust priorities. These inevitably inspire the most heated efforts of the Israel lobby.

5 · Conclusions

The survival of the editor of *The Nation* after the Gore Vidal episode tells us that anti-Semitism with Israel as its focus is no longer professionally suicidal. Granted, some would argue that because the editor of *The Nation* is himself Jewish, he enjoyed an immunity that would not have been extended to the Gentile.

But what explains, five years later, the survival of Pat Buchanan? Here was a Gentile who said things about Jews that could not reasonably be interpreted as other than anti-Semitic in tone and in substance. His conduct precipitated, as we have seen, pressures on newspaper editors and program managers to discharge him. As far as I can tell, these pressures were of no avail: Buchanan's reach is as extended today as in the fall of 1990, when he was suggesting that, in America, only satellites of Israel favored military action against Iraq. He thus, with a dozen keystrokes, transformed a majority of Republican legislators and a plurality of Democrats, to say nothing of independent warmongers like me and *National Review*, into satellites of Israel.

As noted, Pat Buchanan survived. He would not have done so, in my opinion, ten years ago; which is why I speak of Auschwitz having become a senior citizen, fading away as the dynamic arbiter of the nation's moral reflexes. This development is welcome in one sense, unwelcome in another. If it intimates a creeping cultural–political insensibility to anti-Semitism, then it is both wrong and alarming. If it suggests only that the public feels free to react against intimidation on the subject of Israel, then it is healthy.

John Judis, writing in *The New Republic* (August 11 and 18, 1986) on the subject of "The Conservative Wars," describes the quarrel between conservatives and neoconservatives—a "war" more written about than engaged in. It is correct that there are disparate impulses within the schools of conservatism. But factionalism of this kind is quite general; we find it within socialism, liberalism, social democracy, Catholicism, Protestantism, Judaism. The division that interests us here has to do with the public identification of neoconservatism with Jewish scholars. Mr. Judis writes about a meeting in 1986 of the Philadelphia Society, an old-line conservative intellectual forum (I was its co-founder) that brings off an annual meeting and two or three regional meetings every year. "Some of the themes voiced in Chicago," Judis says,

> struck even some conservatives as at best "anti-cosmopolitanism" (Burton Pines's term) [Mr. Pines is senior vice president for research at the Heritage Foundation, and Jewish] and at worst "anti-Semitic." The speech that most troubled the neoconservatives was by Stephen Tonsor. What one neoconservative described as a "hooded" version was printed in *National Review*. Like [Professor M. E.] Bradford and the others, Tonsor attacked the neoconservatives for being interlopers. Referring to their leftist pasts, he remarked, "It is splendid when the town whore gets religion and joins the church. Now and then she makes a good choir director, but when she begins to tell the minister what he ought to say in his Sunday sermons, matters have been carried too far."
>
> Tonsor identified conservatism with Christianity. Ignoring the seminal role played in the 1950s by Jewish or agnostic intellectuals [This is too loose a definition: he should have added "Gentile." There are many agnostic "Christians" who nevertheless identify themselves with conservative-Christian politics, France's Charles Maurras the most conspicuous in recent times.] such as Henry Hazlitt, Willi Schlamm, James Burnham, Frank Meyer, Max Eastman,

Eugene Lyons, Ralph de Toledano, Leo Strauss, and Milton Friedman, Tonsor declared that conservatism's "world view is Roman or Anglo Catholic." In contrast, Tonsor identified neoconservatism with the "instantiation of modernity among secularized Jewish intellectuals." Commenting on Tonsor's speech and the articles in [an issue of] the *Intercollegiate Review* [focusing on the neocons], Midge Decter said, "It's this notion of a Christian civilization. You have to be part of it or you're not really fit to conserve anything. That's an old line and it's very ignorant."

Indeed it is an old line and indeed it is ignorant. But this is not the place to explore that question. Instead we ask only whether the *asseveration* is inherently an act of anti-Semitism. It is not: To claim that all the pillars of conservatism are Christian is not racially or ethnically invidious, though it may be chauvinist. It is a historical and philosophical misreading, in particular given that Christian thought is Judaeo-Christian in origin.

Judis went on. At the Chicago meeting, he wrote, there were intimations that neoconservatives were more loyal to Israel than to the United States—"a charge of 'dual loyalty' that the anti-Semitic Right of the late 1940s and early 1950s (when Zionism was a liberal cause) had leveled against Democratic supporters of Israel." Judis interviewed several of the participants who, he said, made these charges "explicit."

> Russell Kirk, who tried to calm the tempers at the Chicago meeting, said in a telephone interview: "What really animates the neoconservatives, especially Irving Kristol, is the preservation of Israel. That lies in back of everything." Paul Gottfried said, "I don't think one can differentiate the neoconservatives from the very large Jewish composition of the movement, and the fact that many of the Jewish leaders of the movement broke from the Left precisely over the question of Israel and other Jewish issues and therefore are going to take a very strong pro-Israeli position." He added, "I happen to think that position corresponds to American interests, but I think the neoconservatives would make it appear such no matter what."

We should all know that when examining political declamations in search of venality ("What's good for General Motors is good for the country"; "For he today that sheds his blood with me shall be my brother"), it is a good rule to peel away a few storeys of rhetoric to make room for the convention of hyperbole, the tall-tale gristle of American humor. "I swear he is taller than the Eiffel Tower" translates idiomatically as that he is, oh, six feet six. Russell Kirk, an eminent scholar who has written fifty books, five thousand scholarly essays, and five million columns (allow me the hyperbole), suddenly trips into the anti-Semitic spotlight for saying that the preservation of Israel "lies in back of everything" the neocons believe in. Obviously if one is seeking the point, as distinguished from impaling a polemical target, it makes sense to transcribe that as, "The preservation of Israel is important to the neocons, many of whom are Jewish Americans." So handled, the statement is not really very inflammatory, and has the benefit of being correct. So also would it be correct to say that the preservation of Israel is important to most non-Jewish Americans. Gallup did a poll after the OPEC cartel went into action in 1969, tripling the price of gasoline at the local gas station. It asked whether support for Israel was costing us too much and whether therefore we should diminish that support. The pollsters found no difference in public support for our Mideast policy (about 70 per cent in favor) even after the cartel's heavy imposition on the American consumer. It is mischievous to assume that because Tonsor wants to put a Christian-religious pedigree on conservatism as he understands it, and Kirk believes that neocons are (mostly) pro-Israel, therefore anti-Semitism is creeping into the Kirk–Tonsor Division of American Conservatism.

At this point it is useful to isolate one cause of tension. Although this deals formally with religion, it is less a question of religious than of civic contention. I prefer to quote Irving Kristol on the question (*NR*, December 30, 1988) than to say it myself, though our thoughts on the subject are the same. There is the obvious advantage that Kristol is himself Jewish; the other advantage, unhappily equally obvious, is that I cannot surpass him in lucid social analysis. "The kind of tension that is now building up between Jews and Christians," he wrote in *National Review* three years ago,

> has very little to do with traditional discrimination, and everything to do with efforts by liberals—among whom, I regret to say, Jews are both numerous and prominent—to establish a wall between religion and society, in the guise of maintaining the wall between church and state. The major Jewish organizations proceed from the correct proposition that legally and constitutionally we are not a Christian nation, to the absurd proposition that we are in no sense at all a Christian society. They are aware, of course, that the overwhelming majority of Americans are Christians, but insist that their religion be a totally private affair, one that finds no public expression and receives no public deference. Such insistence shows a lamentable ignorance of history, sociology, and psychology.

Kristol brings up the matter of religious practices in the State of Israel, but to make other than the easy point that Israel is in a formal sense a Jewish state:

> Today, in Israel—still theoretically that strange hybrid: a secular but Jewish state—there is no debate over the separation of church and state, only a debate over where one draws the line in the involvement of religion with both society and state. There is every bit as much religious toleration in Israel

as in the United States,* and Christians and Moslems are free to practice their religion without let or hindrance. But the Israeli government closes down on Yom Kippur, not on Christmas.

And, of course, in America, the government closes down on Christmas:

> I see nothing wrong with that, just as I see nothing wrong with the public schools in New York City closing down on Yom Kippur. It is common sense and common prudence for a secular government not to put itself unnecessarily at odds with the religious sensibilities of its citizenry. Diplomacy and tact is called for, not ruthless self-denial, which is what the American Civil Liberties Union calls for. Unfortunately, many Jews seem to think that the extreme secularism of the ACLU is their best guarantee of religious, social, and political equality. Since I believe that such extreme secularism is *contra naturam*—except in a nation of atheists or agnostics, which the United States is not—I also believe that the American Jewish community is misguided in its now-dominant dogmatic view of how the relations between the two religions are to be structured.
>
> The Jewish view, that religion ought to be an exclusively private affair with no public involvement, is the understandable view of a religious minority with long and vivid memories of official anti-Semitism, discrimination, and persecution. But the inescapable truth is that Jews are not going to be able to impose this view on the Christian majority of the United States. It is just too extreme—so extreme that, even now, the major Jewish organizations stop short of arguing against the status of Christmas as a national holiday, or school closings on Yom Kippur in some localities, or all sorts of other, traditional intrusions of religious expression and ritual into public life.

Mr. Kristol makes now a shrewd observation having to do—notwithstanding his point about the dominant Christian culture—with the dilution of Protestant dogma during the critical period of secularization:

> One reason American Jews were able to take seriously the prospect of a near-total divorce between religion and society was the attitude of the major Protestant organizations, whose liberal Protestantism was more keenly inter-

---

*Not quite so, and thereby hangs a tale. The *New York Times* of June 10, 1977, reported that in his effort to form a coalition government, Menachem Begin pledged to the Orthodox religious bloc to seek legislation "to prohibit Christian missionary activity among Jews." An effort to ascertain whether such legislation was passed took me first to an American scholar who has been helpful in checking facts pertaining to Israel, on which he is an authority. He confessed ignorance on this question and referred me to the Israeli Consulate in New York. A call there also elicited ignorance on the question, together with a promise to fax Israel to get the information. But notwithstanding a couple of prods with promises of cooperation, the question was never answered. One report—from a scholar who relies on his memory—is that the legislation was indeed passed, but restricted itself to making it unlawful for any missionary to "bribe" an Israeli citizen, intending to proselytize another religion. If so, this would make illegal the free distribution of the New Testament. In the absence of protests from the missionary wing of the Christian churches, one assumes that either the law is a dead letter, or else that it is so effective as to eliminate evangelization.

ested in social reform than in religious belief. Jews prefer Christians whose Christianity is lukewarm and therefore, they feel, less likely to lead to Christian anti-Semitism of a kind our Jewish ancestors experienced for centuries in Europe. This is perfectly understandable. But it is also a parochial perspective, out of tune with current realities, and this for two reasons.

He distinguishes now between contemporary sources of anti-Semitism, and foresees a revival in Protestant faith.

First, the anti-Semitism that has been so dangerous to Jews [in this century], and is still so dangerous today, is not Christian anti-Semitism. It is neo-pagan anti-Semitism (Nazi and Fascist), or Moslem fundamentalist anti-Semitism, or Marxist anti-Semitism, or simply nationalist chauvinist anti-Semitism of a kind one now finds in Japan (of all places!) or Latin America. Our major Jewish organizations are oriented, almost hypnotically and surely atavistically, to the past rather than to the present or future.

Secondly, it is ridiculous to think that liberal–modernist–secular Protestant Christianity would remain forever "the wave of the future," and that never again would Christians want to be devout. Ever since World War II and the Holocaust, large numbers of American Jews have felt impelled to become "more Jewish," in one way or another. But the American Jewish community as a whole—always excluding the ultra-Orthodox, who are uninterested in Christians—was surprised to discover, was positively alarmed to discover, that something like a Christian revival was also occurring, primarily among the evangelical wing of Protestantism. So the Jewish organizations keep anxiously looking for signs of anti-Semitism among "born-again" Christians, exaggerate the few such expressions they do find, and wait for this phenomenon to pass. I don't think it will pass. I believe the secular era is fading, that Jews (at least those who remain Jews) will become more Jewish, Christians more Christian, Moslems more Moslem, Hindus more Hindu, etc.

I do not from personal experience know whether what then follows, in Kristol's analysis, is so, in part because of course he is Jewish and better equipped to interpret the signs about us; but I find it important because of the keenness of his social sense, and his special powers to draw interesting and seductive conclusions:

American Jews are utterly unprepared for this new world, in which Christians wish to be more Christian without necessarily being anti-Semitic. They doubt the very possibility of this happening. I am willing to contemplate such a possibility. Which is why I refuse to get excited about a crèche being erected outside a town hall, or students in public schools singing Christmas carols or even putting on a Nativity play. In those communities that are predominantly Christian, this is to be anticipated and Jews can live with it. . . .

Tact and prudence: the recovery of these virtues, by both Jews and Christians, seems to me the key to decent relations between these two religious groups. I think it is foolish in the extreme for Jews even to appear to be anti-

Christian, just as it would be wrong for Christians even to appear to be anti-Semitic. . . .

This Christmas, as in all Christmases past and future, there will be no Christmas tree in my home. But I am not anti-Christian and see nothing wrong with the Christian majority erecting Christmas trees on public property. Indeed, I have what I regard as a theologically positive view of Christianity. Like the greatest Jewish theologian of this century, Franz Rosenzweig, I see Christianity as a sister religion to Judaism, as a form of "Judaism for the Gentiles."

In his essay, Irving Kristol touched on the question of the minority, the outsider. I have thought for many years about the phenomenon, in part because as a Roman Catholic I have always thought myself something of an outsider. I have to confess that when, at a Protestant boarding school, I announced (age 15) that I would not be attending Sunday Protestant services at the school chapel, going instead with two or three other Catholic students and one faculty member to the Catholic church five miles away, I found the experience other than self-isolating: I think I actually got something of a kick out of it, as many Catholics did during those decades when, for instance, they would politely decline to eat meat served to them on Fridays. For this reason I read with special empathy Michael Kinsley on a subject I have never myself written about:

"On a practical level [Kinsley is quoting a document of the American Civil Liberties Union], a child whose family does not believe in the Divinity of Christ must view the public crèche as a symbolic representation of his or her status as an outsider. The child will question . . . his identification with the American culture."

I think that's right. But I also think this child had better learn early on to question his identification with the American culture, because it's a tough question that will follow him all his life no matter how successful the ACLU is in banning nativity scenes. There is a majority culture in this country. It is Christian, white, middle class. Jews and nonbelievers (I am both) are outsiders to some extent in that culture. So are blacks, homosexuals, Orientals, and so on. This is so even though we are a society that is constantly remaking itself, and a society committed to protecting the civil rights and economic opportunities of minorities. The battle for minority rights goes on, of course, but does final victory require eradication of the majority culture? And is every manifestation of that culture an insult to those who aren't fully a part of it? . . .

In theory, there is a difference between the society and the polity. In practice, the difference is impossible to police. The majority culture needs some degree of government sanction, and attempts to prevent the government from recognizing this are futile. December 25 has to be a national holiday. If we are going to get any work done at all we can't add Chanukah and Ramadan.

Mr. Kinsley closes with an animating thought that exactly reflects my own experience as a Catholic:

> Far from being a handicap, a sense of "outsiderness" can be a great asset in a society that does, in the end, try to protect the rights of cultural outsiders. It energizes, promotes skepticism, gives perspective. I would not want my child to grow up completely comfortable in his surroundings, never forced to "question . . . his identification with the American culture." The enormous literary contribution of homosexuals, the prominence of Jews in courageous social causes of all sorts, the creation of jazz by blacks all derive in part from the discomfort of being outside the majority culture. I am happy to be a bit of an outsider in my own country. I am no less an American for it, and may even hope to be a better one as a result.

A Case Study

So the ongoing debate over the religion clauses in the First Amendment no doubt generates anti-Semitic resentment to the extent that the fundamentalist separationists are thought of as predominantly Jewish. Here is a source of tension, but not comparable to the divisiveness of the question of Israel, a tension that climaxed as these words were written in September 1991. It savages reality to suppose that such differences as do divide us over Israel's policies in the occupied territories will always be transacted in hygienic democratic circumstances. No, notwithstanding that the Israeli government's policies (under Yitzhak Shamir) are themselves supported by only a bare majority of Israelis, the government of Israel governs Jewish American organized sentiment in these matters. Here is the headline in the *New York Times* (September 15, 1991—as it happens, on the day these words are being written):

Pro-Israel Lobby Readies for Fight
In Opposing Quick Action on Backing for Loans,
Bush Faces a Powerful Foe

By Adam Clymer
Special to The New York Times

—And the story, excerpted:

> Israel's supporters in American politics put at least $4 million into last year's election campaign, sent at least 1,000 volunteers to Capitol Hill last week, and are trying very hard to sign up sizable, perhaps veto-proof majorities in Congress to back the loan guarantees, which are meant to help Israel provide housing for its large influx of Soviet Jewish émigrés.
>
> President Bush, who wants consideration of the guarantees delayed until January, portrayed himself at a news conference on Thursday as "one lonely

little guy" contending against "powerful political forces" who want Congress to act without delay.

Those forces are indeed powerful. Last winter, they pushed a reluctant Administration into supporting an outright $650 million grant to Israel when Israel said the Persian Gulf war had cost it that much. . . .

The strength and depth of the forces backing Israel go far beyond the influence of any particular lawmaker making the case for guarantees.

The campaign money is one factor. About 60 political action committees are committed to helping lawmakers who support Israel. The $4 million they gave to House and Senate candidates during the 1989–1990 campaign period made them the "biggest ideological group" among such committees, said Larry Makinson, research director of the Center for Responsive Politics.

The $4 million was about as much as real estate or oil and gas interests gave. In contrast, abortion rights and [pro-life] groups gave only $750,000. Moreover, many pro-Israel political action committees often aid the same candidate, [Larry Makinson] said. Senator Howard M. Metzenbaum, Democrat of Ohio, got $245,000 from them in 1987 and 1988, he said.

But people matter at least as much. The 1,000 or so visitors who descended on the Capitol on Thursday were a dramatic example. . . .

The one-day visit was one showy project of the Task Force on Loan Guarantees, which was set up several months ago by about 25 especially active members of the Council of Presidents [of Major American Jewish Organizations], Mr. Hoenlien [the Council's executive director] said. But the task force sponsors a wide variety of activities to broaden support for the guarantees, he said, and this issue has created "a unique level of consensus and cooperation among Jewish groups." . . .

The center of that national voice is the American Israel Public Affairs Committee, known as Aipac, one of the most determined, single-minded, and effective lobbying groups in the capital. . . .

He [director Thomas A. Dine] and the other registered lobbyists at Aipac can get Congressional attention in a hurry. They talk with Congressional leaders and help devise strategies and round up support. Few lobbies do it as well. Few are also as reluctant to be quoted in the press, which may provide a mystique of power.*

The shoot-out between President Bush and the Israeli lobby was termed by Abba Eban the most serious Israeli–American confrontation in forty years. Bush stood his ground; AIPAC walked up to the brink, and then stepped back. It was a politically important engagement, whatever one's sympathies on the point at issue.

It does not follow that all critically situated American Jews submit to AIPAC's conscriptive drag on the issue, though citing, for instance, Leslie Gelb doesn't altogether substantiate the point. Mr. Gelb writes the Foreign

---

*The headline the following day in the New York Times, page 1: "Israeli Loan Dispute Turns Ugly; / Rightist Calls Bush 'Anti-Semite.'"

Affairs column for the *New York Times* op-ed page. In the same issue in which the lobbying powers of AIPAC were discussed, Gelb writes:

> . . . the President took his case directly to the American people on Thursday and headed toward a showdown for far-reaching reasons: to break the back of the Israeli lobby in Congress and put himself in the negotiating catbird seat. From that perch he will demand that Israel first freeze further settlement activity in the occupied territories and then relinquish these territories to the Palestinians in exchange for peace.
>
> I, too, oppose further Jewish settlement in the West Bank and Gaza Strip. I also believe that land for peace is the right goal for the U.S. and for Israel— but at the end of the bargaining process and only after an extended series of limited agreements empowering Palestinians and giving them a chance to demonstrate their intent to live in peace with Israel.

Mr. Gelb then goes on to say that for this reason he too opposes Mr. Bush's call to freeze the loan guarantees.

We have seen above the pride AIPAC takes in unseating congressmen and senators who defy its resolutions. In 1988 John Chafee, senator from Rhode Island, found that AIPAC was backing his opponent lustily. Why? Because Senator Chafee had voted in favor of selling AWACS airplanes to Saudi Arabia. Undifferentiated political persecutions of this kind—reflexes of policy decisions of a foreign government—are rightly tolerated under our laws, and rightly resented. And since the targeted agents of Israel's government are American voters, their submission to foreign muscle, so exercised, is regrettable. The purpose of "registering" American citizens and American organizations as agents of a foreign government is to alert voters to the possibility that interests other than America's are being served by such people and organizations. But nobody doubts the successes of AIPAC, even when its intrusiveness is brought to light. (I learned about Senator Chafee from watching *60 Minutes*. And of course he was re-elected, but by narrower margins than would have been the case without AIPAC's activity.) The political-action committees are effective—they would not, after all, survive if they were ineffective—and manifestly their success is here and there resented, especially if, in opposing them, one runs the risk of being charged with anti-Semitism. The suggestion that the President of the United States should think himself "one lonely little guy" even when 74 per cent of the American people think he is doing a good job suggests an imbalance in (our old friend) the Correlation of Forces. It is probably an historic political event that he won that showdown against the Israeli lobby handily.

To the Barricades

In a conversation before Labor Day, 1991, Edward Koch made a dramatic point. "Last week at Crown Heights, the first killing of a Jew because he was a Jew took place since 1946 in Poland." Indeed, the killing of the young Hasidic Jew by a young black (the product of 48 hours of frenzy brought on by the accidental killing of a black child by a Jewish motorist) was just that, a ritual execution—any old Jew would do.

It is wrong to suppose that that bleak episode was other than an apostrophe in the long narrative that began with slavery, traveled through Reconstruction and Jim Crow, on to the civil-rights era, headed, we all hope, to truly civilized interracial relations. But even though it was an anomalous act, this first Jew-*qua*-Jew killing in 45 years, the clouds darken as anti-Semitic excesses go unreproached. Leonard Jeffries, a black professor at CCNY, inveighs against white people in general and Jews in particular. Efforts to get from any member of the congressional Black Caucus a rebuke of Professor Jeffries's animadversions are unavailing, four weeks after they were first published. Congressmen being above all political animals, one has to suppose that they believe any rebuke of Professor Jeffries would bring punishment by the voters. Voters whom AIPAC, or the Anti-Defamation League, cannot reach.

But here a distinction is appropriate, one that understands the difference between anti-Semitism by white Christians and anti-Semitism by blacks. Once again, Irving Kristol:

> It is my strong impression that, while relations between Christians and Jews as individuals are far better today than ever before, tensions between the two religious communities are being exacerbated. [But] it is not a matter of a "resurgent anti-Semitism," as some major Jewish organizations claim. Only within the black community is there evidence of any such resurgence, and since this phenomenon is as inexplicable as it is irrational, given the extraordinary Jewish commitment to the struggle for equality of civil rights, no one really has any idea of what to do about it. In any case, there is nothing even superficially Christian about black anti-Semitism, which is a peculiar, home-brewed racism that has little appeal to white Christians.

But wherever it comes from, the same protections are needed, foremost among them a consistent pressure for sensitive behavior. When Joe Sobran went cuckoo (the term we used in-house, never "anti-Semitic") on the subject, he was not again asked to write, in *National Review,* on the subject of the Mideast; a man of intellectual grace, he didn't apply to write for us on the Mideast, nor complain about those editorials on the Mideast that gave voice to views with which he took issue in his columns, the single exception being when he invoked his right of access, as a senior editor, to "The Open Question."

It would not have been inappropriate for newspaper editors who publish Pat Buchanan to decline to publish those of his columns that touched on Jewish or Israeli questions, pending evidence that he would more carefully observe the civilized distinctions. *The Nation,* by sponsoring the

Vidal piece, moved more deeply in toward the fever swamps of political thought. But the principal malefactor of the season was unquestionably President James Freedman of Dartmouth College, whose exultant efforts to transform the mischief of one unidentified student into a racist plague was irresponsible at the outset and, in the light of reflection, progressively inexcusable.

History brings on the need for fresh dispensations. It ought not to be considered racist to remark differences in IQ scoring by blacks. And, *pace* Norman Podhoretz, it ought not to be considered racist to speak of group characteristics. We are familiar with the paradox that group characteristics are tolerable when beneficent ("Jews are brighter than non-Jews"), racist when censorious ("Jews are a greedy lot"). Michael Kinsley put it nicely in *The New Republic* (October 14, 1991): "Ethnic traits are a sensitive subject, and rightly so. I don't even object to the unwritten rule that you—especially if you are an outsider—can ascribe good traits to an ethnic group (music, humor, intelligence) but not bad ones. Logically, though, the possibility of the one category existing suggests the possibility of the other." The trouble with all compound characterizations is that they leak terribly, and tend to get leakier all the time—a second's reflection is all that is needed to bring to mind a dumb Jew or a Jew utterly indifferent to material possessions. But it is incorrect and damaging to resist group characterizations—*unless there is evidence that such characterizations are motivated by a desire to disparage.*

And finally, those who believe that the main reason for resisting race prejudice is the commitment to respect one's neighbor (to love him is perhaps too exacting a mandate to guide fallen men) should, in regard to containing anti-Semitism, warn against the undesirable effects of ideological hostility to the public practice of religion, born of a fanatical application of the religious-freedom clause in the First Amendment (as described above by Irving Kristol), and enlivened also by that fear of "outsiderness" mentioned by Michael Kinsley. Religion has been abused in the past as a vehicle to justify discrimination, but it is the light of the gospel of a common brotherhood that mostly illuminates our brighter moments on earth. The single most powerful engine, striving always to haul us up to a vision of equality, was dispatched by Him who made us, children of God, with a common ancestry. "Let not mercy and truth forsake thee: bind them about thy neck; write them upon the table of thine heart. Happy is the man that findeth wisdom, and the man that getteth understanding."

PART TWO

W hat follows is material provoked by the publication of the essay "In Search of Anti-Semitism: What Christians Provoke What Jews? Why? By Doing What?—And Vice Versa." The essay was in five parts. It attempted, by examining complaints against Joseph Sobran, Patrick Buchanan, *The Dartmouth Review*, *The Nation*, and Gore Vidal, to explore the contemporary faces of anti-Semitism and of anti-anti-Semitism. The fifth part attempted to delineate some moral and political perspectives.

What is it that John Doe actually said that gave rise to the charge that he is anti-Semitic? Did it have to do with a single utterance by Mr. Doe, or is it that Mr. Doe appears to be fixated on questions that relate primarily to Jewish interests? In the context in which Mr. Doe spoke, are we enlightened as to his purposes in speaking as he did? Is it possible that in fact Mr. Doe is not anti-Semitic (three dozen people who know him well swear to it that there isn't a bigoted bone in his body), but that those who do not know him as John, but need to make judgments based on what he says and writes as John Doe, plausibly think him to be anti-Semitic? In such a situation, what can Mr. Doe do to efface the impression he has made, which impression he wishes he had not made? Or does he care?

Is one's attitude toward Israel a reliable index of one's attitude toward Jews? Many writers have complained that opposition to Israel is regularly misinterpreted as betraying anti-Semitic sentiment. Some Jewish writers and thinkers will say that to criticize policies of the government of Israel isn't anti-Semitic, but to question the right of Israel to exist may be and probably is motivated by hostility to Jews. When such questions arise, the job becomes to scrutinize the way in which hostility to Israel is expressed, in an effort to reason to whether that hostility is probably motivated by generic opposition to any corporate Jewish purpose. Why should the effort be made? Because the reaches of anti-Semitism are an all but contemporary memory.

The essay brought in a great deal of commentary. We received about two hundred letters, and the ratio was 3 to 1 critical of the essay. Many of these criticisms, however, were based on the presidential candidacy of Pat Buchanan (For heaven's sakes, why get in the way of a genuine protest candidate?), notwithstanding that we had made it plain that the essay was written before Mr. Buchanan announced his candidacy. Some critics seemed to be saying that because he decided to enter the race, we should therefore have put off publication of an essay in the research and writing of which almost an entire summer was spent. Some readers complained that I had not got around actually to defining anti-Semitism. That is formally correct, I did not: though I thought it pretty plain that a definition crystallized in what I said, and in the language I quoted. Anti-Semitism has different energy levels. One reader wrote that he defined anti-Semitism as a dislike or disapproval a) even of Jews one has never met and b) of any corporate objectives identifiable as of special concern to prominent and vociferous Jews—a pretty good definition, which would account for the casual anti-Semitism of someone who reacts in opposition to whatever organized Jewry is seen to be up to because organized Jewry desires that end. The manifestations are many and varied. They are sometimes signaled in that little exclamation, the single comment direct or oblique, the blurt, the cocked eyebrow, which can be the equivalent of addressing an uppity Negro in the old South as "Snowball."

Why should we care? The subject is important for moral as well as intellectual and analytical reasons. The Holocaust is one of the great nightmares of history, and just as the Catholic Church has spent a hundred years agonizing over the Spanish Inquisition, it is inevitable that the poisoned wells that generated Auschwitz should continue under microscopic scrutiny by those who do not understand, but seek to do so, how the anti-Semitism of the Twenties and Thirties, largely social and cultural, metastasized into the Holocaust. Might such lackadaisical anti-Semitism have been the culture impregnated by the "scientific racism" of such as Gobineau and Houston Stewart Chamberlain, itself an atheistic bastard child of late-nineteenth-century rationalism? The essay declares that Auschwitz has now become, so to speak, a senior citizen: Most present-day Germans were not even alive when the ovens were working. What they and others are left with is a historical memory, even as we have a historical memory of the age of slavery. That memory enjoins careful supervision of undisciplined thought and commentary. On the other hand, if we are intimidated by unreasoned or opportunistic denunciations, useful thought is impossible.

Our critics addressed these and other themes. They were columnists, editorial writers, academicians, clergymen, and of course *National Review*'s great body of readers. We reproduce some of this material. A word about what criteria I used in deciding what to publish in space that accommodates less than one-tenth of the volume of commentary the essay generated:

We have given first priority to persons specifically named in the essay. Joe Sobran comes in with a vigorous essay taking vigorous exception to my own. I comment, in turn, on his, which appears in full. Patrick Buchanan was invited to respond, but pleaded the burden of his political engagements. President James Freedman of Dartmouth, heavily criticized in the essay, has not written, nor has Gore Vidal, to defend his essay in *The Nation*, a magazine also criticized.

Norman Podhoretz, the editor of *Commentary*, figures prominently in the essay. He published a six-page "Open Letter to William F. Buckley Jr." in the February issue of his magazine, and it is substantially reproduced here. Irving Kristol, heavily quoted in the essay, addressed a letter to us which is important if only because he wrote it. William Pfaff, the syndicated columnist, who writes from Paris, undertakes to clear up a misunderstanding in the essay which he attributes to Mr. Podhoretz. So do columnists Edwin Yoder and Robert Novak. A. M. Rosenthal of the *New York Times* gave his opinions in his column and in a supplementary letter. Alan Dershowitz is the author and professor of law at Harvard; David Frum is an assistant editor on the *Wall Street Journal*'s editorial page. Eliot Cohen is Director of Strategic Studies at the Paul H. Nitze School of Advanced International Studies at the Johns Hopkins University; he is a strategist whose name appears on the mastheads of both *The New Republic* and *National Review*. Manfred Weidhorn is a professor of English literature. Professor Hugh Kenner's views were solicited. Henry Hyde, the prominent conservative representative from Illinois, has also written for *NR*. John Roche's syndicated column appeared in *National Review* for several years, until he discontinued it; he is a prominent author and political scientist, and was a sometime aide to President Lyndon Johnson. Jeff Nelligan was an associate at *National Review*; currently, he is a speechwriter at the Agency for International Development. Eric Alterman is Senior Fellow of the World Policy Institute. Professor Christopher Ricks of Oxford is currently teaching literature at Harvard; he is the author of *T. S. Eliot and Prejudice*. We are grateful to other writers we have quoted, and of course to all those who wrote (well, practically all those who wrote).

I most deeply regret that there simply isn't time to answer the letters that flowed in, and stormed in.

W. F. B.

1 · An Essay by Joseph Sobran

When a man shouts "Wolf!" it's not really necessary to remind us that the wolf is a dangerous animal, or to inform us that its Latin name is *Canis lupus,* or to discourse on its breeding and migratory patterns. We just want to know if there's really a wolf there. And if we can find no trace of a wolf, it may be helpful to know whether the man doing all the yelling uses the word "wolf" to include, say, terriers and spaniels.

The uninitiated reader, seeing the title of Bill Buckley's essay, "In Search of Anti-Semitism," might assume he was going to read about racial theories, vandalism, legal discrimination, cross-burnings, riots, mass expulsions, expropriations, persecutions, lynchings, massacres, and genocide—or, at the very least, the snobbish exclusion of Jews from polite society.

That reader might be surprised to find that Bill isn't writing about any of these things, or even their advocacy. He's hardly writing about anti-Semitism at all.

He is actually writing about charges of anti-Semitism—charges leveled against a few journalists, charges made in the context of disagreement over Israel, charges that have the odor of political ideology about them. And though he announces that he will examine both sides ("What Christians Provoke What Jews? . . . And Vice Versa"), the "Vice Versa" never really shows up. He doesn't even provide us with a helpful definition of anti-Semitism for purposes of evaluating the charges.

Bill's whole essay has a curious tone. It's as if a particularly scrupulous judge were presiding at a show trial, without realizing that the verdict had been decided in advance.

Throughout the chapters on Pat Buchanan and me, Bill seems to take for granted the good faith and sanity of our accusers. They are never put on the witness stand for cross-examination. The entire burden of proof seems to be on the accused, even though the accusation remains vague. (John O'Sullivan's attempt to paraphrase the charge is tellingly nebulous: Pat and I are "suspected of harboring anti-Semitic feelings." Suspected of harboring feelings?) Bill doesn't ask whether the accusers have an obvious interest of their own in discrediting critics of Israel whose arguments they can't refute on their own terms.

Worst of all, Bill never suggests any penalty for making false or loose charges of anti-Semitism. This omission makes it hard for me to credit the rest of his argument. If there's no penalty for falsely making serious charges (and all "anti-Semitism" seems to be equally serious), it's open season for slander—as, in fact, I happen to think it is. The graver the crime, the more culpable the false witness. But Bill doesn't even acknowledge this as a problem.

I submit that anyone can see that it's not only a problem in this country today, but a far more pressing problem than anti-Semitism—real anti-Semitism, that is—which has been properly discredited. In a society where Jew-hating was rife, charges of anti-Semitism would have no bite. But what, in the current atmosphere, is to discourage the Rosenthals and Podhoretzes from defaming and trying to ruin anyone who says openly that the U.S.–Israeli alliance is detrimental to this country's best interests?*

The chief polemical project of modern Zionism has been to forge an ideological high redefinition of anti-Semitism that puts criticism of Israel on the same plane with Nazism—as if these were merely different degrees of the same metaphysical evil. And once this bogus continuum is established, even differences of degree don't seem to matter much. The point of the devil-term is not to distinguish, but to conflate. A Buchanan somehow gets no credit for confining his supposed animus to verbal criticism of Israel; there are no venial sins in this department. On the contrary, he is attacked with as much fury as if he'd called for a nuclear first strike on Tel Aviv. Yet we all sense something unreal about the accusations: Buchanan's foes would be as amazed as his fans if he were arrested for actually harming a Jew.

Everyone heatedly denies equating "legitimate" criticism of Israel with anti-Semitism, but somehow the equation keeps popping up. Everyone makes devout obeisances to free speech on the matter, but somehow critics of Israel keep finding their careers at stake. *Time* observed recently that Buchanan had "survived" Rosenthal's attack on him. You don't have to "survive" a debate, a discussion, a difference of opinion. You only "survive" an attempt to destroy you.

Measure Israel by the same yardsticks you apply to other regimes, and you'll get more than an argument. You'll find your reputation and sources of income under attack. This has been not only Pat's and my own experience, but that of many journalists; a number of them—Fred Graham of CBS, Jeremy Levin of CNN (a former hostage in Beirut), columnists Georgie Anne Geyer and Bob Novak—have told me their stories, which usually don't reach the public. The average American has no conception of how the range of opinion about Israel in the media is constricted by backstage pressures. When I began questioning Israel's value to the U.S. as a "reliable ally" and "strategic asset," my employers, editors, and syndicate were all besieged with demands for my dismissal.

I am grateful that most of the people I write for were as firm as they were; I must specially mention the dauntless Lee Salem of Universal Press Syndicate, who politely told Richard Cohen where to get off when Cohen was calling for my head. I have some pity for those who were less firm: it can be unnerving to a civilized man to be suddenly confronted with fanaticism—in the form of people so committed to a cause as to be incapable of detachment or irony about it, unable even to imagine an alternative

---

*Since Bill wrote his essay, Abe Rosenthal has upped the ante by likening Pat Buchanan to David Duke, and offering a seven-point plan to stop them.

view of it, and possessed with a powerful urge to punish anyone who disagrees.

Such vindictive zeal is so incommensurate with the ordinary give-and-take of civil society that one hardly knows how to cope with it. Israel, as my sociologist friend Jack Cuddihy, a profound student of Jewish–Christian relations, observes, is "the issue that makes strong men tremble." Everyone in journalism knows you criticize Israel at your own risk.

This is not a two-way street. There is no hyphenated cussword in general use to stigmatize hostility to Christianity. Popes and cardinals come in for abuse when they speak of the rights of Palestinians. Leon Wieseltier can call a cross on a convent at Auschwitz "sickening," and nobody condemns him. Norman Podhoretz doesn't hesitate to publish, in *Commentary*, long essays by Henryk Grynberg and Hyam Maccoby blaming Christianity for the Nazi extermination of millions of Jews; no uproar ensues, nobody tries to get Podhoretz fired. Israeli soldiers can beat up a priest on the West Bank, then shoot up his church during Mass, and only the Catholic press takes note. (I called attention to the story at an *NR* editorial conference; nothing came of it.) If Christians had done such a thing to a synagogue, anywhere, it would have been front-page news, everywhere. This is the "Vice Versa" Bill never gets around to discussing. In controversy over Israel, the ad-hominem argument is the norm—for one side. The motives of Israel's critics are always fair game for discussion. No matter how cogent their arguments, their inner lives become the subject of unflattering speculation. (The motives of Israel's partisans, on the other hand, are assumed to be honorable.)

Now it's one thing to reproach a man who makes an anti-Semitic argument, one that arouses or appeals to hostility toward Jews. If he argues against American aid to Israel only on the grounds that it's a Jewish state, he is in the wrong. But if he argues against such aid because he opposes foreign aid in general, or because Israel has dealt ungratefully with the U.S., or simply because Israel has nothing to offer this country that justifies the costs of supporting it, his argument has to be met on its own grounds, and it's irrelevant, and unfair, to accuse him of ulterior motives. Besides, those who make glib and cynical judgments about the motives of people they disagree with (and whom they have an obvious interest in discrediting) ought to be distrusted. Those who object to anti-Semitism in principle must also object to Israel's injustice to its own minorities.

An "anti-Semite," in actual usage, is less often a man who hates Jews than a man certain Jews hate. The word expresses the emotional explosion that occurs in people who simply can't bear critical discourse about a sacred topic, and who experience criticism as profanation and blasphemy. The term "anti-Semitism" doesn't stand for any intelligible concept. It belongs not to the world of rational discourse, but to the realm of imprecations and maledictions and ritual ostracisms. And woe unto him, even in this modern secular world of ours, upon whom this curse is pronounced.

The word "anti-Semitic"—like its cousins "racist," "sexist," and "homophobic"—has become a monotonous expletive, like the obscenities in action movies. It's tempting to ask whether the people who constantly resort to it have ever learned how to use a thesaurus. Can't they describe the behavior they object to in vivid nouns and verbs?

No. Not without losing the effect they desire. To say, for example, that Buchanan overstates his case against Israel here and there would be much less dramatic than uttering the formulaic malediction. And in pronouncing the curse, as in performing an exorcism, it's vital to adhere strictly to every syllable of the prescribed formula.

We're not being asked to show merely reasonable respect and consideration for minorities these days. We're being required to internalize their ethnocentrisms, to make ourselves satellites of their indomitable self-absorption—a mentality perfectly expressed by Meyer Lansky, whose notoriety was such that Israel refused to accept him under the Law of Return. "When you're a Jew," Lansky moaned, "the whole world's against you." If Abe Rosenthal and Norman Podhoretz talk in their sleep, this is probably what they say.

Any reasonable and decent man must reject anti-Semitism, or any other irrational and unfair prejudice, especially when it becomes, or threatens to become, state policy. The whole idea of the rule of law is that the state should treat everyone alike. This is not only my sentiment but my guiding principle, as anyone who knows my work understands.

But if you apply this simple principle consistently, the Orwellian minority lobbies will accuse you of hating minorities. Oppose special government favor to any special interest—the race-quota lobby, Zionists, homosexuals, feminists, "artists"—and you are tagged as racist, anti-Semitic, homophobic, sexist, or Jesse Helms.

Replying to Bill's essay in the February issue of *Commentary*, Podhoretz all but equates opposition to Israel with anti-Semitism. And in his mind, "opposition" to Israel seems to mean rejecting any of its claims and demands against the American taxpayer. In other words, desiring merely normal relations with Israel is anti-Semitic!

But there is no reason why the American taxpayer should be forced to subsidize any foreign regime. He is already overtaxed to pay for his own government's constant pandering to domestic interests.

In the mental prison of his self-absorption, the minoritarian polemicist can only understand criticism of Israeli "democracy" (or of "civil rights," or federal grants to artists) as the expression of a special animus. It never occurs to him that the critics may be speaking out of their own principles, and he senses that he can't afford to subject his own interest to the scrutiny of principle.

So his endeavor is to sow suspicion against the critics. He has no other defense against them except the accusation. If he had to make his case on the presumption that others could disagree in good faith, he would be speechless.

I'll tell the full story of my own encounter with the Israel claque, and answer Bill's observations in detail,* someday soon. For now, this abridged account will have to do.

I had been pro-Israel—emotionally pro-Israel, in fact—for some years after the 1967 Six Day War. That changed with the 1982 Lebanon War, when the ruthless bombing of Beirut, and the attendant slaughter of Palestinian refugees, became too much for many of Israel's former admirers. I was disgusted with the trite phrases and revolting excuses that were being made for our "reliable ally." Menachem Begin, moreover, had lied to Ronald Reagan about his intentions in Lebanon. Some friend. We were being implicated in Israel's crimes. What were we getting out of this dubious alliance?

My mind really changed when I reread some old columns and editorials by James Burnham in, of all places, *National Review.* By then Jim was no longer with us—a stroke had forced him to retire in 1978—but his writings on the Middle East held up well. He had written that American and Israeli interests were basically divergent; that when push came to shove, the chief American interest in the region was access to Arab oil, which was threatened by American patronage of Israel, a relation that catered to the Israel lobby in America.

The more I reflected on this, the more obvious it seemed. I asked various pro-Israel conservatives for their views, but none of them made nearly as much sense as Burnham.

Taking his logic further, I concluded that it was in the interests of Israel to set the U.S. in opposition to the Arab world. But it was not in our interests. Such an alignment could only please the Soviet Union, which was seeking it for its own purposes. The idea that Israel was our "only reliable ally in the region," when it was alienating friendly Arab nations

---

*One point won't wait: Bill seems to misremember the Thomas Friedman incident. Nobody disputes that Friedman (and his colleague William Branigin of the *Washington Post*) described the Israeli bombing of Beirut as "indiscriminate," or that the *New York Times* excised this damning adjective from his report. It remains a cause célèbre in American journalism. (Friedman recalls the incident on page 73 of his book *From Beirut to Jerusalem.*) I had mistakenly ascribed the editorial tampering to Abe Rosenthal; that's all I was apologizing for in the letter Bill quotes. I hadn't invented the bombing of Beirut.

from us, recalled the old joke illustrating chutzpah: the man who kills his parents, then asks the court for mercy as an orphan.

An alliance is a hard-headed affair; your interests may require an alliance with someone you'd never want for a friend, just because you have a common enemy. Stalin is the notorious example. First you have enemies, then you form alliances. But in the Middle East, it seemed to be the other way around: first we got the "ally"—then we got the enemies.

The claim that Israel was our "strategic asset" died an embarrassing death during the Gulf War, when the Bush Administration had to beg Israel to stay out of the fighting, lest the anti-Iraq coalition fall apart. I never thought the Israelis wanted to fight, when the U.S. could dispatch their chief enemy for them; I predicted, though, that they would later demand American money for what was fulsomely called their "amazing restraint" in letting the U.S. do the fighting. Sure enough, they were soon demanding $10 billion in loan guarantees. And when President Bush stipulated conditions, an Israeli cabinet minister accused him of guess what.

I knew, nearly a decade ago now, that to write in this vein in my syndicated column would be to antagonize various Jewish neoconservatives, such as Norman Podhoretz and his wife, Midge Decter. I respected the neocons in those days, but I thought of them essentially as New Dealers who were beginning to see the light. I really had no idea how central Israel was to the Podhoretzes' politics. I figured that though we would differ on Israel, we agreed on most other things, so Israel wouldn't matter too much. I was yet to learn that they reasoned the other way around: if we differed on Israel, nothing else mattered.

The neocons could tolerate criticism of Israel from liberals and socialists, whom they dismissed as bleeding hearts. But criticism from a conservative—precisely on the grounds that Israel was neither a "reliable ally" nor a "strategic asset" to the U.S.—undermined the very basis on which they promoted American patronage of Israel.

By the spring of 1986, the Podhoretzes and their set were in full cry. They never argued with me; they accused me, publicly and privately, of "anti-Semitism," and they took their complaints to Bill and other editors, whom I gather they urged to fire or drop me. This is denied all around, but Bill's essay shows at least that their modus operandi is to communicate primarily with the editors and employers of writers who incur their wrath.* (In his reply to Bill's piece, Podhoretz complains that Bill broke his "promise" to prevent me from writing about Israel and Jewish topics

---

*The only time I heard from them directly was when Midge wrote me an accusing letter, copies of which were also sent to most of my principal editors. She told a reporter that she had tried to "keep it private," but circulating the letter among journalists proved an unsuccessful method of keeping it out of the papers.

in *NR*. What "promise" is he referring to? This comes as news to me. But whether or not any such promise was in fact made to him, we see here how he does business.)

Bill was very rattled. He published the strange statement he quotes in full in his essay, denying that I was anti-Semitic but saying it was perfectly reasonable to conclude from my columns on Israel that I was, with a pointed digression on the relative retaliatory powers of Jews, blacks, and homosexuals. (The statement appeared, as impish fate would have it, just below an editorial plangently affirming that free speech must never be squelched by pressure groups.)

Naturally, I was upset. But Bill discouraged me from writing a reply, arguing that I'd only be hurting myself; better to let the whole thing blow over. I accepted this unwise advice, assuming that I'd be vindicated by the letters from our readers in my behalf. The mail was pouring in, angry, eloquent, and overwhelmingly on my side. I was moved and gratified by those letters; some of them brought me close to tears. I never felt so proud of *NR*'s readers.

But Bill gave orders that none of those letters were to be published.

The result was that everyone got the false impression that our readers took no interest in the affair. I think I was more disheartened by that than by anything else in the whole episode. It's amusing that Bill now begins his essay by quoting a single letter critical of me. Vox populi . . .

The ultimate target of the silencing campaign, it should be remembered, is not the relatively few writers under attack, but the public. Israel's little helpers want not so much to prevent us from speaking freely as to prevent us from being heard by people who may be listening intently. Israel's subsidies depend on maintaining an illusory monopoly of opinion in the media that will keep American taxpayers uninformed and passive. It's not enough that one side should be heavily overrepresented; no other side should even seem to exist.

It pains me to reflect that *National Review* came into being precisely to counteract such lopsidedness and false unanimity in public discussion.

Bill Buckley is lovable, brilliant, funny, generous, and innumerable other endearing things, but he is not always the keenest listener. He can make distinctions that would dizzy Bertrand Russell, but when he's determined not to see your point, a team of logicians armed with red-hot pokers can't make him see it. So when he summarizes my views on Israel, he fatally omits something obvious and central to them. What he calls "my burgeoning case against Israel"—as if I were likening Israel to North Korea or Uganda—is really my burgeoning case against Israel as an ally of the United States.

I don't know how I could have made this plainer than I have over the years. It's not that Israel is such a horrible state, as modern states go; it's a farrago—rather typical of the Middle East—of socialist, ethnic, and religious elements. We have no stake in its feud with its Arab and Moslem neighbors. This is just the sort of quarrel America has successfully avoided at home for two centuries. Why should we plunge into one on the other side of the world?

We live in an age so intent on motive-hunting that it has forgotten how to argue. Before Bill undertakes to grapple with my motives and purposes, I wish he would at least get straight what I've actually said. Anyone who has read as much Burnham as he has shouldn't find my meaning impenetrable. If I were wrong on every detail he has collected against me, my general argument would be unaffected.

For example, he writes: "Joe Sobran never spent a lot of time blasting apartheid." Well, I've never blasted bribery in Mexico, polygamy in the Moslem world, or female circumcision in sub-Saharan Africa either. Deplorable as these things are, they don't affect American global interests.

Bill is right to call Israel's domestic policies "analogous" to South Africa's. But this is hard to square with his fantastic assertion that non-Jews (he says "Arabs," as if there were no other restricted minorities in Israel; Christian Armenians, for example) enjoy virtually "equal rights" with Jews in Israel proper—where Jim Crow laws and quasi-legal arrangements, enforced by the agriculture minister, forbid non-Jewish residence on more than 92 per cent of the land. Bill once sent me a propaganda sheet from the Zionist outfit FLAME (Facts and Logic About the Middle East) to assure me of this supposed equality, apparently not realizing that FLAME is to Israel roughly what Corliss Lamont was to the Soviet Union.

Does he, or anyone else, seriously believe that Arabs can be equals in a polity officially dedicated to Jews, and in which the total expulsion of Arabs is a live topic of discussion? In his book *Chutzpah,* even Alan Dershowitz admits that Arab equality in Israel is a fiction. The *New York Times* has recently carried several stories about Arabs being driven from their homes to make way for Jews; such news items ought to catch the eye of champions of private property. They illustrate the warnings of von Mises and Hayek about the malign uses of socialist state power. Socialism is a lousy system for producing wealth, but it's an excellent system for controlling a subject population. Ask any Ukrainian.

The South African analogy fails on several key points.

1. We aren't taxed to support South Africa. We are taxed to support Israel. We're usually free to find fault with that which we are forced to pay for.

2. There is no shortage of critics of apartheid; whereas Israel has not only a powerful lobby in America, but a big claque in the press constantly repeating its propaganda claims.

3. Most pertinent here, no journalist takes a risk to his career by criticizing apartheid. The power of the pro-Israel forces not only siphons off American tax money, but seriously impedes free discussion of Israel in this country.

Bill himself has sometimes noted ruefully that there is more freedom to criticize Israel in the Knesset than in the American press. For some reason, he doesn't address this problem in his essay. Not only is it pertinent; the essay itself is indirect proof of how serious the problem has gotten. Pat Buchanan and I are far from the only journalists whose livelihoods have been threatened because we criticized Israel. Everyone in the business knows you mention Israel's shortcomings at your own risk.

Very well, then; but must I criticize Israel so much? Must I be so . . . "obsessed"? I note that this word is applied exclusively to pundits on the wrong side of the unwritten law. If I were writing frequent columns faulting (say) Mali, when nobody else was even defending Mali, I'd have to say, Yes, it looks as if I'm a little obsessed with Mali.

But take a quick inventory (only the Census Bureau could do the job exhaustively) of the commentators who constantly defend Israel: Podhoretz, Rosenthal, Dershowitz, Martin Peretz, George Will, Mortimer Zuckerman, Morton Kondracke, Jeane Kirkpatrick, Kenneth Adelman, Amos Perlmutter, Eric Breindel, Cal Thomas, Max Lerner, Ben Wattenberg, Charles Krauthammer, William Safire, Fred Barnes . . . Peretz and Zuckerman have bought three major magazines—*The New Republic, U.S. News & World Report,* and *The Atlantic*—and turned them into organs of pro-Israel apologetics. The U.S. Government and the news media give enormously disproportionate attention to Israel, which gets the lion's share—more than a quarter—of U.S. aid. (How much goes to Mali, which has twice the population and fifty times the acreage of Israel? Where the hell is Mali?)

Please! *I* don't put Israel on the front pages of the *New York Times* and the *Washington Post. I* don't make Dan Rather and Tom Brokaw talk about it. *I* don't fly Secretaries of State to Jerusalem every few weeks.

The truth of the matter is that I'm responding to an obsession—a more or less official national obsession with a tiny, faraway socialist ethnocracy, which, I agree, ought to be a very minor concern of American policymakers, but isn't. The orthodox view that Israel is a "reliable ally" is so brittle that a single maverick can ignite a frenzy. The reason, I repeat, is not that critics of Israel are so numerous, but that even one, as far as Israel's claque is concerned, is one too many. There is the terrible danger that the public may be more interested in what he has to say than in the party line the rest of the chorus is emitting.

I'm also responding to a very loud silence. Obsession is not always overt. It can also take the form of evasion, of a jittery refusal to face a thing that cries out for frank discussion. I find this obsession in people who suspend their professed principles when it comes to Israel: in liberals who damn discrimination everywhere but in Israel, and in conservatives who overlook everything from socialism to espionage when Israel is the perpetrator. I guarantee you, I'll criticize Israel a lot less when other conservatives criticize it a little more.

Or when they feel free—really free, as an American should always feel free—to criticize it at all. It's really the silence that bothers me. Above all, I'm responding to the fear that creates that silence. Anti-Semitism, as the term is used by honest people, is contemptible. But so is the dishonest imputation of it. Not long after the Podhoretz crowd's attack on me, Midge Decter accused the most venerable of American conservatives, Russell Kirk, of "anti-Semitism" for a perfectly harmless quip: he had remarked that some neoconservatives appear to think the capital of the United States is Tel Aviv. Her smear was neither reported nor rebuked by *National Review*. I think *NR* finds it easier to stand up to Saddam Hussein than to Midge Decter. It can be witty and sassy on every subject but one.

I very much mind the tens of billions of dollars Israel and its partisans have taken from us. But I mind much more the freedom they have taken from us—the full freedom to discuss our own country's best interests. And I mind that it's a freedom Bill and *National Review* seem indisposed to exercise, or even to lament having lost.

WFB's Commentary

1. I don't understand Joe Sobran's saying that in my essay I never write about the "Vice Versa." In the essay I deplore a) unwarranted imputations of anti-Semitism; b) the intimidating activity of the American Israel Public Affairs Committee (AIPAC); c) heavy pressures, some Jewish in origin, by the abuse of the First Amendment, to cultivate an unnatural secularism (the essay even quoted at some length two Jewish critics, Irving Kristol and Michael Kinsley, who deplore this practice). Longtime readers of the magazine will remember that d) back when the Anti-Defamation League was tempted to identify American conservatism with fascism and racism, we regularly gave the organization hell. (We welcomed its reformation at the hands of the late Nathan Perlmutter, who was a contributor to *National Review*.

2. It is true, and should not surprise anybody, that as often as not there are no penalties imposed on minorities who abuse majorities. Associate Justice Thurgood Marshall referred to President Reagan as the "greatest racist" in the history of the White House and nobody except Reagan seemed to notice (President Reagan invited him over to the White House and they had a nice chat). The head of the NAACP said roughly the same thing about Reagan, more or less repeatedly. Anti-Christian and especially anti-Catholic abuse is everywhere engaged in, notably in Hollywood, and everywhere tolerated. Our own religion editor, Richard John Neuhaus, commented some time ago that in the view of the *New York Times* "the only good Catholic is a bad Catholic." And it has been suggested that no Catholic or Christian fundamentalist should be heard in public debate on those questions where their opinions derive from their underlying religious philosophy.

But this does not mean that the reputations of fanatics don't suffer. Professor Dershowitz is taken less seriously by serious people since the publication of a rabid book. President Freedman of Dartmouth is in effect disavowed in the *Commentary* piece quoted below. One must assume that such folk can be "hurt," even if nobody sues them for damages or puts them in the pokey, or in Coventry.

3. It is true that to criticize Israel is often to invite critical biopsies by people a) looking out for Israel and b) looking for anti-Semitism. That there is a hard lobby working for Israel is nowhere denied; on the contrary, it is stipulated in the essay. There are other lobbies. Is it more dangerous for a congressman to antagonize AIPAC, or the National Rifle Association? A draw, I'd guess. We spend $3 billion per year on Israel. The Grace Commission showed how we might save annual expenditures of $400 billion. To blow one's stack over that relatively small part of the budget that goes to Israel is only absolutely safe to do—if fiscal husbandry is the objective—if one has a whole lot of other stacks lined up to blow, in protest of other federal expenditures. If it isn't the money, but the moral question, indignation over expenditures in countries with unsavory governments should be consistent (how much did we invest in the Philippines when Marcos was in charge?). Otherwise the suspicion can and will arise that there is animus behind the objective of trimming the budget at the expense of Israel.

4. It does not occur to Joe to meditate on the exchanges with his colleagues during the period in question: three protracted sessions, two of them lasting over two hours, at which the other Senior Editors, plus the Managing Editor, plus the Publisher, endorsed the analysis that went into the editorial he classifies as "strange," and the action to which that analysis pointed. All five of us joined in warning him that what he was then writing inevitably gave rise to conclusions that what burns up Joe Sobran

is the Jewish operation in Israel. Joe does not call attention to his praise of *Instauration* magazine (later withdrawn), or to some of the language used in his column ("Holocaust Update" for the *New York Times*). Dammit, people who provoke—and that often includes *National Review* and its Editor-at-Large—have got to face up to the consequences of provocation: people get mad and they fight back. The question here is whether they fight back fairly—in this case, by alleging anti-Semitism. It was precisely the purpose of the essay to probe that question. When Pat Buchanan said that only the Israeli Defense Ministry and its "amen corner" were in favor of resisting Saddam Hussein's war of aggression he certainly provoked me, by God: I'm neither an Israeli Defense Ministry nor an "amen corner," and I and fellow editors had written several columns and editorials backing Bush's tough response to Iraq. So Joe and Pat should be surprised that some people suspect, others proclaim, that Sobran and Buchanan are bent on provoking friends of Israel? Well, they succeeded in their provocations and have to live with the hounds they unleashed. This is hardly an endorsement of such as A. M. Rosenthal, who indefensibly situated Pat Buchanan alongside David Duke, or of Richard Cohen, who goes so far as to contend that no anti-anti-Semite should consent to appear on the same television program with Buchanan. And of course it is supremely deformed to suggest that Pat Buchanan's campaign in New Hampshire was in any significant way related to the question here being discussed.

5. When the editorial about the disavowal of Joe's columns was published in *NR*, this was not an invitation to our readers to comment on who was right, who wrong, in the adjudication. In the first place, none of our readers (that we knew of) had studied the scarlet dozen of Joe's columns. They could not have known the hours of thought given to the decisions arrived at by a unanimous senior staff whose responsibility it is to make policy and personnel decisions. I did not elect to embarrass Joe in the editorial I wrote—by reproducing the offensive columns. Nor did I dilate on the number of times I had told him about the minefield he was electing to kick up his heels in. And it is critical to recognize that we are talking about a minefield the editors of *National Review* substantially approve of: alarms that go off when people venture, inadvertently or by design, toward a dark and toxic house, whose identity becomes decipherable only after one has trod too far. There is a graffito there that reads: EZRA POUND SLEPT HERE.

6. I do not understand Joe's extraordinary suggestion that Israel is immune from critical attention by me or by *National Review* (or, for that matter, by the *New York Times*, CBS, or Garry Trudeau). We reproduce, on pages 106–8, brief excerpts from published criticisms of Israeli practices which *did not* provoke charges of anti-Semitism. But any useful com-

mentary on the Israeli phenomenon has got to begin by understanding that an explicitly Jewish state isn't going to be a multicultural state. Much that goes on routinely in Israel, and certainly in the West Bank, would be forbidden under the U.S. Constitution. Accept this, and much else is merely derivative. Christians are not free to proselytize in Israel. Israel isn't a state within which there is civil equality. On this subject I have written, if I may say so, vividly. I have also written (the phrase is reproduced in the excerpts of criticisms of Israeli policies) that our concern for Israel is "one part geopolitical and nine parts moral"; and that was written even before the cold war ended. In 1946 the feeling in America among the morally alert was that something should be done to revive Jewish hope, to help to remoralize a people wounded and humiliated by the Holocaust. That sentiment, so widely held, diminishes today because of the excesses of the Shamir government. But although our help over the years was largely that, a benefaction—even as we exercised charity toward Japan and Germany—Israel was, also, over a particular period, a strategic asset whose government reflected majority opinion. It is absolutely incorrect to suggest, as Joe does, that South Africa's apartheid policies lay outside his interest inasmuch as South Africa was never a strategic asset. On the contrary, it was: the source of minerals not elsewhere procurable, and the Gibraltar of the South Atlantic. The embargo on South Africa, at the time it was imposed, imperiled our strategic interests; which is why *National Review* opposed that embargo even while disapproving of apartheid.

7. *National Review* came into existence to endeavor to speak the truth and to encourage discriminating thought. It continues to be proud of one of its primary achievements, namely to have encouraged Joe Sobran to harness up and come on into our tent, where he is much admired, much beloved; and, as should certainly be evident, much prayed over.

* * *

Some examples of critical assessments, done by WFB in his column and in *National Review*, of past Israeli government practices.

". . . the present danger is that Israel's history and Begin's fanaticism may merge. [That fanaticism] threatens to infect the basis of Israel's support, which has all along been one part geopolitical and nine parts moral. The essence of the Israeli case has always been the right of a people to a homeland . . . But the right of a people to a homeland is, at root, impartial. The Palestinians are also entitled to a home."

—Column, February 9, 1982

". . . the top leadership of Israel decided to get huffy. They took the position: 'Your Eminence, you can visit us in our offices or not at all.' In putting it that way, the Israelis give the impression of opportunism and of insincerity."

—Column, January 1, 1987

". . . there is the other position held nowadays by some American Jews, expressed by Rita Hauser, the prominent attorney and stateswoman: 'Israel runs the risk of losing its soul.' She meant by this that democracy is one of the ideals with which Israel is associated. But Israel is right now engaged in colonizing the West Bank, never mind that Israelis are outnumbered there 10 to 1. And there are no plans, warns Miss Hauser, to give equal rights to Arabs . . ."

—Column, January 7, 1988

"[Amos] Elon began by telling interrogator Harry Reasoner that it was nonsense for Americans, particularly Jewish Americans, to take the position that they should keep their hands away from Israeli policy. Israeli policy, said Elon, is very much a matter of concern to America. The trouble with many American Jews, said Elon, is that having conquered their environment and won a secure place in the American scene, they 'live like WASPs, but vote like Puerto Ricans.' It is too much the fashion to suppose that because a policy is sanctioned by the government of Israel, it is a policy that should evoke loyalty from Jews around the world . . . Elon told his vast audience that under existing policies, Israel faced one of two futures: 'I really do not see that there is a third alternative.' One future is the transformation of the area into one more Lebanon, which is what would happen if Israel annexed the West Bank and the Gaza Strip. The second alternative, which is a continuation of present policies—occupation and suppression—would mean simply that Israel had become another South Africa, with one law for citizens of one race, a second law for others. To go in either of these directions, Elon said, is to abort the dream that guided the founding of Israel."

—Column, April 19, 1988

"Israel has a way of driving its friends mad, which gives us some idea of what it does to its enemies. The latest is the imposition by Israel of censorship to cover the emigration of Soviet Jews into the West Bank. Israel is engaged in breaking all the rules . . ."

—Column, March 6, 1990

". . . the riots also show the morass into which Israel, as a result of its own policies, has sunk . . ."

—Editorial, January 22, 1988

". . . The issue is that Israel continues to occupy, as it has for 22 years, territory to which it has no claim and no title. The totalists in Shamir's party and beyond it—the Sharons and the Kahanes—want the occupation to continue *in saecula saeculorum*. Shamir . . . has bowed to their pressure . . . It is endlessly said that there is only one democracy in the Middle East. Considering the constipation of Israeli politics, it might be better to say, in the manner of the Unitarians, that there is at most one democracy in the Middle East. The Labor Party of Shimon Peres is more exasperated by Israeli bitterendedness than any critic in America, but the Israeli political system, which is based on proportional representation of the most fragmented sort, prevents any major party from proposing a coherent program of change. Peres lacks the votes, Shamir lacks the guts, and so the country remains hostage to religious and expansionist fanatics . . ."

—Editorial, August 4, 1989

". . . the Shamirites have grown so accustomed to thinking of the Palestinian problem as one that can be bluffed away or denied that their capacity to deal with the problem's actual manifestations, whether in the occupied territories or in Israel itself, has virtually eroded . . ."

—Editorial, November 5, 1990

". . . since the United States is also a sovereign state, we have our own decisions to make, based on our own interests. When Israel takes actions which snarl our diplomacy on the eve of a major push . . . then our interests are not served. We should make it clear to our friends in Jerusalem that if they insist too hard on going it alone, we could conceivably let them do so."

—Editorial, August 7, 1981*

2 · An Interrogatory From Ronald R. Stockton†

Item 1. You take Sobran to task for reporting that a Friedman story non "indiscriminate" bombing was modified stateside. You say Thomas

---

*For the benefit of those with very large appetites, see also columns by WFB 6/13/81; 2/22/83; 10/15/85; 1/15/87; 3/4/88; 9/8/89; 4/6/90. And NR editorials 10/2/81; 4/16/82; 10/1/82; 9/30/83; 4/20/84; 12/31/85; 1/30/87; 2/5/88; 4/16/90.

†Mr. Stockton is a professor of political science at the University of Michigan–Dearborn.

Friedman wrote an article in *Columbia Journalism Review* correcting facts.

Observation: I spoke with Tom Friedman and asked about the "indiscriminate" story. He said he *had* used the word and it *had* been cut stateside. He said the story in the Roger Morris article in the *CJR* (November/December 1982) was an accurate depiction of what happened, that he told *you* the facts and "Buckley got it wrong." He said he himself had *no* article in *CJR*.

Item 2. While Israel does not allow mixed marriages, a marriage contracted overseas "yields equal rights upon return."

Observation: It would take a lawyer to sort this one out, but my understanding is that the children of such marriages are illegitimate *(mamzer)* under Israeli law.

Also, by way of anecdote, a colleague, Sandy, who is Jewish, married Sue, who is not. When Sandy took his sabbatical in Israel a few years ago, Sue was not allowed to work because they would not give her a spouse work permit for this reason (at least that is what Sandy understood).

Item 3. You discuss the anti-inducement law and observe that "In the absence of protests from the missionary wing of the Christian churches, one assumes either that the law is a dead letter, or else that it is so effective as to eliminate evangelization."

Observation: *Arrrrgh!* My first thought was that this is the logic whereby Syrian Jews who do not tell TV reporters they are being harassed are not being harassed. My second thought is that you need a better informant. Do you know the problems the Mormons had, getting permission to build in Jerusalem? Or the problems of Jerusalem's Baptist church? It burned down in the early 1980s, waited over an hour for a fire truck to come from a few blocks away, waited most of the decade to get a permit to rebuild, then had to put in expensive soundproofing when neighbors protested against Christian songs. I personally met a "secret missionary" registered as a bookseller. He says that he has a rabbi in his group: the rabbi says if he acknowledged his faith he would be ruined. The missionary fears expulsion. Talk to some Christian Palestinians.

Item 4. Abe's mother is Jewish. Under the Law of Return he has a right to citizenship—unless he renounces his faith.

Observation: Murky is too mild a word, but apparently Abe's *descendants* have a right to citizenship even if Abe converts. Clause 4Aa guarantees citizenship to "the child and grandchild of a Jew" exempting only the "person" who converted. This looks like citizenship by descent as well as faith. Zucker, *Coming Crisis in Israel*, discusses some court decisions.

Item 5. Vidal says "a small number of American Jews made common cause with . . . the TV studios of the evangelical Jesus-Christers." You say "I am genuinely at a loss as to what Vidal means here."

Observation: The close relationship between Revisionist Zionism and the Televangelist Right was a bit of a scandal in the 1980s among progressive Jews. Falwell received the Jabotinsky Award in 1981 and was reportedly the second American called by Begin after the bombing of Iraq (after the President). I was told by someone in the Evangelical movement—not involved in Middle Eastern affairs—that the Israelis gave Falwell a private jet. (See my article on Christian Zionism, *The Middle East Journal,* Spring 1987.)

Item 6. The Pollard case would be different if Israel had given secrets to Russia.

Observation: Did you read the Weinberg brief (sensitive sections were deleted)? It suggests exactly that (although he cannot say so directly). Also see the *MacNeil–Lehrer* interview with DeGenova the day of sentencing. He came as close as possible to saying it without saying it.

Item 7. You say there is no move to expel "Israeli Arabs."

Observation: Are you aware of the positions of rightist Israeli parties? Check the platforms of Tehiya, Molodet, and Tsomet, and the public statements of their leaders. Remember these are (or were) in the Israeli cabinet.

Item 8. "A fierce anti-Semitism exists among Palestinians. Probably a higher percentage of them hate Jews than did the Germans."

Observation: This may be the oddest statement in the essay. It comes from nowhere, is unconnected to anything before or after, and offers no evidence. On the face of it, it seems part of the Israel-linked rhetoric wars. I have seen Palestinian public-opinion studies, have read official PLO documents, have spoken to Palestinians in Jerusalem, in the territories, in Israel, and in Dearborn, and see no evidence for your conclusion. A few months ago the Bishop of Jerusalem told my class how he had been a 'Sabbath boy' to a beloved neighbor in Haifa in 1948. A Nazareth pastor told me last summer how he invited Jews from Tel Aviv to take refuge in his church until the war ended. And Father Chacour told a Detroit congregation recently of his determination to have peace between Jews and Palestinians. You mentioned a "percentage." Would you share your data?

Comment by WFB

Re Item 1. I regret the confusion. Here is the PS in a letter I sent to Joe Sobran on September 29, 1990: "I called Thomas Friedman. He told me 1) Abe Rosenthal was not on duty when the adjective 'indiscriminate' was excised—Seymour Topping was. 2) Friedman never wrote a piece on the subject for the *Columbia Journalism Review,* Roger Morris did. 3) Not all the facts in the Morris account are accurate. He would be glad to tell the entire story to anyone at *NR* who wants to call him." In my essay my memory slipped, but in no important detail: I had forgotten that it was Roger Morris who had written up the story in the *Columbia Journalism Review*. My memory of what Thomas Friedman said over the telephone is distinct, and the reason I published the story is made clear in the context.

Re Item 8. I don't understand why you find this perplexing. Organized Jewry in Germany was never hostile to Germany. The Palestinians have been fighting the Jews since 1948, fighting directly on five occasions, indirectly on other occasions. They are most definitely hostile to the state of Israel, which they believe began by taking their territory and continues, expansively, to colonize outside the pre-1967 borders. It should not surprise us that there are Palestinians who are friendly and hospitable to individual Jews, and vice versa. It was so in Nazi Germany, between Jews and (yes) even some Nazis.

3 · An Open Letter to William F. Buckley Jr. From Norman Podhoretz*

I have just read "In Search of Anti-Semitism" and I am, quite frankly, relieved. The reason is that it did not confirm my deepest apprehensions upon first hearing the top-secret rumor that you were writing a very long essay by that title which would take a new look at the charges of anti-Semitism against Joe Sobran, Pat Buchanan, Gore Vidal, and *The Dartmouth Review*.

No doubt you are wondering, perhaps a little testily, why this rumor should have made me so apprehensive. Well, our mutual friend George Will once observed that one does not call a conference on "Whither Incest?" in order to reaffirm the prohibition against incest. Just so, it is reasonable to suspect that one does not necessarily go in search of anti-Semitism in order to find it. Anti-Semitism is, after all, easy enough to

*"What is Anti-Semitism? An Open Letter to William F. Buckley Jr." is excerpted from *Commentary*, February 1992.

unearth without a search warrant; conversely, if one needs to search in order to find it, the possibility arises that it may not be there at all.

But I am being a little disingenuous here (though no more than I admit—see below—I have sometimes found you to be on the subject of anti-Semitism). The truth is that, after discussing the issue with you several times over the past ten years—first in connection with the response to Israel's invasion of Lebanon in 1982, and then more recently in connection with Sobran and Buchanan—I had come away with the sinking feeling that (forgive me, even though I can hardly forgive myself, for borrowing from the feminists) you just didn't get it.

But, you are fully entitled to ask me, what about your past record not only in spotting anti-Semitism when it appeared in your own immediate environs but also in fighting to expunge it? In your new essay, you remind us of that record, and the pride you take in it shines through. So it should; it is a very honorable record indeed. You begin with a casual shocker: "I have some credentials in the area, among them my own father's anti-Semitism." You also confess that in 1937, at the age of 11, you "wept tears of frustration at being forbidden by senior siblings" to accompany them on an adventure that consisted of burning a cross outside a Jewish resort. But later in life, putting away childish things, and having come to see in the wake of the Holocaust that "The age calls for hypersensitivity to anti-Semitism, over against a lackadaisical return to the blase conventions of the prewar generation, which in one country led to genocidal catastrophe," you set your face most resolutely against anti-Semitism. When you founded National Review in 1955 and became its editor, you recall, the magazine

> declined association with anti-Semites, and indeed on one occasion went a generic step further. When it became clear, in 1957, that the direction The American Mercury was headed was anti-Semitic, I ruled, with the enthusiastic approval of my colleagues, that no writer appearing on the Mercury's masthead, notwithstanding his own innocence on the subject, could also appear on National Review's.

There can be no doubt that this was indeed a "generic step." Before you took it, the American Right had provided a rather comfortable home for anti-Semitic ideas, attitudes, and feelings, even if many on the Right were themselves, as individuals, "innocent on the subject." Thanks to you, however, a process of purgation, of cleansing, began. It is a process that still remains to be completed, but so far has it already gone that—as your successor to the editorship of National Review, John O'Sullivan, puts it in his introduction to your essay—"When anti-Semitism appears today outside the restricted confines of the country club . . . , it is almost invariably a left-wing phenomenon."

Nearly thirty years later came the case of Joe Sobran, which you review at length in the first part of "In Search of Anti-Semitism." The salient points are that in 1986, Sobran, then a Senior Editor of *National Review*, wrote a number of syndicated columns which many people regarded as unambiguously anti-Semitic. Complaints were made both orally and in writing to him, to you, and to some of your colleagues. You responded in due course with an extraordinary editorial in *National Review* denying that Sobran was anti-Semitic but acknowledging that

> Any person who, given the knowledge of the reigning protocols, read and agonized over the half-dozen columns by Joe Sobran might reasonably conclude that those columns were written by a writer inclined to anti-Semitism.

Invoking the precedent you had set in connection with *The American Mercury* in 1957, you concluded by dissociating yourself and your colleagues "from what we view as the obstinate tendentiousness of Joe Sobran's recent columns" (even though those columns had not appeared in *National Review* itself). While you did not go so far as to drop him from your board of Senior Editors (that would come in 1991, over the Gulf War), you did forbid him to write in *National Review* on Jews, Judaism, or Israel.

As for my own role, which you now rehearse in great—perhaps too great—detail, it consisted at first only of being among those whose complaints had led to this outcome. Later I wrote an article for *Commentary* entitled "The Hate That Dare Not Speak Its Name" [November 1986], which was mainly about Gore Vidal and *The Nation* (a case you take up in Part 4 of your essay) but which concluded with a section about Sobran and *National Review*. Later still, you and I had a rather sharp two-round exchange of unpublished letters about a piece by Sobran in defense of himself against me and some of his other critics that you published in *National Review*. "In Search of Anti-Semitism" contains extensive quotes from that exchange (with more space devoted to your letters than to mine—but who's counting?), and you naturally give yourself the last word with seven points in rebuttal. My guess is that any reader of that section of your essay who is unfamiliar with "The Hate That Dare Not Speak Its Name" will get the impression that I had been one of those who, you report, were dissatisfied with the way you handled "the Sobran crisis." Curiously enough, in spite of the praise I lavished upon your behavior in "The Hate That Dare Not Speak Its Name," you seem to lapse at moments into that impression yourself. So let me make things Kristol clear (pun intended, naturally).

I thought then, and I think now, that you acted nobly in confronting a "beloved" (your word) disciple and colleague and trying to set him straight in private on a matter of great delicacy and difficulty. I thought then, and I think now, that going public with your chastisement of him when he remained obdurate was an act of high statesmanship. Had you lacked the courage to perform it, grave damage would have resulted to the reputation of your magazine and of the conservative movement it has done more than any other single force to establish as an influential presence in the mainstream of our political culture. I wondered then, and I wonder now, whether I would have had the stuff to acquit myself so well in an analogous situation.

In short, I have no hesitation in including your handling of Sobran on the list of your accomplishments in fighting anti-Semitism on the Right. (Until, that is, you tarnished that accomplishment by deciding to publish what I called his "unrepentant and disingenuous" rebuttal in *National Review*—about which more below.)

Finally, to complete the list of your struggles to cleanse the conservative movement of anti-Semitism, we come to the case of Pat Buchanan. To my mind, the section on him in "In Search of Anti-Semitism" is the best, and politically the most important, news about the essay. Here, to my gratified surprise, you conclude another long and careful review of the record by stating simply and clearly, and without any fancy dancing, that you

> find it impossible to defend Pat Buchanan against the charge that what he did and said during the period under examination amounted to anti-Semitism, whatever it was that drove him to say and do it . . .

Again, if you are wondering why I should have been surprised, I would refer you to the column you wrote on the subject after Abe Rosenthal, in his column in the *New York Times*, had (as you put it) "gone ballistic" in charging Buchanan with anti-Semitism. Your own judgment at that time was that Buchanan was merely "insensitive to those fine lines that tend publicly to define racially or ethnically offensive analysis or rhetoric." You also seemed to endorse the view that what others took to be anti-Semitism was in reality an attraction in Buchanan to "mischievous generalizations." Worse yet, you concluded with a peroration which in my opinion came perilously close to falling into the abyss of moral equivalence in its assessment of the debate:

> The Buchanans need to understand the nature of sensibilities in an age that coexisted with Auschwitz. And the Rosenthals need to understand that clumsy forensic manners are less than a genocidal offense . . .

You now reveal that you were uneasy with the points left unexplored in this column, and that this is what prompted you to investigate further and eventually to write "In Search of Anti-Semitism." Yet to tell you the truth, I saw little sign of any such uneasiness at the meeting of conservatives you called around that time to discuss Desert Shield. Inevitably, a good part of that meeting was devoted to the Buchanan question, and whereas a number of the non-Jewish participants were willing to say unequivocally that Buchanan's pieces on Desert Shield—along with some of the remarks he had made on television and in other columns dealing with Israel, American Jews, and Nazi war criminals—added up to anti-Semitism, you were conspicuously reluctant to join them. You kept raising questions and introducing distinctions that struck me (see above) as disingenuous and logic-chopping and that served more to darken counsel than to advance understanding.

Hence my gratified surprise when I read the results of your subsequent investigation of and reflections on the case of Buchanan. And I was all the more gratified to discover that Joshua Muravchik's scrupulously documented article in *Commentary*, "Patrick J. Buchanan and the Jews" [January 1991], had helped you resolve some of your earlier doubts and reach your new conclusion.

In the cover letter accompanying the advance copy you sent me of "In Search of Anti-Semitism," you wrote: "I have a feeling you will agree with 95 per cent of my own conclusions, nuanced though they are—which means to run special risks . . ." As it happens, 95 per cent may be a little high, since I would have to deduct at least 5 per cent alone for your positively talmudic (or should the word be Jesuitical—as from before the Jesuits went left, of course?) whitewash of Russell Kirk. I acknowledge that he deserves your deepest respect as one of the founding fathers of the contemporary conservative movement. But that does not remove the anti-Semitic stench from his crack that "not seldom has it seemed as if some eminent neoconservatives mistook Tel Aviv for the capital of the United States."

Still, I do agree with a great deal of your essay. On your conclusions about Gore Vidal and *The Nation*, for example, there isn't a dime's worth of difference between us—though that may not be saying much, given that we have long seen eye to eye where the growth of anti-Semitism on the Left is concerned.

On the other hand, it may perhaps strike you as more significant that I am with you all the way in your section exonerating *The Dartmouth Review* of the charge of anti-Semitism. Some people are always complaining that false charges of anti-Semitism are just as bad as anti-Semitism itself. I doubt it, but even stipulating that in certain circumstances it may be so, it remains the case that for these people, virtually all charges of anti-Semitism are false. The reasoning seems to be that the accusation of anti-Semitism is so damaging that not even those who make blatantly anti-Semitic statements should be subjected to it. (Remember when the press refused to call even outspoken members of the Communist Party Communists?) For some, nothing short of releasing the gas into the showers of Auschwitz constitutes anti-Semitism; and even that may not be enough—assuming (they quickly go on to add) that such a thing ever really happened; or if it did happen, that it resulted in as many deaths as "the Jews" claim it did.

Yet for once, in *The Dartmouth Review*, we have a genuine example of false charges of anti-Semitism doing damage to innocent victims. I see no good reason to rehash your excellent summary of the particulars of this case here, but there is one crucial point that needs to be extended and stressed.

In dealing with *The Dartmouth Review* you return to the question you raised earlier in discussing Sobran and Buchanan of whether there is "a nexus between anti-Semitism and opposition to the policies of Israel." But this time—because *The Dartmouth Review* defended itself against the charge of anti-Semitism by emphasizing that it had always been a supporter of Israel—you raise the question in order "to probe the contrapositive assumption, namely that friendship toward Israel exonerates one from any suspicion of anti-Semitism." Your own position is that

> this is as a practical matter true, though not conclusively so. It is difficult to imagine someone who is anti-Semitic and pro-Israel. But such could exist, e.g., the (hypothetical) man who wishes Zionism to flower so that Jews in the rest of the world would be attracted to emigrate; so to speak, inaugurating an anti-diasporization.

Now, to be fair, your hypothetical man is not hypothetical at all; in the nineteenth century, the founder of political Zionism himself, Theodor Herzl, used this very argument with some success to enlist gentile support. But that was in another country, and those wenches have long since died. Today, I for one would insist, it *is* impossible "to imagine someone who is anti-Semitic and pro-Israel." But what about Solzhenitsyn, who is thought by many to be anti-Semitic and yet is certainly pro-Israel, possibly for the very reason that he wants all the Jews of Russia to go there? In an essay on Solzhenitsyn a few years ago, I grappled with this question, and came up with the following answer:

> Solzhenitsyn has always defended Israel, even to the point of invidiously comparing the courage of the Israelis in the face of their Arab enemies with the appeasement of the Soviet Union by the Western democracies. To be sure there was a time when it was possible for an anti-Semite to be a Zionist of sorts. . . . *But in our own day Israel has become the touchstone of attitudes toward the Jewish people, and anti-Zionism has become the main and most relevant form of anti-Semitism.* So much is this the case that almost anything Solzhenitsyn may think about the role of Jews in the past—or even in the post-Communist Russia of his dreams—becomes academic by comparison.

This was published in February 1985, and pausing for a minute to express my awe at the realization in so short a time of Solzhenitsyn's dreams, which then seemed so far off, I want to call your special attention to the sentence I have now put in italics. For it is here that you and I have our sharpest disagreements, and it is here that I come to the bad news about "In Search of Anti-Semitism."

As between the two of us, the story goes back to "J'Accuse," the article I wrote for *Commentary* [September 1982] about the response to the Israeli invasion of Lebanon, and the two columns you then wrote in response to it.

I recall this old controversy not because I have any desire to awaken sleeping dogs, but because you yourself dig it up in your essay—and in a most peculiar way. Instead of tackling it directly, as you do with the other instances of debate between us which you describe in other parts of "In Search of Anti-Semitism," you drag it in via endless quotations from a piece by one Allan Brownfeld attacking "J'Accuse," as well as a speech I made a few years later at a conference of Jewish journalists in Jerusalem.* Brownfeld you identify as "a syndicated columnist who is himself Jewish," which is true as far as it goes but omits the more relevant information that he is violently anti-Zionist (being, in fact, the editor of an American Council for Judaism newsletter) and hence violently anti-*Commentary* and me.

Be that as it may, in one of the passages you reproduce, Brownfeld repeats the widely circulated lie that in "J'Accuse" I equated any and all criticism of Israel with anti-Semitism. You then make this comment:

> The episode to which Brownfeld refers is well remembered by readers of *Commentary*. It was the general judgment of the concerned community (I was among the critics, devoting a column to the subject) that Podhoretz's fears and condemnations were exaggerated. . . .

---

*I spoke, as I usually do, from notes, but the account of the speech in the *Jerusalem Post*, on which Brownfeld relied, was reasonably accurate. Which is more than I can say for Brownfeld's interpretation. Though you for some reason see fit to transcribe this piece of disinformation, you do at least assume that my speech, "coming to us third hand, contained qualifications . . . that Mr. Brownfeld either is not aware of or else is disinclined to quote." Indeed it did. Thus, you would not know from Brownfeld that the question I was asked to address was whether the editors of and contributors to local Jewish papers had any special Jewish responsibility. My answer was that they were free to disclaim it, but *insofar as they accepted such a responsibility*, it was to defend Israel rather than to join in the ideological campaign against the Jewish state—which I took (and take) to be a war against the Jewish people as a whole. What Brownfeld did with this was use it to show that no one, not even "Israeli critics of Israel's policy in Lebanon," was safe from my reckless accusations of anti-Semitism.

Here either your memory is failing you (if so, welcome to the club) or you are once again slipping into disingenuousness (ditto). Whichever, there are three errors in the second of the two sentences quoted above: 1) The mail on "J'Accuse" showed that the "concerned community" overwhelmingly endorsed my thesis that the coverage of and comment on the Israeli invasion of Lebanon went far beyond unfairness and gave witness to "an eruption of anti-Semitism." 2) You devoted, as I have already indicated, not one but two columns to the subject, in the second of which you answered me and others who had complained to you about the first. 3) Neither you nor the other critics of "J'Accuse" thought that my "fears and condemnations were exaggerated," as you now so blandly phrase it. What you all thought, or at any rate said, was summed up in a letter I sent you on the day your first column appeared. Instead of paraphrasing that letter, I will follow the example you set in "In Search of Anti-Semitism" of quoting from private correspondence when it serves to illuminate. Here, then, are a couple of the relevant passages from my letter:

> Nearly 15 years ago, I began earning the enemies you congratulate me on having by pointing to the prevalence of anti-Americanism on the American Left. This charge elicited ... vituperation and evasive action: "Podhoretz smears anyone who criticizes America as anti-American." To this I would reply: "Yes, to be sure, there is such a thing as legitimate criticism of America, but the phenomenon I am pointing to is more properly called 'anti-Americanism.'"
>
> Now you, of all people, come along and make an analogous charge against an analogous argument ... I was careful to say in "J'Accuse" that *not* all critics of Israel's incursion into Lebanon are anti-Semitic; I specifically mentioned the *New York Times* editorial page as an example. Yet like my own critics on the Left ..., you charge—and the *Washington Post* delightedly highlights the charge in bold type—that I "label as anti-Semitic the critics of Israel's campaign against the PLO in Lebanon."

Your response to this appeal was to write in your second column about two weeks later that

> although Podhoretz did not accuse every opponent of Israel's policies of being anti-Semitic, he was mistaken to the extent that he suggested that any of those he quoted (this side of the fever swamps inhabited by such as Alexander Cockburn) is motivated by anti-Semitism.

But I was never talking about *motivation;* I was talking about words on paper, and I said that both in the interest of intellectual honesty and for the sake of social hygiene, those words could, indeed must, be characterized as anti-Semitic. About five years later, in arguing with you about Joe Sobran, I again emphasized that the question of whether he was an anti-Semite could be left to those who presume to know the secrets of the human heart; as for me, it was enough to observe that he had written anti-Semitic articles.

To clarify the distinction further, I will add that any person not motivated by anti-Semitism who wishes to avoid being called anti-Semitic need only refrain from voicing anti-Semitic ideas or sentiments. And might we not expect that such a person would be appalled if shown, through careful documentation and analysis, that he has blundered into anti-Semitism? For example, Nicholas von Hoffman, whose anti-Semitic remarks I cited in "J'Accuse," had the decency to be thus appalled at the sight of what he had said.

Sobran, however, was not only unrepentant, he was defiant. Like Pat Buchanan after him, who would declare, "I don't retract a single word," Sobran stuck by his guns; and, again anticipating Buchanan, he represented himself as an innocent victim of Jewish pressure, a courageous speaker of forbidden truths who, if the Jews had their way, would be censored.

You agreed when I said that Sobran was unrepentant. But you became (in your own word) "peevish" when I expressed my dismay at the fact that, in violation as I saw it of your promise to keep him from writing on Jewish themes, you nevertheless had opened the pages of *National Review* to his counterattack. Although you declared that I was mistaken in viewing this as a violation, what seemed to bother you most was not my public statement [in *Commentary*'s correspondence column, March 1987] that you had thereby "tarnished your previously honorable record on this sorry episode." What really riled you was my private remark (in a letter to your colleague Jeff Hart) that the publication of this counterattack lent "credence to all those like Marty Peretz who have attacked me for being too easy on Buckley."

You felt then, and you evidently still feel, that I had committed a double sin against you here. First, I had shown excessive "docility" toward Peretz's criticisms of *National Review*; but more seriously, I had conspicuously failed to dissociate myself from his statement in a *New Republic* editorial that "the old Catholic Right has always had trouble with the Jewish problem. This explains why Buckley has made things so cozy for an unabashed bigot like columnist Joseph Sobran."

We differed then, and we continue to differ, on whether I had a duty to do unto Peretz (who after all neither worked for me nor spoke for me) what you had done unto Sobran. Indeed, you were not even mollified when I informed you in a letter that I was so outraged by the *New Republic* editorial in question that "I hung up on [Peretz] when he too remained unrepentant in response to my call of protest." All you knew was that I should have made a public disavowal comparable to the one you had made of Sobran's columns.

All right, then, I will make one now—of Peretz's allegations 1) that you were in effect letting Sobran off the hook, and 2) that you have "trouble with the Jewish problem" (a euphemism, I suppose, for a residual degree of anti-Semitism). In my judgment—a judgment richly confirmed by "In Search of Anti-Semitism"—the only trouble you have with the Jewish problem is that it will not let you rest, and that you feel called upon over and over again to struggle with it and think about it and talk about it and write about it. (I have the same trouble myself.)

But this does not mean that I agree with you that Peretz is guilty of "blind intolerance of nuance in any discussion of Israel." For my money he is all too tolerant of such nuance when it comes from his friends on the Left, especially Irving Howe and Michael Walzer. Furthermore—to throw you a nuance of my own of which I trust you will be tolerant—I myself have been upset by the irritable and needling editorials on Israel which have appeared from time to time in National Review. This is not because I have regarded them as anti-Semitic. It is because on general conservative principles I would have expected National Review to be friendlier to Israel than it seemed to be—as friendly, say, as some other Christians of conservative political bent (Jeane Kirkpatrick, Michael Novak, Bob Tyrrell, George Weigel, and George Will, to name only a few).

Marty Peretz, is, of course, Jewish, but I have to tell you that, as I honor the likes of Kirkpatrick, Novak, Tyrrell, Weigel, and Will, I honor Peretz as well for his championship of Israel at a time when it takes real courage in liberal circles to stand up for that besieged and beleaguered country against the relentless ideological assault to which it is being subjected.

I also have to tell you in all candor that I cannot in all conscience disavow Peretz's charge that—to repeat, present company excepted—the old Catholic Right in general "has trouble with the Jewish problem." For in spite of the laudable efforts which have been made by the Church in recent years to eliminate anti-Semitism from Catholic teaching, the Vatican still refuses to recognize the state of Israel. If this is not a symptom of trouble with the Jewish problem, what is it?

Which brings me back to the role of Israel in anti-Semitism today. "In searching out the meaning of contemporary anti-Semitism," you observe, "it is useful to ask whether in order to qualify as a contemporary anti-Semite one needs to be anti-Israel." The answer is, Not necessarily, but it certainly helps—though I reiterate that I would put it in terms that stress ideas and attitudes rather than motives or conscious intentions.

Here again, instead of paraphrasing myself, I will follow your example and quote freely from what I have written in *Commentary* on this subject in the past. First, on why and how Israel has become the main focus of anti-Semitism in a post-Holocaust world:

[It] is a testimony to the persisting vitality of anti-Semitism [that], expelled more or less successfully from domestic society in the countries where once it flourished, [it] now reappears, suitably translated into the current language and modalities of international life, to deal with the phenomenon of a Jewish state among other states as it once dealt with Jewish individuals and communities living in states dominated by other religious or ethnic groups ["The Abandonment of Israel," July 1976].

Or, putting the point in another way:

. . . it is perfectly true that anti-Zionism is not necessarily anti-Semitism. But it is also true, I fear, that the distinction between the two is often invisible to the naked Jewish eye, and that anti-Zionism has served to legitimate the open expression of a good deal of anti-Semitism which might otherwise have remained subject to the taboo against anti-Semitism that prevailed . . . from the time of Hitler until, roughly, the Six Day War ["A Certain Anxiety," August 1971].

Lastly, on how the process of refocusing works:

Historically anti-Semitism has taken the form of labeling certain vices and failings as specifically Jewish when they are in fact common to all humanity: Jews are greedy, Jews are tricky, Jews are ambitious, Jews are clannish—as though Jews were uniquely or disproportionately guilty of all those sins. Correlatively, Jews are condemned when they claim or exercise the right to do things that all other people are accorded an unchallengeable right to do.*

As applied to the Jewish state, this tradition has been transmuted into the double standard by which Israel is invariably judged . . . [A]ll other people are entitled to national self-determination, but when the Jews exercise this right, they are committing the crimes of racism and imperialism. Similarly, all other nations have a right to ensure the security of their borders; when Israel exercises this right, it is committing the crime of aggression. So, too, only Israel of all the states in the world is required to prove that its very existence—not merely its interests or the security of its borders, but its very existence—is in immediate peril before it can justify the resort to force ["J'Accuse," September 1982].

---

*You refer to this passage no fewer than three times. The first time you astonishingly misinterpret it to mean that I classify "as anti-Semitic anyone who ascribes to Jews characteristics uniquely Jewish." The second time you summarize it accurately. But by the third time, you have forgotten the second and are back to the first ("*pace* Norman Podhoretz, it ought not to be considered racist to speak of group characteristics"). Is it any wonder, then, that you so often leave me feeling that, where anti-Semitism is concerned, you are uncharacteristically capable of obtuseness?

This point you now do get; you even call it "logically sound." But even though you now defend me against the canard that in my eyes "mere opposition to an Israeli policy constitutes anti-Semitism," you still seem to resist what logically follows from my "logically sound" point—namely, that criticisms of Israel based on this particular double standard, rooted as it is in the ancient traditions of anti-Semitic propaganda, deserve to be stigmatized as, quite simply, anti-Semitic.

I live in hopes that you will some day get that point as well.

4 · A Letter from William Pfaff

Hit a glancing blow in the course of Mr. Buckley's article on anti-Semitism, allow me to complain that in writing about me Mr. Buckley addresses what Norman Podhoretz says that I have said, not what I have actually said. My name occurs first in his article in connection with the Gore Vidal–*Nation* magazine affair. I have never said that Mr. Vidal was an "innocent 'critic'" of Israel. I consider what he said about the Podhoretzes in *The Nation* unacceptable. Mr. Podhoretz does not tell you that in my column on the affair I wrote that I "knew the Podhoretzes, and respect[ed] Miss Decter in particular, as a writer of high, if humorless, seriousness." I said that I believed that she and her husband had every right "to give particular support to Israel out of commitment to Judaism or to the Jewish community and cultural tradition . . . without having imputed to them a lack of patriotism . . . or divided loyalties." I went on to make a second general, and I would think self-evident, point, that one should be free to criticize Israel's policies without having an anti-Semitic motivation imputed.

Out of that Mr. Podhoretz drew a defense of Gore Vidal. Mr. Buckley, describing this as "solemn and responsible criticism," goes on to quote the charge of anti-Semitism Mr. Podhoretz first made against me in connection with a newspaper column critical of Israeli policy written after the massacre of Palestinians by Christian militiamen in Beirut in September 1982.

Mr. Podhoretz first attacked this column in the *Commentary* article he entitled (with characteristic modesty) "J'Accuse." As I did not see this article until months later, and considered the accusation preposterous, I did not reply.

In 1986, after the Gore Vidal affair, Mr. Podhoretz returned to the attack. This time I thought an answer necessary. I wrote a letter to the editor of *Commentary* saying, "As the matter is grave, I trust that you will do me the justice of publishing what I actually wrote, so that *Commentary*'s readers may form their own conclusions, either of the newspaper column to which you refer (. . . which I enclose), or at least to the following paragraphs from that column, which are the relevant ones."

Mr. Podhoretz replied that my letter quoting myself was "totally out of line" and would not be published. He said that if I wished to write a letter in which I disputed his interpretation of a column the actual words of which his readers were not to be permitted to read, he would "of course make every effort to publish it." I protested that if "your interpretation of what I wrote is right, lengthier quotation can only more convincingly damn me. To refuse to allow me to convey to your readers exactly what I said . . . would seem an admission that you now recognize that your charges against me are not sustainable." He nonetheless refused.

As Mr. Buckley's article does reiterate the Podhoretz accusation, permit me to deal with it very briefly. Mr. Podhoretz describes me as "predicting" that Hitler might "find rest in Hell" through "the knowledge that the Jews themselves, in Israel, have finally accepted his own way of looking at things." This, when I wrote it, said the following: "Hitler had killed the Jews and driven the survivors to Palestine. The Jews killed Palestinians, and thousands fled to Jordan and Lebanon. The Palestinians nearly wrecked Jordan, were expelled, and then did destroy Lebanon, while going on killing Jews. The Israelis, in their turn, continued to kill Palestinians. The chain of murders goes on, reaching its most recent climax in the Israeli invasion of Lebanon, and in new killings. . . .

"Hitler's work is not complete. Three nations in turn have been wrecked—European Judaism, Arab Palestine, Lebanon. What will bring it to an end? Must a nation somewhere be exterminated before Hitler's work is done?

"[George] Steiner says Jews made themselves hated because they kept telling everyone: 'Wake up! God's eye is upon you. Has he not made you in his image? Lose your life so that you may gain it. Sacrifice yourself to the truth, to justice, to the good of mankind.' The world was sick of that message. When Hitler turned on the Jews, no one seriously objected. Steiner puts into Hitler's mouth the belief that the world was 'glad that the exterminator had come. Oh, they did not say so openly. I allow you that. But secretly they rejoiced.'

"What would, of course, allow Hitler to find rest in Hell would be the knowledge that the Jews themselves, in Israel, have finally given up their troublesome message and accepted his own way of looking at things. That would seem to be the issue now before the government of Menachem

Begin." Thus did the column end. Hard criticism indeed; but where is the anti-Semitism?

It is again on the basis of what Mr. Podhoretz has written that Mr. Buckley describes me as saying that Jewish-Americans attempt to "manipulate" U.S. policy. Nonsense. That is paranoia language. I have never said it. They try to influence policy—as well they might; why shouldn't they? So do I.

My complaint aside, of the great deal more to be said on the larger controversy Mr. Buckley admirably addresses, the issue of selective criticism of Israel strikes me as fundamental. Israelis, and Israel's friends, often complain that Americans (and Europeans) attack Israel for faults they ignore in the conduct of other countries. This is true.

I do so myself because I consider Israel part of the political and moral community in which I live, to which I am committed, and for which I feel a responsibility. I am surprised that anyone would wish Israel to be judged by any other standards than those of the liberal democratic Western community.

I write critically about Israel—and even more often about France, Britain, Germany, etc., and above all, the United States—because I expect much of them. These are my people, democrats, members of Western liberal culture, part of a civilization and a moral inheritance to which I, as an American and a Catholic Christian, belong, and which is shared by a very small minority of those alive in the world today.

The survival and success of this community is by no means assured. One reason for that is its amply demonstrated tendency toward abandonment of its own standards and hence toward suicidal conduct. Its values must be defended internally as well as externally, or we all risk sinking. On the other hand I don't often write columns deploring the failure of Syria or Sudan or Burma or China to meet Western standards of behavior because I don't expect much of their political conduct to begin with. To say that is, I know, highly "incorrect" in the United States today, but I have been politically incorrect all my life and am too old to change now. That of course is exactly my problem with Mr. Podhoretz.

5 · A Letter from Irving Kristol

My first reaction to Bill Buckley's article was that it was very long. Even the quotations were long, though the quotations from me seemed not so long.

My second reaction was one of surprise. I am certainly not insensitive to anti-Semitism, but it has been my distinct impression that there is probably less of it today than at any other period in my lifetime. I grew up in the shadow of Hitlerism and was disturbed (to put it mildly) by the echoes of Hitler's anti-Semitism to be found on the fringes of the America First movement—and sometimes not only on the fringes. When I went into the army, it was in a Midwest regiment recruited mainly from Chicago and Cicero, and the anti-Semitism I encountered was blatant, often brutal. So I have vivid memories of the "bad old days" and I therefore have been inclined to be rather dismissive of the current intermittent, marginal symptoms that one occasionally reads about. After all, today something in excess of one-third of all Jews marry Gentiles, and I have been more interested in this fact, as a portent for American Jewry, than in some young punks defacing a Jewish cemetery or vandalizing a synagogue. But then I recall that the intermarriage rate in Germany, under the Weimar Republic, was just about as high as that, and I begin to wonder whether there is a kind of auto-immune response within a body politic still overwhelmingly Christian.

Bill's essay has persuaded me that I have indeed been too complacent. Some months ago, *The New Republic* sent around a questionnaire asking respondents their opinion as to whether Pat Buchanan's columns were anti-Semitic, as some were claiming. I said then that I did not believe that Buchanan—whom I have known for some years—was personally or politically anti-Semitic but rather had allowed his irritation with the liberal commitment of the majority of the Jewish community to spill over into remarks that, if uttered by someone else, could easily be taken to be anti-Semitic. I would now revise that judgment.

I still cannot find it in my heart to say that Pat Buchanan is personally anti-Semitic, but he definitely is politically so. There is no other way of explaining his newfound compassion and concern for Palestinians on the West Bank, or his harsh judgments for Israeli policy there as being "unjust" and morally reprehensible. Whatever one thinks of that policy, it makes no sense for Buchanan to single it out as his sole, moralistic venture into international compassion. The whole tenor of his approach to American foreign policy has been narrowly "realistic"—too narrow and simplistic, in my view. Yet when he talks about Israel he sounds as one would expect him to sound were he talking about Saddam Hussein, about whom, in fact, he is so reticent. A reasonable interpretation is that this is a rhetorical sublimation, for reasons of political expediency, of a deeper anti-Jewish impulse.

But how important is Pat Buchanan, anyhow? As a national political figure, not important, I would confidently assert. But so far as American conservatism is concerned, he is very important. Pat Buchanan is ostensibly running for President, but in truth his ambition is to assume leadership and to reshape the American conservative movement. Should he succeed, this movement will have suffered its greatest defeat since the election of 1964, which set the liberal tone for American politics for the next 15 years.

Pat Buchanan is not a conservative, he is a reactionary. Now, I am fond of *cultural* reactionaries, because the reactionary impulse can be so creative and fruitful in its cultural dimensions. After all, the three greatest poets in the English language this century—W. B. Yeats, T. S. Eliot, and Philip Larkin—have been reactionaries. So have been some of our finest novelists (e.g., Evelyn Waugh). But in a dynamic, capitalist society, being a *political* reactionary is a ticket to oblivion. We have seen this happen with some of our Southern novelists, poets, and critics—among our finest—who tried, back in the 1920s, to translate literary nostalgia into a sort of pseudo-agrarian social program. This was, and remains, little more than a cultural oddity. Similarly, Pope Pius IX's *Syllabus of Errors* ought to be studied by all liberals, who would benefit from the challenge to their basic beliefs. But political conservatives who take it too seriously are doomed to irrelevance.

Pat Buchanan is seeking to shape the conservative movement along reactionary lines. And behind him there has formed a curious coalition of what have been called "paleo-conservatives"—i.e., conservatives of the 1930s–1950s vintage. These include Taft Republicans, America First isolationists, passionate anti-statists, and a sprinkling of "Southern" intellectuals who admire Jefferson Davis at the expense of Abraham Lincoln. But the basic thrust of this mini-movement is, in a profound sense, radical and anti-political. These people really do want to turn the clock a long ways back—a proper aesthetic agenda but never a serious political agenda. Only a revolution can turn a society's clock back to any substantial degree, and the "paleos" may have revolutionary enthusiasm but nothing of great interest to say to the live human beings who constitute the American public.

It is important to note that we are not dealing here with a pro-Reagan reaction to George Bush's centrism. Though Pat Buchanan has too much political sense to say so, the quasi-official view of the "paleos" is that Ronald Reagan betrayed conservatism because he didn't simply abolish the welfare state, lock, stock, and barrel. Admirers and supporters of Ronald Reagan understand that, while reforming the welfare state is a proper conservative goal, abolition is not in the cards—as the experience of Margaret Thatcher, with her Conservative majority in Parliament, conclusively demonstrates. One might leap to the conclusion, as many "paleos" have, that the people in our Western democracies are all in a sad state of corruption. But abolishing people who get in the way of a political agenda is a left-wing idea, not a conservative one.

And how does anti-Semitism fit into all this? It is a symbolic issue, a signal light that holds this radical coalition together. It is, after all, a coalition with many internal stresses and contradictions. The Jews provide—as they always do—a scapegoat, which is also a unifying force for people of various frustrations. I do not believe for a moment that these people really have it in mind to persecute Jews (though they may decide to persecute Israel as a proxy). But who knows what fires a few random sparks can set off? In any case, by importing into American conservatism a set of anti-Semitic innuendoes, they are debasing the conservative movement and robbing it, in the eyes of the public, of its political legitimacy.

That is why I think, in the end, that Bill Buckley's essay is so important. It is a forceful statement, by our leading American conservative, as to what kind of political body and what kind of political soul American conservatism is to possess.

6 · An Editorial by James M. Wall*

William Buckley, who first achieved fame with his book on the antireligious environment at Yale University, recently addressed the issue of secularity in a lengthy and carefully nuanced essay on anti-Semitism in *National Review*. Acknowledging the difficulty of identifying anti-Semitism, Buckley nevertheless boldly concludes that he has found anti-Semitism in the writings of some of his colleagues on the political Right as well as among those on the Left such as Gore Vidal.

National Review Editor John O'Sullivan points out that Buckley's essay is "ten times as long as the average cover story," but he says the topic was important and sensitive enough to dictate printing the entire article. It was a good decision. As one of the chief figures in American conservatism, Buckley is well situated to address a topic which has unfortunately been introduced into the 1992 presidential campaign by Republican candidates David Duke and Pat Buchanan. Buckley's careful treatment is especially

---

*Mr. Wall is the editor of *The Christian Century*, from whose January 15 issue this editorial is excerpted.

valuable because Buchanan and conservative writer Joseph Sobran are among his close friends. Much of his article focuses on whether it is possible to criticize the state of Israel without being labeled anti-Semitic. Buckley believes it is, but he argues that Buchanan and Sobran have gone beyond such criticism.

The essay will no doubt become án important guide in the public debate on Israel and its critics, for it outlines the complexity of an issue that touches upon politics, human rights, and religion. In a concluding section Buckley turns his attention to the religion clauses in the Bill of Rights, which, he believes, provide a second point of tension in our current concern for properly identifying anti-Semitism. Buckley quotes from an essay by Irving Kristol published three years ago in *National Review*, because, he admits, Kristol is Jewish, and because "I cannot surpass him in lucid social analysis." Kristol points to the "tension that is now building up between Jews and Christians," a tension that "has very little to do with traditional discrimination, and everything to do with efforts by liberals—among whom, I regret to say, Jews are both numerous and prominent—to establish a wall between religion and society, in the guise of maintaining the wall between church and state."

Two hundred years after the adoption of the religion clauses, Kristol argues, the prevailing liberal mindset is far more concerned with avoiding religious establishment than in encouraging religious expression. Specifically, Kristol says, "the major Jewish organizations proceed from the correct proposition that legally and constitutionally we are not a Christian nation, to the absurd proposition that we are in no sense at all a Christian society." Even though the overwhelming majority of Americans are Christians, these Jewish organizations insist that Christians' religion "be a totally private affair, one that finds no public expression and receives no public deference. Such insistence shows a lamentable ignorance of history, sociology, and psychology."

Kristol offers a devastating critique of the liberal Protestant organizations that have been "more keenly interested in social reform than in religious belief." Lukewarm Christianity, Kristol suggests, is more attractive to Jews because they assume, incorrectly in his view, that social-minded religious people will be less likely to produce the sort of anti-Semitism "our Jewish ancestors experienced for centuries in Europe." He thinks this is a faulty assumption because vicious anti-Semitism is not Christian anti-Semitism, but neopagan (Nazi and fascist), Muslim fundamentalist, Marxist, or "simply nationalist chauvinist anti-Semitism, of a kind one now finds in Japan (of all places!) or Latin America."

The Framers of the Bill of Rights could not have anticipated the rich pluralism of contemporary America, but they give us a framework in which pluralism is something to cherish, not to fear. We must be vigilant in protecting minority rights. But we must also be careful not to read the "no establishment" clause so as to restrict all public expressions of faith and hence dilute the meaning of "free exercise."

The "free exercise" clause applies to all faith groups equally and should not be seen as a threat to those that are in the minority—precisely the groups that the "no establishment" clause was designed to protect.

7 · A Letter and Column by A. M. Rosenthal

One point I would like to clear up for your readers has to do with the mysterious three weeks between the time Mr. Buchanan made his comments about the "amen corner" and the time I attacked him in my column.

Mr. Buchanan, as you knew when you brought up the issue in your article, made this time-lapse the basis for saying that the Anti-Defamation League and I had been parties to some kind of plot—which I am sure you recognize as the old Jew-conspiracy bit.

You did not say that directly, of course, but you did call attention to the "whole three weeks," suggested orchestration, and left it all in an air of mystery.

All you had to do to clear up this mystery was to lift up the phone and ask me; you never did. I would have been happy to tell you that I was out of the country when Buchanan made those cracks on NBC. I was on vacation in Majorca and previously in Oslo, attending a conference on hatred.

So I did not know a thing about Buchanan's statements that only the Israeli Defense Ministry and its American "amen corner" wanted war in the Gulf until I returned to the United States.

I found waiting for me communications from the ADL, an admirable and useful organization, which I believe were sent to other journalists they hoped would pay attention but who did not and from a couple or three readers sickened by Buchanan's nastiness. I played one of the tapes of the broadcasts I received. Thereupon I pulled out my file on Buchanan and anti-Semitism, a plump one, and decided the time had come to do a column on the man, overcoming my distaste at the idea.

Later, an executive of the ADL sent out a memo to his board rejoicing in and taking credit for the ADL part in calling my attention to the broadcast. I am delighted to thank the ADL for alerting me, as I thank others who did so.

The only real mystery in the affair is why in those "whole three weeks" no other columnist, to my knowledge, wrote about the Buchanan performance and why it has taken you a year and some months even to dance gingerly up to what should have been obvious at once—that what he has had to say could only come from the mouth, mind, and motivations not of somebody who just said "anti-Semitic things" for reasons you cannot seem to fathom, but from an anti-Semite, whose reasons grow out of his very condition.

Comment by WFB

Sorry, I fail to see your point. 1) It is obvious that an Anti-Defamation League should protest to its principal constituency evidence of anti-Semitism. 2) Whether that protest ignited your column, or whether you'd have noticed the inflammatory comments by Pat Buchanan if you had been in America, isn't especially important. 3) It is above all interesting that the question of Buchanan's anti-Semitism became a national question only after the publication of your column: If Buchanan were as conspicuously evil as you take him to be, one must suppose that someone else would have raised an alarm. Otherwise we are required to deduce that every time you go to Oslo or to Majorca, the conscience of America sleeps.

Column by AMR, "New York Times," January 21, 1992

After more than a year of study of the abundant record, William F. Buckley Jr., columnist, novelist, television host, lecturer, and distinguished sailor, finally has delivered the judgment that Patrick Buchanan, Republican candidate for the Presidency, really has said "things about Jews" that are anti-Semitic.

For this discovery, part of a voyage for which he felt it his duty to skipper first his intellectual ship and now the readers of his magazine through 40,000 words, Mr. Buckley is receiving the applause of those editorial writers, columnists, and friends who had worried about him while he was pitching so far out at sea.

He devotes a whole issue of his *National Review* to the article, which he calls "In Search of Anti-Semitism" and will preserve as a book. Obviously he considers he has made landfall after an arduous and significant exploration, although it may surprise many that anti-Semitism is so very difficult to find.

Mr. Buckley is considered the delineator of American conservatism. Mr. Buchanan now is thoughtfully trying to transfer this weight from Mr. Buckley's shoulders to his own.

So the judgment by Mr. Buckley is understandably welcome to Americans—conservative or otherwise—who have long regarded Mr. Buchanan as an anti-Semite, even though Mr. Buckley still cannot bring himself to use so blunt a noun about him.

Also, Mr. Buckley's article will buoy those who felt they had to wait for somebody certifiably both conservative and non-Jewish to lead before they spoke up about Mr. Buchanan's "things."

But unfortunately Mr. Buckley's pronouncement is not likely to change the minds of readers inclined toward Mr. Buchanan, in New Hampshire or anywhere else. One reason is that Mr. Buckley does not even try to make sense of Mr. Buchanan's anti-Semitism by dealing with its roots—and particularly its political motivations. And he does not even suggest to fellow Republicans that Mr. Buchanan's anti-Semitic comments might be a reason to vote against him.

Moreover, the Buchanan section is so genteel about him, written with such absence of real censure, with such contradiction and evasion, and is so late and tortuous that politically and intellectually it destroys itself—a pity.

Mr. Buckley's only outrage is for those who had previously attacked Mr. Buchanan as an anti-Semite. For instance, Mr. Buckley was ballistically annoyed when on September 14, 1990, I wrote that Mr. Buchanan's demeaning of Holocaust reality, his lie that only Jews wanted war with Saddam Hussein, and so on, were anti-Semitic and dared suggest that anti-Semitism could lead to Auschwitz.

In the current article, Mr. Buckley reprints his column denouncing the idea. He now assures us that "an anti-Semitic crack like Buchanan's isn't of the kind that threatens" what Mr. Buckley delicately calls the "discrete territory of Auschwitz." In the post-Hitler world, he says, "workaday" anti-Semitism is not genocidal.

Workaday.

But then he writes about people trying to distinguish between "country club" anti-Semitism and "naked anti-Israelism and genocidal indifference." And he adds that the "pain"—whose?—comes from the "historical knowledge that prejudice of the first kind can metastasize—and has done so, to be sure by mutation—into Auschwitz."

So what does he really believe about Mr. Buchanan? Not much. In 1990 Mr. Buckley found Mr. Buchanan guilty of nothing worse than "clumsy forensic" manners. Even now, musing on the mystery of Mr. Buchanan's anti-Semitism, he suggests graciously that it may be an "iconoclastic temperament," which implies bravery.

No: anybody who keeps saying anti-Semitic "things" is no mystery, just one more anti-Semite. Over the centuries, as now, that has taken no iconoclastic daring, just hate and cowardice.

Since the 1990 explosion about his anti-Semitism Mr. Buchanan has refused to retract a word. But he keeps his obsession about Jews better zippered. Temporary, but it does demonstrate that the best weapon against anti-Semitism is to spot it and expose it fast and plain.

Mr. Buckley has often shown himself a man of intellectual clarity and good heart. So I hope he gets back in the boat and keeps sailing and searching. If he makes true landfall he can send us a more helpful log.

8 · A Letter from Alan M. Dershowitz

William Buckley observed that "even Harvard Professor Alan Dershowitz, ordinarily an outspoken advocate of the First Amendment, declared that Buchanan should be removed from the national media." Here is precisely what I said:

"If the issue were whether the government should censor Buchanan's bigoted views, I would fight for his freedom of speech as forcefully as I fought for the rights of Nazis to march through the city of Skokie, Illinois. But the question is whether private American newspapers and television stations should continue to give Buchanan a mainstream platform for his anti-Semitism."

Not only is my approach entirely consistent with the First Amendment, it is precisely the approach taken by William Buckley, in dissociating *National Review* from right-wing bigots. Private publications have a First Amendment right *not* to publish objectionable views; there will always be enough bigoted publications that are willing to.

Mr. Buckley also neglected to mention my criticism of the ACLU for not defending the rights of the *Dartmouth Review* students.

9 · A Letter from David Frum

My reaction on reading your brave essay on anti-Semitism was apprehension that you might be about to encounter the form of ingratitude that the late Isaac Bashevis Singer described to Sanford Pinsker, who retells it in Toronto's *Idler* magazine:

"Singer was once invited to read a story to a group of Yiddishists in Brooklyn. They begged him to come, even though they were too poor to be able to pay him. But, their spokesman argued, at least he would be among *landsmen*, people who understand Yiddish, not like when he visits fancy-shmanzy colleges and people make fun of his accent.

"'What could I do?' Singer told me. 'These are old people, so I went. The cab ride to Brooklyn cost me $35. And when I finally arrived, who was there? Maybe 12 people all together. So I read them a new story. No sooner am I finished than the first person gets up and says the following: This is not a good story. This is not a Zionist story. I spit on your story. And he proceeded to spit on the floor in anger, and then to sit down.

"'At that point the next person gets up and says: This is not a good story. This is not an orthodox story. This is a dirty story, so I also spit on your story. And like the first man, he spat on the floor in anger and sat down.

"'Others objected that the story was not a socialist story or a nice story or even a properly Yiddish story; but about one thing they agreed: it was definitely not a good story. In fact, one man spat on the story twice—once because it was not a Zionist story and once because it was not an orthodox story. So from 12 people I collected 13 spits.'"

Just in case some tiresome self-appointed defender of the faith like Alan Dershowitz or Richard Cohen has been spitting on the floor and complaining that your essay was not written exactly as he would have it written, I wanted you to know that in this house it was greeted with applause and thanks.

10 · A Letter from Robert D. Novak

William F. Buckley's exploration of anti-Semitism leads, I fear, into a trap where any criticism of Israel exposes the critic to being branded with the scarlet A as an anti-Semite.

Let me begin with the reason why I have been invited to contribute to this discussion: my response to David Frum's attack on Pat Buchanan published in *The American Spectator*. Mr. Buckley misrepresents me as follows: "Novak had made a vulnerable point when he wrote that Buchanan has after all written millions of words that do not even touch on Jewish questions (the classic antecedent of this form of casuistry is the legendary Irishman being tried for murder who volunteers to bring in thirty people who did not see him commit the crime)."

What I actually did write was quite different, that "the body of his writing" does not "support the indictment" of anti-Semitism. But even that arguable contention has to be placed in perspective. Mr. Frum's long assault on Buchanan as a "bully-boy" outside the mainstream of conservatism does not allege anti-Semitism by other than insinuation until the last paragraph, when he asserts that Buchanan's "real message is inseparable from his sly Jew-baiting."

My position on the danger of this mischief was spelled out in this response:

"It is particularly reprehensible that an article that starts by questioning Buchanan's criticism of neoconservative funding ends with a gratuitous accusation of 'Jew-baiting.' The connection is ludicrous. The two targets most vocally unhappy about Buchanan's [anti-]neocon column—[Bob] Tyrrell and Bill Bennett—are, like Buchanan, Roman Catholics . . .

"A final word on anti-Semitism. In the wake of Hitler's Holocaust, it is unpardonable and impermissible. But the very unacceptability of the offense mandates that any accusation must be founded in fact, not in surmise or fancy. Buchanan is no anti-Semite, as anybody who knows him well will avow. Nor does the body of his writing support the indictment."

Unlike the case of Mr. Buckley's Irishman, that is not merely a case of Buchanan now and again failing to attack Jews. If it can be stipulated that no supporter of Israel is by definition anti-Semitic, how can Buchanan's previous writings in support of Israeli policy be explained? Did he awake one morning and suddenly find himself a full-blown anti-Semite compelled to attack Israel? On the contrary, he simply changed his mind about Israeli government policy.

Yet, Mr. Buckley decrees that Buchanan's writings "could not reasonably be interpreted as other than anti-Semitic in substance." But there is nothing in those writings that degrades Jews or calls for their exclusion from this or that activity.

Buchanan's specific sin that caused all the commotion was to state an indisputable fact: that Israel and its American-Jewish supporters were uncommonly anxious to commence the war against Saddam Hussein, while the amount of Jewish-Americans in the fighting force was quite small. Buchanan stated that fact with characteristic hyperbole, but it is quite a stretch to call it anti-Semitic.

His overriding sin, since he changed his mind a few years ago, has been to seem "anti-Israel." Mr. Buckley implies that is prima facie proof of anti-Semitism, while he excuses what seem clearer cases of hostility toward Jews by conservatives Stephen Tonsor and Russell Kirk. Mr. Buckley calls it "mischievous" to ascribe creeping anti-Semitism to Tonsor's claim that conservatism must be Christian and to Kirk's allegation that the neoconservatism of Irving Kristol is just a ploy to help Israel. You could have fooled me.

Mr. Buckley similarly seems far less concerned by country-club anti-Semitism than "naked anti-Israelism." Yet over the centuries hatred of Jews has been expressed by exclusion: exclusion from the country club at the lowest level ranging up the scale to exclusion from Yale University, exclusion from the old German general staff, exclusion from Spain for half a millennium, and, ultimately, in the case of Hitler, exclusion from the living.

The very notion that "naked anti-Israelism" connotes anti-Semitism charges into a semantical thicket. Anyone who opposes the idea of Israel's existence today has made a good case for calling him anti-Semitic. General George Marshall was no anti-Semite when he opposed the creation of the Jewish state a half-century ago because of what he perceived as threatened U.S. interests, but he could not continue to take that position today without being presumed guilty of bias. If on the other hand a writer recognizes Israel's right to exist (as Buchanan surely does), his culpability as an anti-Semite is markedly reduced.

But Elie Wiesel brands Buchanan as an anti-Semite "because he is a man who is constantly critical of Israel." Thus, it is not necessary to be anti-Israel, only critical of Israel. But is criticism of the current government of Israel really being critical of Israel? If so, Abba Eban and even Yitzhak Rabin would, absurdly, qualify for Mr. Wiesel's anti-Semitic condemnation.

Mr. Buckley correctly suggests the existence of taboos in writing about Israel and incorrectly implies that observance of these taboos will avoid allegations of anti-Semitism. Here, I must refer to the experience of the Evans & Novak column, whose criticism of Israeli government policy dates back to the aftermath of the 1967 war. A note on why we have written so much about the subject: the Middle East has been both an incubator of war and a vital area for U.S. economic and strategic interests, which we do not feel are inconsistent with the health and security of Israel.

We have carefully scrubbed every one of the hundreds of such columns we have written to eliminate all wording that might be deemed offensive. For example, when the Israeli government complained years ago that our reference to it as "Tel Aviv" (as the American government is called "Washington" and the former Soviet government was called "Moscow" in journalistic jargon) came straight out of Arab propaganda, we instantly stopped the practice even though few states recognize Jerusalem as the Israeli capital.

To no avail. We have been continually accused of anti-Semitism, even though our criticism of Israeli government policy mirrors the position of many prominent Israelis. When A. M. Rosenthal says, "I didn't attack him [Buchanan] because of what he said about Israel and Iraq but because he put in anti-Semitic language," he is disingenuous. When we recently published new information about the 1967 sinking by Israeli forces of the U.S.S. *Liberty* in language that contained no taint of anti-Semitic rhetoric, Mr. Rosenthal assailed us vigorously (and unfairly). He is the journalistic cop on the beat guarding against any criticism of the Israeli government's conduct.

Making accusations of anti-Semitism is a serious business. In the nearly 29-year run of the Evans & Novak column, we have been attacked, properly, by those we attack. But the only sustained, serious, and organized effort to silence us has come from the pro-Israel lobby. Attempts have been made, often by advertisers, to remove our column from newspapers—occasionally with success.

It is distressing to see Mr. Buckley, whom I so greatly admire as one of this nation's great forces for good during my lifetime, ally himself with those who feel that views contrary to the Israeli government must be suppressed. "It would not have been inappropriate," Mr. Buckley writes, "for newspaper editors who publish Pat Buchanan to decline to publish those of his columns that touched on Jewish or Israeli questions, pending evidence that he would more carefully observe the civilized distinctions."

But what are the "civilized distinctions"? When AIPAC urges readers to write editors to remove columnists opposed to its views, it is trying to prevent full discussion of the Israeli question. This intent is only obscured when criticism of the Israeli government's policies is equated with the evil, immoral sin of anti-Semitism.

11 · A Letter from Hugh Kenner

The points on which I agree with Joe Sobran are 1a) that the state of Israel is mighty arrogant in its presumption of entitlement to U.S. handouts and general compliance; 1b) that a large & influential U.S. Jewish population shares this presumption (and of course must be taken stock of by U.S. Administrations); 2) that "anti-Semitism" is a rather facile label for habitual objection to 1a and 1b. Also, I did think that in your *NR* piece you were rather freely pasting the anti-Semitic label on people whom Jewish opinion calls anti-Semitic because they balk at 1a and 1b.

I note from a recent *New York Times* that Abe Rosenthal (whose company, by the way, I've enjoyed on two occasions) was not satisfied with your treatment of Pat Buchanan. It is surely evident that such as he will never be satisfied by anything short of a casting of whoever annoys them into outer darkness, and I think it is a mistake to let them control the terms of discourse. "Anti-Semitism"—here I agree with Joe—has no stable meaning; it can run all the way from gas ovens to a mere wish that Abe R. would moderate his frenzies. And a term that has no stable meaning is simply not a profitable head for rational discussions.

12 · A Letter from Edwin M. Yoder, Jr.

As one named as a party to earlier discussions of the subject of anti-Semitism, I must invoke a personal privilege. Mr. Buckley has unintentionally mislabeled me as one of those who share "the conviction . . . that

U.S. policy is manipulated by Jewish Americans who are hell-bent on serving Israeli interests and are prepared to use the weapon of alleged anti-Semitism to immobilize their opponents."

In fact, I have never stated any such view and do not hold it now. Perhaps such an inference could be drawn from my intervention in the Vidal–Podhoretz controversy. My two cents' worth on that matter was prompted by a historical point: the curious report or allegation that Norman Podhoretz had said the American Civil War was as unengaging to him as the War of the Roses—a view which, I am assured, he did not and does not hold.

After long and vigorous support of Israel, I suddenly find myself mistaken for one possibly hostile to its interests. This is positively Kafkaesque. I have written critically of Israeli leadership and policy on occasion—I was irritated by the Pollard affair and abhorred the invasion of Lebanon. For the rest, I have written favorably of both scores and scores of times over more than three decades.

I confine myself to a single example. As editorial-page editor of the *Washington Star* in 1981, I wrote our lead editorial endorsing Israel's bombing strike on Iraq's nuclear facility—an act harshly condemned in the press and at the UN. (I am pleased to think that later developments tended to vindicate our judgment.) . . .

Just to be crystal clear on the main point: in my view, Israel enjoys strong support in virtually every sector of American opinion for exactly the right reasons—its redemption of a shattering crime against a people; its democratic traditions and creeds; its loyalty to Western interests; and the vision and civility of such leaders as David Ben-Gurion, Moshe Dayan, and Teddy Kollek. This support has been frayed a bit, in my judgment, by the exasperating policies of Mr. Shamir. But it cannot be accounted for on any theory of "manipulation" by lobbies—not even by AIPAC, though AIPAC enjoys extraordinary and perhaps excessive influence on Capitol Hill . . .

Anti-Semitism is a heavy term, fraught with the darkest history. I am in agreement with Bill Buckley that we should not trivialize the word or the idea (as "racism" is today being trivialized) by brandishing it in every petty dispute.

13 · A Letter from Murray Reswick

This letter is written in the hope that it will be directed to your attention. Hope bolstered by the fact that a letter requesting my release from

Vichy France, once written by my nobody-special father to Marshal Pé-
tain, was not only read but favorably acted upon.

I do not entertain the slightest hope of improving on today's Rosenthal
column in the *New York Times*. But I do believe that my credentials in
respect of the ability to distinguish a fun-loving iconoclast from an anti-
Semite are unrivaled.

I am a highly recognizable Jew with the physiognomy of a Hittite cam-
ouflaging the mindset of an atheistic cosmopolite. Molière might have
described me as a Juif Malgré Lui. I also happen to be a Médecin Malgré
Lui but that is beside the point. Growing up in France, I swam, with no
discernible discomfort, in a world replete with people harboring multiple
hues of antagonism toward Jews. I've always known that you cannot
shoe-horn all anti-Semites into one foul box. I also knew that many of
my friends would mouth anti-Semitic utterances that they did not truly
believe and that most such utterances were unfraught with any possibility
of serious mischief. Having said all that, may I now tell you flat-out that
Buchanan is an anti-Semite. Oh, a jovial one to be sure—but unmistakably
a vicious one, whether or not you or he believes this to be the case. And
to arrive at this diagnosis, the cumulative effect mentioned in your study
need not be considered. There is only one of his statements that truly
counts. It is the crack about the names of the boys slogging up the road
to Baghdad. A purely factual observation, since there are so few black
Jews in the armed forces of this country, but consider how potentially
damaging had we suffered heavy casualties. At the risk of appearing im-
modest may I state that my own skirts are unsullied by this particular bit
of mud-slinging, since I served in the armies of France and the United
States of America, during WW II, without waiting to be drafted.

I fully understand and accept that, as the father of the conservative
movement in this country, you carry responsibilities that by far outweigh
any consideration of an objective and dismissive assessment of Buchanan's
misdeeds, so that there are good and just reasons for you to dilute a feeble
paragraph about his anti-Semitism in the midst of your exhaustive survey
of the current dimensions of the problem in our country. Moreover the
text as a whole was enlightening about things I did not know, such as the
rejection of the neoconservatives by the original crew (country-club anti-
Semitism?) and the finely reasoned Michael Kinsley condemnation of the
Jewish bigotry regarding Christmas trees and crèches.

14 · A Letter from Eliot A. Cohen

Let me express my admiration for the thoughtfulness with which you address this issue, and the courage you have shown in confronting it, now and in the past. Parts of this must have been very painful to write, dealing as they did with friends, allies, and even family. Indeed, I read the article not to find out your position—it is as well known as could be—so much as to see how you expressed it, and it was gracefully done.

You began your article by describing some of your personal experiences in this matter, and so should I. I have not been exposed to much in the way of anti-Semitism, really: some taunts and bullying when walking home from the Hebrew day school I attended; casual insults—most thoughtless—from a variety of persons some of whom did not realize they were speaking to a Jew; more recently, a guarded suspicion about my loyalties hinted at by government officials preoccupied, I suppose, by Jonathan Pollard. In my parents' generation it was different, of course, but anti-Semitism did not prevent them, or their immigrant fathers and mothers, from making their way, protected by a regime that, as Washington said to the Jewish community of Newport, "gives to bigotry no sanction, to persecution no assistance."

That is at one level. Yet at another level any religiously and historically conscious Jew lives with an awareness of anti-Semitism. Not just the Holocaust but all that preceded it: the rabbis teach the Biblical story of the Amalekites who attacked the stragglers of the Israelite camp in the desert as a prototypical and enduring story of malice. That kind of hatred is *not* ascribed to the non-Jewish world in general, but to that small part of it (which includes some of Jewish birth) which despises the Jewish faith and people. It is the kind of irrational loathing that manifests itself in such bizarre phenomena as "anti-Semitism without Jews," or such grisly deeds as the massacres of Jews in Poland in 1945—*after* the Germans had been driven out.

Curiously, perhaps, this view of anti-Semitism as an evil and rather mysterious disease disinclines me to probe the origins of anti-Semitic behavior in America. In what I have seen of Joe Sobran's, Pat Buchanan's, and Gore Vidal's writings on this subject, there is a tinge of this madness. Now in these cases it is not a violent kind of craziness, and their venom is not directed solely against me and my people, but sickness is how I think of it. I am only glad that their cases are mild and that the great majority of my fellow-citizens are inoculated against the disease.

Let me suggest two reasons why Jews are sometimes hypersensitive about anti-Semitism. One has to do with the historical character of Jewish religious practice, for Judaism leads its adherents to ponder their history long and hard, and not merely contemplate that past, but live in it. The destruction of two Temples; the massacres that marked the routes of march of the Crusaders to the Holy Land; the expulsions from Spain and other European countries; the pogroms which my grandparents' generation fled—these are all more vivid in the consciousness of many Jews than one might think. My point here is that it is not the Holocaust alone that makes American Jews, who have had such an extraordinarily easy time of it, touchy about anti-Semitism.

Consider further that for Jews who care about their Jewishness, survival is at stake, even in America. Anxiety about survival is only partly reflected in an intense reaction to anti-Semitism, and is often conflated with it—even by Jews. The survival of the Jews is at risk in the United States, not because of hostility but because of the very reverse—Jewish readiness to abandon our traditions and beliefs in an environment that has been uniquely welcoming. That this may be hard to appreciate was driven home to me in a conversation with a sophisticated non-Jewish friend who simply could not understand what it was to have a collective (not an individual) fear of extinction, be it through physical annihilation or assimilation.

There are Jews for whom anti-Semitism ends by defining their Jewishness. That this is unhealthy and sterile goes without saying—what Jewish child would want to live a Jewish life if the chief characteristic of such a life were the search for (and occasional discovery of) mortal enemies? The greater one's belief in the wealth and richness of Judaism, the less tragedy defines one's Jewishness. But to be a Jew is also to be aware that Jewish existence is tenuous.

A few words about Israel. The Jewish affinity for Israel *is* something deep and abiding. "If I forget thee O Jerusalem let my right hand forget its cunning," said the Psalmist, and the love of Zion is woven through our daily prayers. I will not rehearse for you the story of Israel's precarious geopolitical position, or the history of the attacks launched against it, or the way in which its enemies have not distinguished between Jews and Israelis in their deeds of terror. Nor will I expand on the peculiarly high standards that are often applied to Israeli conduct. But I will say that for better or worse Judaism, including all but the fringe elements of Orthodox Judaism (and Jews have their would-be Ayatollahs), is now tied up with the existence of a healthy state of Israel. Were it to perish I doubt that the Jews could survive as a faith or as a people. I say that knowing well the many problematic aspects of Jewish life in Israel, and its depressing divide between obstinate varieties of religious fanaticism and secular emptiness. And I say that believing as well that the Jewish experience in the United States is blessedly unique; in this country, unlike any other save Israel, full citizenship was not the grudging gift of a ruling class but a birthright.

What I suppose all this means is that your analysis, which was sensitive and careful, did not fully capture some elements of anti-Semitism as felt by a Jew, or by Jews. It would have been quite extraordinary if it had, because it would require more empathy than anyone could expect. But I thought that I might try to convey, in words that I see are inadequate, some of those thoughts and emotions.

One concluding word, along lines already alluded to above. It bothers me deeply that so much attention is devoted to anti-Semitism that the beauties and richness of Judaism are not even mentioned. I hope that we might help rectify that, in some small way, with an open invitation. If you are ever in Washington on a Friday night and can bear the presence of four lively small children, Judy and I would be honored if you and your wife would come to our house for dinner as we welcome the Sabbath. Judaism is not a proselytizing religion, as you know; we would merely like you to see some of its traditions and warmth—and, if you wish, to continue this conversation.

15 · An Essay by Manfred Weidhorn*

Mr. Buckley's painstaking survey of the state of anti- and anti-anti-Semitism is marked not only by candor (e.g., about his father) but by a scrupulousness that is rare. Right- and left-wing ideologues—that is, most of us—are more concerned with saving the system (or saving face) than with finding the truth. In his assay at extirpating any traces of anti-Semitism among reputable conservatives instead of scoring easy points off the anti-Semitism on the Left, he has not only shown courage but also carried out the function of criticism as Matthew Arnold saw it. For Arnold's ideal critic the solecisms and hypocrisies of one's enemies are obvi-

---

*Mr. Weidhorn is a professor of English literature and author of the forthcoming *A Harmony of Interests: Explorations in the Mind of Sir Winston Churchill.*

ous and expectable, but the defects in one's own camp are too easily ignored or excused. A true patriot wants to clean up his own nest before setting out to enlighten the rest of the world.

Since one good turn deserves another, here, in the spirit of the ecumenism and good-faith dialogue which Mr. Buckley has conjured up, is an attempt at similar candor by a Jew.

Christianity bears a heavy responsibility for the prevalence of anti-Semitism, but not an exclusive one. Anti-Semitism existed before Christianity (Apion, Tacitus, Juvenal) and exists today outside it (in certain circles in Japan and in parts of the Moslem world). The ubiquity of this moral plague can be smugly written off by Jews as the jealousy all peoples have of the one people doing things right. Or it can make conscientious Jews ask themselves whether they are not doing something wrong. All that smoke, and no fire?

Jews are not, in fact, entirely blameless.* The concept of the "chosen people" has played a mischievous role in history. Rabbis are always quick to explain that chosenness bears no relation to notions of Aryan supremacy, racial superiority, American exceptionalism, or any of the garden-variety chauvinisms that exist in Japan, France, Russia. Chosenness, they insist, means rather for Jews an extra set of moral obligations: Gentiles only have to observe a few Noahide principles, but Jews are saddled with no fewer than 613 commandments, the majority of them, to boot, beginning with the unfortunate "Thou shalt not." Jews accordingly are not in any sense superior but more burdened.

Modern psychologists and novelists have, however, noted how a burden of this sort has an insidious way of turning into an unacknowledged sense of superiority. "I am more constrained morally than you," some inner voice says, "because I am more worthy of such a mission than you are. Besides, an all-just God would not inflict sacrifices on one set of persons throughout history without rendering some sort of compensation elsewhere or later." Pay now, enjoy later. Expecting such a possible future reward may be seen as a sort of pulling rank.

Being burdened or victimized, moreover, begets its own form of hybris,

---

*Lest I be accused of "blaming the victim" and exculpating the victimizer, let me clarify this delicate point with an incident from recent history. Taking a jog in the outer reaches of Central Park at 11:00 P.M. is a hazardous enterprise. So is being the beneficiary of chosenness. The believing Jew takes that lonely jog in a perilous world under orders from a higher authority. That someone does jog in a dangerous time and place may well flout worldly wisdom—and which religion does not flout worldly wisdom?—but in no way excuses a mugger, rapist, or murderer. Whatever the temptation offered by the otherworldly jogger, a crime is a crime, and the book should be thrown at the criminal. In other words, I understand but in no way condone any act of anti-Semitism, down to the slightest graffito.

or at least of clannishness. Joseph Sobran's remarks on the invidious distinction in expressions like "goyish kopp" ("gentile head," i.e., dumb) touch on such tribalism. The tribal reasoning goes something like this: We are morally and ritually far more burdened than you; therefore we are purified by self-sacrifice and heavenward gazes; therefore we are wiser—and probably nobler—than the spiritually virginal, the naïve and untested, gentiles.

Jews may not speak or even think (consciously, at any rate) in this fashion, but *some* Jews certainly betray such logic by their actions. A joke: A monk lies on his deathbed. His colleagues are seated at a nearby table writing his eulogy. After arduous work, they lean back, saying: "Let's see, we mentioned his charitableness, self-sacrifice, piety, etc. Did we leave anything out?" The dying monk sits up and exclaims: "Don't forget my humility."

In any case, the official rabbinic interpretation of chosenness is not the one that most gentiles, or even many non-Orthodox Jews, are familiar with. To the world at large, the phrase "the chosen people" implies a special status. One can, of course, be "chosen" for extermination, but in everyday parlance, "chosen" connotes "favored," "elect," "privileged." Jealousy—and its attendants, resentment and hate—cannot be far behind. Most people have but to recall the annoyance they felt in elementary school with the classmate who was the "teacher's pet." Whether one buys the rabbinic or the normative understanding of chosenness, the Jews are "God's pet." No favors from those left out need be expected. Nor should one forget that the teacher's pet is likewise a burdened soul; he receives a larger proportion of questions from a teacher confident that one student at least will give the correct answer. Being burdened and being favored are, clearly, not opposites.

Whatever the meaning of chosenness may be, the content of the laws placed on Jewish shoulders is an invitation to trouble. The mandate to be exclusive—the dread of intermarriage, the tradition of looking and acting differently, the fear of contamination by gentiles (see Shylock), the apparent reluctance to participate in that most civil of ceremonies, breaking bread with outsiders, because the food may have non-Kosher elements in it—generates an aura of unintelligibility and haughtiness about Jews and their ways. That which people cannot fathom, they begin to think the worst of. And if religious Jews are raised not to socialize with non-Jews, how can they avoid beginning to feel at some pre-conscious level that non-Jews are leprous or contaminating? And how can such dis-ease not get itself communicated to the non-Jews?

Then there is an irony. The exclusiveness may well be a necessity for group cohesiveness and survival. It also, however, generates aggression in others, and this hostility (as Sartre et al. have noted) in turn is, curiously, beneficial for group cohesiveness and survival. Full-time, professional, chauvinist Jews exist who, in their heart of hearts, cannot regard anti-Semitism (at least in its milder, genteel form) with complete disfavor.

If this sounds too contorted, blasphemous, or paradoxical a thought, consider the United States. As nations go, it has been by far the most receptive, tolerant, and rewarding nation that Jews have come in contact with during their long and often bitter trek through the regions of the Diaspora. And what has been the result? Gratitude, immense and heart-felt, from most Jews but also jeremiads from the rabbis and chauvinist Jews about, of all things, a holocaust, a spiritual holocaust! The dropping of all barriers has meant rampant assimilation, intermarriage, secularism, homogenization—and the ultimate peaceful, quiescent demise of the Jewish people in America. (Read, for example, Rabbi Arthur Hertzberg, and he is but a moderate on this.) Truly, anti-Semitism is a subject that grows more complex every time one looks at it.

The hostility directed at Jews throughout history has, moreover, an ambiguous basis. The Hebrew scripture portrays God as ordering the Israelites to do things His way or He will wipe the floor with them. Doing things His way involves, as we saw, a lot of activity that makes Jews different and bizarre. Now comes a bifurcation. If one is a believing Jew or Christian, God would appear to have followed through on his threat; the Jews did not observe the Law too well, and they have accordingly been punished. This is a classic instance of fulfillment of Biblical prophecy. Jewish suffering at the hands of others is divinely ordained.

If, on the other hand, one is not a believer, one is left with a psychological reading of events: The Israelites dream up a God who favors them but who in return seems to place burdens on them and who, they imagine, wants them to be different from all other people. This difference arouses anti-Semitism among all those "other people," who see in the Israelites only self-delusion and arrogance. The result is a classic case of self-fulfilling prophecy rather than actual prophecy. The Jews are seen to have brought their troubles on themselves by fabricating a very peculiar God. (As a bard says, "How odd / Of God / To choose / The Jews.") The conclusion to all this is, "You pays yer money, and you takes yer choice": Either God's ways are very mysterious, or Jews are peculiarly self-destructive.

Fairness requires, however, the concession that exclusiveness is neither intrinsically evil—it has enabled Jews to survive for millennia—nor specifically Jewish. The Japanese are known for their xenophobia. If the ultra-Orthodox Jews ban TV from their homes for fear of secularization, do not the Amish the same? (And is it such a bad idea?) If the ultras have their own schools and textbooks, do not many Catholics? If the ultras try to sequester themselves from the gentile and even secular Jewish world as much as possible, do not certain Catholic religious orders? If intermarriage is a nightmare in traditional Jewish homes, is it any the less so in traditional Catholic ones? Is even "chosenness" unknown to Catholics and Mormons, to Calvinists and other Christians assured of their salvation? If some benighted Jews actually believe that Jews can do no wrong and gentiles can do no right, has one never run across an American who generalizes similarly about his compatriots as against all those others out there?

Mr. Buckley's observations on knee-jerk anti-anti-Semitism have nothing to do with the concept of "the Chosen People" and little to do with the existence of Israel and the problem of double loyalties. The phenomenon discussed has much more to do with one of the oldest and most ubiquitous impulses, "Kill the messenger."

When faced with a criticism of some policy or action of the Israelis— let us say, alleged torture of Arab detainees—a rational, conscientious Jew would find out whether the charge has merit. If it does and if no convincing justifications are given, he would shoot off an angry letter to those in charge. Such an inquest, however, is time-consuming and extremely taxing. What is worse, if the charge is valid, it calls into question Israel's "most favored nation" status and gives ammunition to Israel's enemies, who can be relied on to exploit it in every unfair manner possible.

How much simpler is it to dismiss the charge by calling the originator of it an "anti-Semite" and resuming one's dogmatic slumber. If the originator of the charge happens to be a Jew and therefore cannot be called an anti-Semite, not to worry! He is, of course, a "self-hating Jew."

A joke: A Jewish boy applies for a job as a radio announcer. He returns home with the news that he did not get the job. "Why not?" inquires his mother. The boy replies: "A-A-Ant-t-ti-sem-m-m-it-t-t-ism-m-m!" Patriotism, we are often and usefully reminded, is the last refuge of a scoundrel. The flag of one's country or the prayer shawl is a handy way of covering one's personal nakedness and shortcomings.

Make no mistake about it, there are real anti-Semites and self-hating Jews out there. Labeling someone in that way just because he raises unanswerable questions is, however, neither good logic nor fine manners. One's first task is to address the charge and either enlighten the interlocutor or revise one's thinking.

Everyone is wedded to the ideology of his choosing or upbringing. When a theory collides with a fact, the iron law of psychology is that the theory will invariably win out. The theory digests and incorporates the fact, as in the case of the leftist who asserted that proof of Trotsky's prophetic insight is that none of his predictions has yet come true.

After Don Quixote's gimcrack armor fell apart in the first testing of it, he rebuilt it and then wisely refrained from repeating the test. Not only that, he even went so far as to call it the best armor that ever was. So do we all operate with our cherished ideologies. How many individuals, Jew or gentile, resist the temptation to take this easy way out when confronted with an embarrassment? "He's a commie!" or "He's a kook!" Mr. Buckley himself has had the honor of being called everything from "fascist" to (just recently) "scary." Killing the messenger is, in short, not a Jewish or neoconservative problem, but a human one. In this case, as in so many other matters, Bernard Malamud's aphorism (adapted actually from Montaigne), "Jews are like other people, only more so," is apposite. In two senses: Jews carry normal forms of behavior to a higher or more intense pitch than do gentiles; and whatever Jews do people will take more notice of than if other ethnics do it.

In line with Malamud's Law, Jews are, like the stuttering would-be announcer, sometimes indeed guilty of over-reliance on the ad-hominem argument. Any sensitive Jew who, on the basis of making a legitimate criticism of black leadership or behavior, is irritated at being called a racist should have some understanding of the annoyance gentiles must feel when labeled "anti-Semitic" as a result of making an objective observation on Jewish affairs. Having been deeply seared by the Holocaust, Jews are understandably on the lookout for signs of any resurgence of evil. But overkill sometimes takes place and is counterproductive. Pat Buchanan, for example, has certainly ventured into a grey area on a number of occasions, but are not A. M. Rosenthal and company perhaps a trifle trigger happy?

Recall the Abe Fortas case in 1967. His nomination for the Chief Justiceship resulted in a Bork-like imbroglio. There were widespread whispers and rumors of anti-Semitism. What held up his nomination, however, was that, at first, conservatives were leery of his liberalism and, later, that he was found to have an unacknowledged conflict of interest.

Anti-Semitism turned out to have been nonexistent. Recall also the groundless fears that Jewish leaders had over the nomination of George Shultz as Secretary of State because of his ties to Bechtel and its ties to the Arab world.

The moral is, when there are other legitimate explanations for a man's behavior or statements, anti-Semitism should be a charge of last, not first, resort. When you have a bona-fide anti-Semite like David Duke on your hands, why add to your problems? The corollary to this rule is that, if you call good-intentioned critics "anti-Semites" frequently enough, they may begin to lose some of their good intentions and you may become a self-fulfilling prophet. Hitler has given anti-Semitism a bad name (hence Mr. Buckley Sr.'s table talk would be out of place in polite company today), but some Jews may be inadvertently allowing it elbow room by mishandling the problem. Recent whispers that President Bush, simply because of legitimate policy differences with the egregious Prime Minister Shamir, is "anti-Semitic" are a definitive instance of disgraceful, whining, self-pitying behavior.

Nor are some Jews, like some or many gentiles, strangers to the use of a double standard, though whether they do so cunningly or unwittingly is best left to the charitableness of the observer. During the Yom Kippur War, Jews were quick to criticize Western Europe and Japan for their reluctance to help Israel (or the U.S.) in any way. Considering that nearly all the oil in those countries came from Arab lands and that a possible retaliatory cut-off of oil would have quickly resulted in paralysis, one cannot so easily blame those advanced industrialized societies, in which oil is the lifeblood, for putting self-interest above principle (if indeed any principle was at stake here for them). Yet one hears little from these principled Jewish critics about Israel's cooperating with South Africa when that nation was a moral outcast; or her building, by hook and crook, nuclear weapons; or her role in human-rights violations.

When not guilty of a double standard, some Jews lapse into something similar—moral deafness or narcissism. Religious Jews who base their claim to the Holy Land (notwithstanding the Palestinians already there) on God's giving it to the Israelites reveal a touching naïveté. They seem not to realize that, in the modern world, many people do not believe in the Bible as a sacred text; that even those who accept the Bible as divine do not interpret it in an Orthodox or even Judaic fashion; that even those who do so are not prepared to settle modern boundary disputes by means of religious documents, at least not until the coming of the Messiah or the Second Coming of Christ.

Jews need also to remember that discrimination and subtlety are required where polemics usually dominate. When apprised of Israeli delinquencies, the hard-liners have three stock responses. 1) The charges come from Arab or UN sources and are therefore highly suspect. 2) Why don't you discuss the far greater offenses of the Arabs? 3) The charges may well be true but you have to look at the whole picture and take into account the extreme position Israel is in; in its quest for survival, Israel may need to break a few eggs.

As to the first response, the matter is akin to the problem raised by the supermarket gossip sheets: The stories there appear in sources that are suspect, but they do sometimes turn out to be true (even if certain editorial boards used to have difficulty deciding whether they were "fit to print"). The second response is often correct but ambiguous. A Jew killing an Arab does get far greater coverage than Syrian soldiers massacring thousands of their fellow citizens. That may indeed be due to pure, old-fashioned anti-

Semitism. Or it may be a compliment: From Syrians, one expects swinishness, but from Israelis one expects civilized behavior. (Is this expectation, by the way, anti-Syrianism? anti-Arabism?) Or it may be due to the marketplace law that violence between ethnic or national groups sells better than violence within a group.

But the third response is the trickiest. If Israel's plight is to be looked at in context and if self-preservation is the shibboleth, have not the Palestinians the right to the same considerations? If mistreatment of detainees and bombing of Palestinian camps with only pro forma concern about civilian casualties is justified by reasons of state, so are terrorist attacks by the PLO. Two can play the same game. After all, the Palestinians have their own Diaspora, their own pogroms (Shatila, Kuwait), and their own Zionism. Before Mr. Podhoretz rushes in to complain about that relic from the cold war, "moral equivalency," he should recall the findings of a British commission (chaired by a prominent Jew) in the 1930s that the contest in Palestine was not between right and wrong but between two rights. That, at any rate, is how the world still sees it, like it or not.

It is an old rule of human behavior that where my enemy's actions are concerned, "the end *never* justifies the means," but when it comes to my actions, well, the law of self-preservation—and only I can interpret the law as it applies to me—supersedes all other principles and rules.

Hence it is that, for Rosenthal and Podhoretz, Jews like Begin and Shamir used to be freedom-fighters, but Arafat is a terrorist; that Jews from Milwaukee and Odessa and Ethiopia have a special claim to the Holy Land, but native Palestinians (faceless Arabs, to too many Jews) can go live in Jordan, Kuwait, or Yemen. Needless to say, Jews have no monopoly on this doublespeak. The statements of Arabs and their sympathizers are rife with a sort of nonsense that is a mirror image of the Jewish one. But the Jewish behavior is under discussion now, and one is not required to accept gobbledygook from one party to a dispute just because the other party is equally delinquent and irresponsible.

The Rosenthal–Podhoretz faction also is a little too complacent on the role of Jews in recent history. Hitler's venom was directed at all sorts of people. Jews were his earliest and most afflicted victims. That makes it seem as if Jews should get credit for manning the barricades for, and before, the rest of mankind; as if, in short, Jews were premature anti-Nazis. In actuality, however, things were not so simple. Jews did not see Hitler for what he was before others did; they were singled out by him and given no choice in the matter.

Let us test that out with a mental experiment. Imagine a different world, one in which Hitler is everything that he was except for a small detail.

He is not anti-Semitic; he thinks as little about Jews one way or the other as about Eskimos or Mormons. What would have happened then? Would Jews have joined the underground, hidden people (Gypsies, Slavs, socialists, dissenting clerics) in the attics, and martyred themselves in great numbers? Probably not. A few saintly (and highly employable) souls like Einstein would have emigrated on principle. Some would have gone into internal exile and avoided cooperation with the state. But many, with jobs and families to worry about, would, like their Catholic and Protestant and agnostic/atheist counterparts, have kept a low profile and done their patriotic duty as good Germans in the war against all those oppressive European peoples. Not manned the extermination camps perhaps, but not done much to stop them either if it involved personal risk. The easy sneer at "good Germans" is inappropriate when coming from those who have not been similarly tested.

Any illusions harbored by the hard-line faction about Jews being immunized against the Nazi virus or being quintessential anti-Nazis have surely been destroyed by recent events: to wit, the flirtation with quasi-Nazi ideas—*Araber raus!*—by the late Meir Kahane (a rabbi, be it noted, a man of God) or by Rabbi Moshe Levenger, by the far-right religious and nationalist sects in Israel, and by the aggressive Jewish-American settlers on the West Bank. No, Zionism is not racism, but, yes, some Zionists definitely are racists.

And why should there not be some racist Zionists? Jews are not saints, not exempt from the laws of psychology and sociology. When impoverished and disfranchised, Jews drifted to liberalism and socialism; when affluent, they think more along conservative lines. The agonizing over whether group characteristics are essential or accidental can be disposed of rather peremptorily. People possessing a linguistic, religious, and cultural tradition are certainly going to have a set of vices and virtues in common. As long as two conditions are met, nothing is wrong with observing that the Scots are thrifty, the Irish dreamy, the Jews studious and money-conscious, the Hispanics laid back, the New Englanders laconic and puritanical.

One condition is that it is understood to be not a genetic but an environmental matter. Look at Jews and the martial virtues. The Biblical Israelites fought a lot of wars, and, during Roman times, the Jews were seen as a fractious, bellicose crowd, ever ready to rebel and to martyr themselves. Then, during the two millennia of the Diaspora, the Jews became passive. As a minority in alien cultures, they had to learn to survive by meekness, bribery, passivity, by being, as Joyce's Bloom is said to be, the only true cheek-turning Christian in a lapsed, or frequently lapsing, Christian society. Hence the well known group characteristic was that "Jews don't fight."

Then came the Holocaust and the consequent resolve of "Never again!" An Israel surrounded by Arab states has produced one of the best armies in the world. In reverting to the style of their ancestors in Biblical and Roman times, Jews—some would even complain—fight too much and too well. At any rate, the arrogance and pugnacity of the aptly named sabra ("cactus"—i.e., native Israeli) is no more a matter of Jewish genes than was the putative physical cowardice in the Diaspora.

The second caveat on the use of group characteristics is that they not be applied mechanically and that each individual must be judged on his/her own. Using group traits is a sort of early science, a lazy man's attempt to make sense of the multiplicity of facts. But always the individual comes first. Juliet had been raised to believe that Montagues are evil. Meeting an attractive but nameless young man, she fell in love with him. She not knowing him to be a Montague, her vision was not distorted by group traits, and she judged him as an individual. Hence her acknowledgment— "Too early seen unknown and known too late"—that experience takes precedence over theory and that with regard to one Montague, at least, group traits are nugatory.

So much at least needs to be said about Jewish culpability in the generation of anti-Semitism. Jews whose toes have been stepped on in the course of this essay will of course dismiss the whole thing as the rantings of a self-hating Jew telling tales out of school to the goyim. Not so; the goal has been Mr. Buckley's, i.e., to rise above partisanship in order to get at the truth. One must therefore add, loudly and clearly, that we have been speaking throughout of the behavior of *some* Jews *some* of the time, behavior which brings opprobrium on all Jews. "Jews are like other people, only more so." *Pace* Mr. Sobran, most Jews do not use expressions like "goyish kopp" or think that way; *pace* Mr. Buchanan, most Jews do not think along the lines of the Rosenthal–Podhoretz polemics. The case is similar to that of American tourists abroad yesterday and Japanese tourists today, who were and are known to speak loudly, flash money, and stay among themselves rather than mix with the natives. These are the traits of certain types, such as some members of the *nouveau riche* class, rather than of the nationalities; most Americans and Japanese never even go abroad.

Once the Jews confront and confess their own role in anti-Semitism, they are morally freed to look elsewhere. The lion's share of the blame can be attributed not to Christ but (in line with the distinctions made by Kierkegaard and by Nietzsche) to Christianity and, above all, to Christendom. And that is a long story which the Second Vatican Council, Mr. Buckley, and other conscientious Christians have started to face up to at long last after nearly two millennia of silence or complicity by Church and flock in the face of the most obscene and profoundly un-Christian behavior by people worshipping the putative Prince of Peace and Love, who happened to be a Jew.

16 · The Political Scene
From a Speech by Murray Rothbard

Following are excerpts, though the ellipses have been omitted, from a very long (ninety-minute) speech by Murray Rothbard, Professor of Economics at the University of Nevada, given to the John Randolph Club, of which he is the president, at its second annual meeting, held in January.

The excerpts raise several relevant questions. The long essay on anti-Semitism is interpreted as a political act designed to discredit Pat Buchanan, the new hero of what, for the lack of anything more precise, one may as well call the John Randolph Right. A second point of interest is Mr. Rothbard's opinion that the American Right can be equally hospitable to anyone who ever had any misgivings about Franklin Delano Roosevelt. (Lenin branded such political indiscrimination as "opportunist"—i.e., the sin of opening Communist Party doors to virtually everyone: the counterpart of the sin of "sectarianism," the practice of denying admission to any but true believers, which practice he held to be too exclusivist.) If it were so, then of course National Review has been wrong over the years in seeking to make such distinctions as were thought necessary to attempt to correct those, e.g., who disdained the political or philosophical company of anyone who believed in God (Ayn Rand); who believed that the beginning of political wisdom was to recognize that Dwight Eisenhower was an agent of the Communist Party (the John Birch Society); or who believed that the Protocols of the Elders of Zion are the ruling surreptitious document within the Jewish community (Allan Zoll). But the enthusiasm here expressed by Mr. Rothbard for Pat Buchanan is not likely to be reciprocated. Mr. Buchanan *isn't going to wage his campaign for the Presidency by denouncing Social Security.*—W. F. B.*

And this, only the *second* annual meeting of the John Randolph Club, celebrates the fact that we have suddenly vaulted from the periphery to a central role in the American Right. The occasion of this dramatic change, of course, has been the entry into the presidential race of our esteemed Randolph Club member, Patrick J. Buchanan. . . .

What has happened is that what I call the Old Right is suddenly back! The terms old and new inevitably get confusing, with a new "new" every few years, so let's call it the *Original* Right, the Right wing as it existed from 1933 to approximately 1955. This Old Right was formed in reaction against the New Deal, and against the Great Leap Forward into the leviathan state that was the essence of that New Deal.

If we know what the Old Right was against, what were they *for?* How far would you roll government back? The *minimum* demand which almost all Old Rightists agreed on, which virtually defined the Old Right, was total abolition of the New Deal, the whole kit and kaboodle of the Welfare State, the Wagner Act, the Social Security Act, going off gold in 1933, and all the rest. Beyond that, there were charming disagreements. Some would stop at repealing the New Deal. Others would press on, to abolition of Woodrow Wilson's New Freedom, including the Federal Reserve System and especially that mighty instrument of tyranny, the income tax and the Internal Revenue Service. Still others, extremists such as myself, would not stop until we repealed the Federal Judiciary Act of 1789, and maybe even think the unthinkable and restore the good old Articles of Confederation.

The proper course for the Right-wing opposition must necessarily be a strategy of boldness and confrontation, of dynamism and excitement, a strategy, in short, of rousing the masses from their slumber and exposing the arrogant elites that are ruling them, controlling them, taxing them, and ripping them. We need a dynamic, charismatic leader who has the ability to short-circuit the media elites, and to reach and rouse the masses directly. We need a leadership that can reach the masses and cut through the crippling and distorting hermeneutical fog spread by the media elites. We need, in short, the leadership of Patrick J. Buchanan.

---

*The personal hostility of Murray Rothbard (it is manifest) traces to a seminar I conducted at Yale in 1962 at which I ventured to opine, referring to an essay by Mr. Rothbard then making the rounds, that the conservative movement could not make out a very persuasive case for privatizing lighthouses. Lighthouses, I said, are primarily useful in circumstances that make it difficult for the sailor to drop his dollar bill into the lighthouse keeper's basket. Mr. Rothbard was greatly offended by this heresy, and cut all ties to *National Review*.

But can we call such a strategy "conservative"? I, for one, am tired of the liberal strategy, on which they rung the changes for forty years, of presuming to define "conservatism" as a supposed aid to the conservative movement. Whenever liberals have encountered hard-edged abolitionists who, for example, want to repeal the New Deal or Fair Deal, they say "but that's not *genuine* conservatism. That's *radicalism.*" The *genuine* conservative, these liberals go on to say, doesn't want to repeal or abolish anything. He is a kind and gentle soul who wants to *conserve* what left-liberals have accomplished.

I must admit that, in one sense, the liberals have had a point. The word "conservative" is unsatisfactory. The original Right never used the term "conservative": we called ourselves individualists, or "true liberals," or Rightists. We want to uproot the status quo, not conserve it. The original Right, the radical Right, had pretty much disappeared by 1963. But now, all of a sudden, with the entry of Pat Buchanan into the presidential race, my God, they're back! The radical Right is back, all over the place, feistier than ever and getting stronger!

What happened to the original Right, anyway? And how did the conservative movement get into its present mess? Why does it need to be sundered, and split apart, and a new radical Right movement created upon its ashes?

The answer to both of these seemingly disparate questions is the same: what happened to the original Right, and the cause of the present mess, is the advent and domination of the right wing by Bill Buckley and *National Review.* By the mid 1950s, much of the leadership of the Old Right was dead or in retirement. Senator Taft and Colonel McCormick had died, and many of the right-wing congressmen had retired. The conservative masses, for a long time short on intellectual leadership, was now lacking in political leadership as well. An intellectual and power vacuum had developed on the right, and rushing to fill it, in 1955, were Bill Buckley, fresh from several years [nine months—Ed.] in the CIA, and *National Review,* an intelligent, well-written periodical staffed with ex-Communists and ex-leftists eager to transform the Right from an isolationist movement into a crusade to crush the Soviet God that had failed them.

Very quickly, *National Review* became the dominant, if not the *only,* power center on the right wing. This power was reinforced by a brilliantly successful strategy (perhaps guided by *NR* editors trained in Marxist cadre tactics) of creating a battery of front groups: ISI for college intellectuals, Young Americans for Freedom for campus activists; moreover, led by veteran Republican politico and *NR* Publisher Bill Rusher, the *National Review* complex was able to take over, in swift succession, the College Young Republicans, then the National Young Republicans, and finally to create a Goldwater movement in 1960 and beyond.

And so, with almost Blitzkrieg swiftness, by the early 1960s, the new global crusading conservative movement, created and headed by Bill Buckley, was almost ready to take power in America. But not quite, because first, all the various heretics of the Right, some left over from the original Right, all the groups that were in any way radical or could deprive the new conservative movement of its much desired *respectability* in the eyes of the liberal and centrist elite, all these had to be jettisoned. Only such a denatured, respectable, non-radical, *conserving* Right was worthy of power.

And so the purges began. One after another, Buckley and *National Review* purged and excommunicated all the radicals, all the non-respectables. Consider the roll call: isolationists (such as John T. Flynn), anti-Zionists, libertarians, Ayn Randians, the John Birch Society, and all those who continued, like the early *National Review*, to dare to oppose Martin Luther King and the civil-rights revolution.

So that's how the dice have been loaded in our current political game. And virtually the only genuine Rightist spokesman who has managed to escape neocon anathema has been Pat Buchanan.

It was time. It was time to trot out the old master, the prince of excommunication, the self-anointed pope of the conservative movement, William F. Buckley Jr. It was time for Bill to go into his old act, to save the movement that he had made over into his own image. It was time for the man hailed by neocon Eric Breindel as the "authoritative voice on the American Right." It was time for Bill Buckley's papal bull, his 40,000-word Christmas encyclical to the conservative movement, "In Search of Anti-Semitism," the screed solemnly invoked in the anti-Buchanan editorial of the *New York Times*.

The first thing to say about Buckley's essay is that it is virtually unreadable. Gone, all gone is the wit and the sparkle. Buckley's tendency to the rococo has elongated beyond measure. His prose is serpentine, involuted, and convoluted, twisted and qualified, until virtually all sense is lost. Reading the whole thing through is doing penance for one's sins, and one can accomplish the task only if possessed by a stern sense of duty, as one grits one's teeth and plows through a pile of student term papers—which, indeed, Buckley's essay matches in content, in learning, and in style.

National Review is no longer the monopoly power center on the Right. There are new people, young people, popping up all over the place, Pat Buchanan for one, all the paleos for another, who frankly don't give a fig for Buckley's papal pronunciamento. The original Right, and all its heresies, is back! In fact, Bill Buckley is the Mikhail Gorbachev of the conservative movement. Like Gorbachev, Bill goes on with his old act, but like Gorbachev, nobody trembles any more, nobody bends the knee and goes into exile. *Nobody cares any more;* nobody, except the good old *New*

York Times. Bill Buckley should have accepted his banquet and stayed retired. His comeback is going to be as successful as Muhammad Ali's.

For Pat Buchanan's race for the Presidency has changed the face of the right wing. It's now a brand new ball game. By his very entry, Pat Buchanan has changed and redefined the entire nature of the conservative movement. He has created a new radical, or Hard Right, very much like the original Right before *National Review.* For all their wealth, media influence, and seeming power, it is now the official conservatives and the neoconservatives who are on the periphery. The right wing shall henceforth only be defined in relation to the Buchananite movement. That movement, neither kind nor gentle, now sets the agenda, and sets the terms of the debate.

17 · Excerpts from Miscellaneous Letters and Columns

• *A Letter from John Kiley*

It tracks like some implacable heat-guided missile to its important target. Beautifully argued and written.

• *A Letter from Christopher Ricks*

Congratulations on the patience, exactitude, and justice of your substantial and substantiated essay on anti-Semitism. It had, if I may say so, all your characteristic virtues, and (I betray my injustice?) some virtues that I'd not thought *characteristic* of you, though I'd not supposed them alien to you. We have a common friend . . . I'm in his debt for letting me be in yours.

• *From a Column by Joseph Sobran*

The conservative reaction to the piece is overwhelmingly negative. "Why did Bill write it?" and "What does he think he's accomplishing?" are the ques-

tions one keeps hearing, along with the adjectives "turgid" and "unreadable."

—*The Wanderer*, December 26, 1991

• *A Letter from Henry Hyde*

1. I hope you and yours have a Blessed Christmas and most fulfilling
1992!
2. Your article on Pat & Joe was painful but essential.

• *A Letter from John Roche*

Wanted to tell you what a splendid piece of analysis your anti-Semitism
study was. One of the things that has always annoyed me was the assertion
that Marshall, Acheson, Rusk, were anti-Semites (Forrestal *was*) in 1947–
48. They simply did not want another loose cannon in the Levant and—
as Rusk told me once—wished "to hell that God had promised them
Nebraska."

• *A Letter from Jeff Nelligan*

Once again, you've demonstrated the Right can look at itself honestly and
even-handedly—something the other side has yet to do.

Superb job.

• *A Letter from Eric Alterman*

I appreciated your use of my Rosenthal/Buchanan argument in your recent
opus and found myself in accord with a surprisingly large percentage of what
you had to say. Two points, however:

1. I think it wrong and unfair to hold "the Left" responsible for Vidal's
mean-spiritedness and Navasky's blind spot—particularly when, in my essay,
I condemned Vidal in the pages of *The Nation*.

2. I wrote Navasky exactly the letter that Podhoretz said he wanted—
without any invitations—when I was being considered for the job of *Nation*
Washington editor. I promised, I think, "to dance the hora for 24 hours
straight if *Commentary* were defunded by the American Jewish Committee,"

but unfortunately, in the Vidal case, "Norman was right, Victor was wrong." I ccd a copy to Norman at the time, as I recall.

In any case, I salute the care and grace you brought to the subject.

• A Letter from Patrick Andretta

In over 25 yrs of subscribing to NR I don't think I've ever read a piece as awful as B. Buckley's screed on anti-Semitism: it was too long, too boring, unconvincing, and misplaced. Mr. Buckley is obviously ready for permanent retirement.

• A Letter from John E. Folan

I have canceled my subscription to your publication. You are, I think, too arrogant to know your sins.

I hold you in total contempt.

• A Letter from Sam Tanenhaus

I've just read Mr. Buckley's essay on anti-Semitism. Its immediate readership may be limited to the cultural-political cloister; but that narrowing is what makes the piece so strong. What seems at first a limitation is instead a spiritualizing discipline. Time chastens, and future readers will demand essences; Mr. Buckley has provided an essence. The essay is narrow as Burton's *Anatomy of Melancholy* is narrow—it opens onto very wide vistas, like a diagnosis of distemper that includes a geography of the central nervous system.

Another metaphor also imposes itself: he has created a kind of music. Instead of simply stating his opinions—and how tiresome opinions become—he has orchestrated voices (Buchanan, Judis, Kinsley, Kristol, Podhoretz, Sobran, etc.) that heard together give us the whole range and register of our political journalism. The essence again. How liberating to hear what it all sounds like—not just the individual diatribes but their cumulative resonance, something to which we are chronically deaf because we overlook, or refuse to acknowledge, that all disputants are, despite themselves, collaborators, united by their passion for the very thing that drives them apart and that compels them into mimicry of one another's words and phrasings, so that an outsider, overhearing the debate, has trouble untangling the strands and determining who stands where. A guess: a future biographer will conclude that this essay is the beautiful synthesis of 1) the many public debates Mr. Buckley has led over the years and 2) his personal "performing" journalism.

• A Current Survey on Anti-Semitism in America (from the "Atlanta Constitution," January 11, 1992)

While anti-Semitism continues to decline in the United States, contradictions in the way people perceive Jews make it difficult to come up with a clear picture of prejudice that remains, according to a new report issued by the American Jewish Committee, a group that monitors bigotry in the United States.

An analysis of recent surveys of perceptions of Jews in America found that the same person may have both negative and positive attitudes toward Jews. Thus, the finding that a person exhibits anti-Semitism in one category, such as viewing Jews as "money-grubbing" or having too much influence, doesn't necessarily predict that the person will have other anti-Semitic attitudes.

. . . On the one hand, they [the studies] show anti-Semitism at "historic lows," with 86 per cent of Americans surveyed saying they hold "warm feelings" toward Jews, said the report's author, Tom W. Smith of the University of Chicago National Opinion Research Center.

On the other hand, Mr. Smith said, responses to some questions involving the wealth, intelligence, and perceived political influence of Jews, as well as feelings toward Jews expressed by blacks and those who are younger and less educated, show those warm feelings could quickly give way to anti-Semitism.

"There is some concern that the documented decline may be only superficial and that, rather than being eradicated, anti-Semitism has only become dormant, retaining its full horrific potential," he said.

. . . Americans rate Jews higher than whites in general and all other ethnic groups when it comes to wealth, self-reliance, peacefulness, and willingness to work hard, but perceive them as less patriotic than Southern whites and whites in general. But, Mr. Smith said, respondents who view Jews as more intelligent, self-reliant, industrious, and wealthier also tend to believe they exercise too much influence in American life and politics. . . .

Mr. Smith said changes in the Middle East could change the perception of Jews by other Americans. "A growth in opposition to treatment of the Palestinians and/or a pro-Arab tilt as a result of Arab control of oil resources would worsen American attitudes toward American Jews, especially if they were seen as favoring Israel over American interests."

PART THREE

1 · Further Reflections, and Commentary

Two months after the second episode of the inquiry into contemporary anti-Semitism in America was published in *National Review*, much had happened, some of it directly affecting the subject under consideration, some indirectly. The candidacy of Pat Buchanan had received enormous publicity, though that coverage dwindled shortly after Super Tuesday established that he wasn't a critical threat to George Bush. Until the votes were counted in New Hampshire it was here and there predicted that Buchanan might even defeat Bush. What would have been the political consequences of such a defeat is not here relevant. But the mere suggestion of this possibility brought the kind of attention to Buchanan that, 24 years ago, leeched onto Senator Eugene McCarthy when he very nearly defeated incumbent President Lyndon Johnson in March, 1968.

The political world held its breath: having got 37 per cent of the vote in New Hampshire, how would Buchanan do in Georgia, where he campaigned heavily, and then in South Carolina and (on Super Tuesday) in the balance of the South? His most optimistic supporters predicted that his full latent strength would here be realized.

And why not? The South tends to be conservative and tends also to oppose the affirmative-action programs against which Buchanan was heavily campaigning. Buchanan reiterated that just as Bush had sold out the party on taxes, so had he sold out when he signed into law a bill that would put the burden of proof on the employer who failed to promote or to hire someone who thereafter complained that he had been the victim of racial prejudice. Moreover, Bush was not faring well. The recession, in midwinter, bit most coldly; and abroad, Saddam Hussein was kicking up his heels. But in Georgia Buchanan didn't make headway, taking only 36 per cent of the vote, and in Maryland, 30 per cent. In the other Southern states he averaged about 30, which is the vote he got in South Dakota, where he did not campaign, a point that would figure heavily in the postmortems.

Before leaving New York in January for my annual book-writing sojourn in Switzerland I was twice questioned on television about the Buchanan campaign. Most specifically about whether, if I lived in New Hampshire, I would vote for Buchanan. I gave studied answers: Yes, I said, I would vote for Buchanan—because of my conviction that a vote for him was the surest way to communicate to George Bush that a body of voters was dissatisfied with his performance as President. I quickly added (without being invited to do so) that if I had to vote either for Buchanan to serve as President or for Bush to serve as President, I would vote for Bush.

Why?—I was asked by both interrogators (Charlie Rose and Gabe Pressman). Because in three areas I was heatedly dissatisfied with Buchanan. He had written about immigration in accents that suggested a disagreeable nativism; on foreign trade he had sided with the protectionists; and in foreign policy he veered toward isolationism. In none of these positions, I said, does he follow in the footsteps of Ronald Reagan, notwithstanding that Buchanan's statements day after day are to the effect that he wished to reorient the Republican Party toward the Reaganism from which George Bush has derailed it.

On the first of these programs I heard for the first time a question the formulation of which would haunt the issue ever after. It was from Gabe Pressman. It is relevant here to add that Pressman ten years ago had given me a remarkable documentary he had done on an anniversary of Auschwitz, concerning which he understandably continues to feel a near-unquenchable horror; and that we became personal friends, of a professional kind, when I ran for mayor of New York and he spent considerable time with me. All of this by way of suggesting that the question he asked was not intended to be personally antagonistic.

"Do you think that how Bush voted on taxes is more important than anti-Semitism?"

I looked up and said with genuine surprise: "Gabe, the contest in New Hampshire is not touching on the question of anti-Semitism. The people backing Buchanan are protesting George Bush's domestic policies, and the question of anti-Semitism simply isn't on the table."

I thought that a dispositive treatment of the question, and I was wrong. It would come up again and again during the next few weeks.

I say again and again: but not in New Hampshire. I could find in no significant outlet in New Hampshire any editorial voice making the point: *A vote for Buchanan is a vote to countenance or even to engage in anti-Semitism.*

The fuel came from out of state. On the understanding that the divisions are blurred, one can say, seeking economy, that there was the "Rosenthal wing" of critics, and the "White House wing" of critics. The Rosenthal wing were aggressive on the subject: *Anyone who votes for Buchanan, whether he desires that result or not, is advancing the cause of racial intolerance.* Charles Krauthammer and Richard Cohen, two Washington-based columnists, were heavy hitters on the Rosenthal wing.

The White House wing consisted of truculent partisans of George Bush whose primary objective (in my judgment) was to discredit Pat Buchanan in order to reinforce Bush. Some of these critics had personal motives (for instance William Bennett, who had been roasted by Buchanan in a column denouncing the work of neoconservatives). Richard Bond, the chairman of the Republican Party, denounced Buchanan as in effect a neo-fascist. And although they were careful not to use the devil-word, Secretary Jack Kemp, Senator Phil Gramm, and Congressmen Vin Weber and Newt Gingrich all disparaged his candidacy, as did the *Wall Street Journal* and *Forbes,* though this last group emphasized Buchanan's fallibilities other than on the question of racism.

A. M. Rosenthal is not the chosen spokesman even for some of the positions he almost owns, given his taste for melodrama. Norman Podhoretz, for instance, labors over distinctions Mr. Rosenthal would not even notice. Even so, I reproduce excerpts from two columns by Rosenthal which give the burden of his argument and the flavor of his rhetoric. Later, I'll remark the more elaborate analysis of Podhoretz; and in between, recount my own experiences and those of *National Review.*

A few days before the first primary, Rosenthal's column was entitled, "Victory for Buchanan."

> Patrick Buchanan already has achieved a remarkable victory in the New Hampshire primary. It will stand no matter what the vote spread. [Remember, Mr. Rosenthal is not here dealing with Buchanan's vote as a demonstration against Mr. Bush's policies.]
>
> He could not have done it alone. He had the help of American journalists and politicians.
>
> Still, it cannot be taken away from Mr. Buchanan that he not only has introduced anti-Semitism into the mainstream of American politics, but has made it acceptable, respectable enough to ignore—and potentially profitable. [We are encouraged to assume that Pat Buchanan's *campaign* was palpably anti-Semitic.]
>
> In New Hampshire, the press paid only fleeting attention to his anti-Semitism. That was better than President Bush and the Democrats, who paid none. [Mr. Rosenthal immediately undermines his own allegation: if Buchanan's campaign rested in any significant way on anti-Semitism, implicit or explicit, one has to suppose that the press would have paid more than "fleeting attention" to this development, let alone the Democratic candidates.]
>
> Political bigots everywhere will correctly draw the lessons. And they had better be learned by all people who consider Mr. Buchanan just one more politician, all politicians who failed to condemn his cracks about Jews and

"Zulus" and those journalists who ran from confrontation with their good old pal. They had better learn damned quick before they hear the bell tolling too close to their ears.

Mr. Buchanan now has earned close attention as a political propagandist. For years he will be using his new prominence, and his regular TV appearances and column to recast American conservatism in his particular mixture of populism and religious and racial divisiveness. If he succeeds, it will change the texture of American life. [One can't here resist the comment, "Yes indeed, if he succeeds in transforming American conservatism into a racist political movement, he will indeed change the texture of American life. As well agree with the Southern barnyard sunburst: "If grandma had balls, she'd be grandpa!"]

But he is just as important as a vivid example of the increasing social and political acceptability of racism and bigotry in the intellectual and political life of the country. [Here—finally—Mr. Rosenthal has a point. Buchanan turned down several opportunities, in New Hampshire, to regret the language he had used, as examined in part one, that was tendentiously anti-Semitic.]

For years now it has been there to see and smell—in anti-Semitic speeches at campus rallies, in college ads denying the Holocaust, in violently bigoted pop and rap lyrics sold to millions and clear except to music critics who left their brains in the piano stool, in TV air time given to skinheads to vilify blacks. [On this subject I am ignorant except in the sense that I know that the hard-rock types are given to indefensible attacks on women, Jews, Catholics, religion, morals, blacks, intellectuals, poets, and non-poets.]

And now we come to the point where a Presidential candidate's record of carefully crafted insults is hardly even discussed during the campaign.

The responsibility for this phenomenon does not rest simply on the bigots—what else did we expect? It rests on blacks who participate in or ignore anti-Semitism, on whites who get all upset when blacks get even a few of the special, essential breaks in life that they themselves always enjoyed. It rests on those journalistic friends—and TV partners—of Mr. Buchanan who tell us he really is a charming fellow even if he talks a little too bluntly. It rests on people like William Buckley who agree now that Mr. Buchanan did after all say anti-Semitic things but then tell us they would vote for him in New Hampshire as a message to Mr. Bush. What message? Anti-Semitism is less offensive than raising taxes? With a few staunch exceptions, Washington columnists and commentators looked straight at Mr. Buchanan's statements and innuendoes—looked, and ran. They stayed friends and admirers right through his trashing of Holocaust truth, through his irritation of Catholic-Jewish sensibilities, through his cracks about how Congress was Israeli-occupied territory and Democrats the poodles of the Israeli lobby. These Washington experts needed no translation: the Israeli lobby gets its money and votes not from Jerusalem but from American Jews legally and morally supporting a cause close to them.

The cesspool was plumbed when Mr. Buchanan said in August 1990 that only the Israeli Defense Ministry and its "amen corner" in the U.S. were beating the war drums. That was a lie—a lie, and as plain a piece of deliberate evil as ever uttered on TV. It meant watch out, the Jews are trying to drag your children into war for foreign purposes. From the Beltway came the sound of silence. [Mr. Rosenthal makes it difficult for his readers. He leaves them here with no choice: Either they must believe that the Beltway—the vital moral and journalistic organ of Washington, D.C.—is brain dead, or else that Buchanan's remark was something less than deliberate evil of *Guinness Book of Records* standards.]

Top politicians matched journalists in courage. Mr. Bush never suggests, heavens no, that Mr. Buchanan's anti-Semitism might be at least one reason to vote against him.

And not one of the five candidates of the other party thought Mr. Buchanan's anti-Semitism an issue worth mentioning. These people—they are Democrats?

So the victory is Mr. Buchanan's, the respectable, acceptable, charming Buchanan's. What's more, he has refused to withdraw, retract or soften his anti-Semitic insults. Please note. This man is keeping his powder dry.

When I first saw this column, for all that I am experienced in hysteria, I thought Abe Rosenthal had simply gone too far. Those of his readers who lived in New Hampshire would be reading probably for the very first time the charge that they were somehow mixed up in a racist, anti-Semitic enterprise, and would be startled to learn that they had been contaminated by it. And startled by this formulation (exactly as used by Gabe Pressman) of the message the Buchananites' were sending to the White House: *"Anti-Semitism is less offensive than raising taxes."* I doubted such a distortion could prosper. Mr. Rosenthal's contention that voting for Buchanan in New Hampshire was tantamount to applauding his (alleged) anti-Semitism was an especially difficult position, as noted, to take in the very same column in which Mr. Rosenthal pointed out that practically nobody in New Hampshire had even raised the question of Mr. Buchanan and anti-Semitism.

But far from retreating from the extremities toward which he was heading, Mr. Rosenthal had just begun. Three weeks later his column, or relevant parts of it, read:

[A]ngry with President Bush's deviations from their vision of economic conservatism, and disgusted with his floundering, conservatives are shutting mouths and eyes to the danger embodied by Patrick Buchanan.

That danger was put forward most plainly by that cool-and-clear-minded columnist Charles Krauthammer. He wrote that Mr. Buchanan's combination of ugliness about immigrants, his fears for the future of "white Americans," his admiration of so many dictators, his contempt for democracy, his anti-Semitism, his adoption of the "America First" slogan so identified with Nazi apologists and now his Peronist denunciations of "vulture capitalism" summon up a word: fascistic.*

---

*We have here a fine example of forensic reductionism. You would qualify for all the elements that, in Mr. Rosenthal's reasoning, add up to the word "fascistic," if you believe 1) that Englishmen are more quickly acculturated here than Zulus; 2) that immigration

The sorrow of current American political life is that many conservatives, in their anger about Mr. Bush and the recession, are tolerating a man whose values dishonor them, their party and the country. That is moral equivalency in emergency-room form.

Case example: The *National Review*, once the healthy pride of American conservative intellectualism, now is wan and pockmarked with the disease. It does not yet match *The Nation*, a carrier from the left, but it is getting too close.

William Buckley, founder and president of the *Review*, wrote that Mr. Buchanan had said anti-Semitic things. Then he promptly backed a protest vote in New Hampshire for the man, stunning friends who thought they would never see the day.

Now he says that since the protest point has been made in New Hampshire there is no use voting for Mr. Buchanan in other primaries. But the point his readers will remember is that Mr. Buckley believes Mr. Buchanan's mouthings acceptable enough to vote for him at least once.

. . . Many Americans who vote for Mr. Buchanan as a protest may not yet have figured through the lasting impact. But the politicians, commentators and intellectual conservatives who know Mr. Buchanan's record and still give him respectability, urge votes for him or even remain silent, these all have made their choice.

Still, a cure exists for the moral equivalency that has stricken conservatives—remembrance of times so recently past. To refuse it is a kind of intellectual suicide, a sin in itself.

To this column I felt obliged to reply, and did so in my own column a few days later:

On the question, "Should I vote for Pat Buchanan, given that he has said irresponsible things about minorities, Jews, and Israel?" there are those who answer, "Do not vote for him, because if you do, you are encouraging racism and anti-Semitism and your own integrity is forfeit."

The avatar of the latter position is A. M. Rosenthal, the *New York Times* columnist who three times now has publicly castigated me for having said, before the New Hampshire primary, that were I a resident of that state I would vote for Pat Buchanan in order to communicate to President Bush the depth of my dissatisfaction with some of his policies. At the same time I recorded that if the vote in New Hampshire were for the next President of the United States, I would vote for Bush, not for Buchanan.

Mr. Rosenthal reacts as if I (and others like me) had made a covert deal with the Ku Klux Klan ("They"—everyone who failed to reject Buchanan in

---

policy can reasonably make some provision for cultural and ethnic homogeneity; 3) that Spain was better off under General Franco than under President Azana, Chile better off under Pinochet than under Allende; 4) that the pro-Nazi element within the America First movement had nothing to do with the cause embraced by such as Phillip Jessup, Norman Thomas, Gerald Ford, and Chester Bowles; and 5) that the junk-bond crowd have done a lot to discredit capitalism.

appropriate terms—"had better learn damned quick before they hear the bell tolling too close to their ears"). He is Rosenthal-mad not only at me but at every columnist who declined to make Buchanan's statements about the Gulf War and Israel the center of their concern in New Hampshire; mad at all the Democratic candidates, none of whom held Buchanan's statements to be critical to the question at hand. Derivatively, Mr. Rosenthal is mad at 37 per cent of the voters in New Hampshire and Georgia.

He does have this problem, namely that there aren't 15 Buchanan voters in either state who understand themselves to be saying anything at all on the subject of racism and anti-Semitism. The people who voted for Clinton didn't understand themselves to be underwriting adultery, and the people who voted for Bush didn't understand themselves to be endorsing his go-slow policies on the Ukraine, the Baltics, and Yeltsin. The people of New Hampshire were asserting themselves not on the issues Abe Rosenthal sits home stewing about. And surely those who did think that anti-Semitism was the principal question before the voters when Buchanan's name came around must have wondered why in the six weeks preceding the primary, the *New York Times* devoted exactly one editorial to that subject.

There are cool thinkers in America who are on the alert to discourage anti-Semitism. Abe Rosenthal isn't one of them. His hotheadedness, his disposition to judge recklessly, set his cause back. I once found myself saying to the late David Susskind, who at his most obnoxious was as obnoxious as any man could be, that the worst setback enlightened race-religious relations had suffered in recent times was that David Susskind had been born Jewish. Rosenthal should guard against encouraging any such judgmental enormity. Democratic candidates for President, columnists, editors, voters are understandably astonished, then outraged, at the proposition that by declining to dwell on Buchanan and anti-Semitism they betray an insensitivity to the question. "The *National Review*," Rosenthal now writes, "once the healthy pride of American conservative intellectualism, now is wan and pockmarked with the disease."

The statement is quite extraordinary, directed at a magazine that in the past three months has published seventy thousand words probing the question of anti-Semitism and concluding, after a fastidious exploration, that indeed what Pat Buchanan had said a year ago was objectively anti-Semitic. If *National Review*'s reputation is pockmarked, what about that of the *New York Times*? Or of Michael Kinsley and Robert Novak, to mention only two Jewish Americans who decline to join in Mr. Rosenthal's blood sport? Or William Pfaff and Edwin Yoder, who complain (in the current issue of *National Review* [part two] of being mishandled by such reasoning as paralyzes Mr. Rosenthal's power to reason, and causes him to be hysterical?

Rosenthal imputes insensitivity to anti-Semitism on a McCarthyite scale. Buchanan's popular support, on the basis of the votes thus far compiled, projects to many millions. To reiterate my finding in the extensive analysis I published last December, "I find it impossible to defend Pat Buchanan against the charge that what he said during the period under examination amounted to anti-Semitism, whatever it was that drove him to say and to do it: most probably, an iconoclastic temperament."

To have said something anti-Semitic does not *necessarily* justify the assumption that the person who said it is anti-Semitic.* Even as to say something stupid does not justify assuming that the person who said it is stupid. It is Abe Rosenthal's good fortune that I shall be guided by that rule in my future dealings with my old friend.

But the major shock was still ahead of me. It came in a letter addressed to *National Review* signed by 13 men—among them scholars, jurists, journalists, theologians, and churchmen—every one of whom I hold in high esteem. They were Peter Berger, Walter Berns, Robert Bork, Terry Eastland, Patrick Glynn, Michael Joyce, Harvey Mansfield, Richard John Neuhaus, Michael Novak, James Nuechterlein, Thomas Pangle, R. Emmett Tyrrell, and George Weigel. They wrote to *National Review*,

> By the time this letter appears in print, the results of the New Hampshire primary will already be history. Nonetheless, we deeply regret the editorial recommendation of *National Review* that conservatives should vote for Patrick Buchanan ["The Week," Feb. 17]. Our objection is a moral one and has two parts:

> First, it is not morally consistent for the editors to recommend that conservatives should vote for Patrick Buchanan, after Wm. F. Buckley Jr., in his courageous dissection of anti-Semitism, publicly admitted that he finds it "impossible to defend Patrick Buchanan from the charge that what he said and did . . . amounted to anti-Semitism, whatever it was that drove him to do or say it."

---

*A classic example of what anti-Semitic impulses do to a working mind is seen in an editorial published in the March issue of *Chronicles* signed, and presumably written, by Samuel Francis, an erudite journalist associated with the *Washington Times*. He cannot believe (he tells us) that I had anything serious to say about Messrs. Buchanan and Sobran. Could it have been . . . a Jewish plot! "Given the triviality of Mr. Buckley's conclusions, the absence of any compelling evidence to support them, and the staleness of the charges themselves, readers are led ineluctably to an overwhelming question: why did Mr. Buckley choose this particular time to secrete so much mental fuid about this immaterial matter?

"Some light on this may be shed by a 'backgrounder' published by the American Jewish Committee more than a year ago, in November 1990, at the height of the controversy about Mr. Buchanan. The backgrounder's author, Kenneth Stern, wonders what 'we' should do about Mr. Buchanan and his decision was suggestive. 'Unless he says something Mein Kampf-ish,' wrote Mr. Stern, 'we should refrain from calling him an anti-Semite. That will only draw attention to him and bring him defenders. Rather, I suggest we approach other people whom Buchanan's adherents see as equally qualified for the title of 'defender of the faith' to write a rebuttal. When it comes to Catholic–Jewish tensions, why not a leader in the church? and when it is an anti-communism-based issue . . . why not a non-Jewish conservative?' If Rasputin and Machiavelli had conspired over cocktails, they could not have concocted a more furtive strategem. The shoe that fits, of course, is Mr. Buckley, a Catholic conservative. Is it too cynical to ask if the American Jewish Committee or someone associated with it manipulated him into launching his insubstantial Scud against Mr. Buchanan and Mr. Sobran?" From there to the Protocols of Zion is pretty steep climbing, to be sure, but the orientation is dead on.

That recommendation, further, sets a bad moral precedent for the future of American politics and the conservative movement. It opens the door for others to make discriminatory remarks against other Americans and then to protest against any censure on the grounds that "Patrick Buchanan did it—and got away with it." In a country such as ours, it is critical to social peace to keep standards for acceptable public discourse high and universal, binding equally on all with respect to all others. Today's anti-Semitism may be tomorrow's anti-Catholicism or anti-white or anti-black speech.

Moreover, conservatives, defending our civilization's ideals, must defend the highest possible standards for public life. *National Review* has played this important role for decades, even at the expense in recent weeks of egregious attacks upon it from Buchanan supporters.

We pass over in silence the politics of the editors' recommendation, in order to focus attention on the essential point.

Finally, so as not to be unjust to Patrick Buchanan, we state that we have long admired his basic moral seriousness and his normal concern for fair, if passionate, expression. These make all the less understandable, and more sad, those lapses which Mr. Buckley (and we) find indefensible.

Editor John O'Sullivan gave his own reasons for acting as *National Review* had done, emphasizing his conviction that Buchanan was not in fact anti-Semitic. My own reply is marked with that impatience one feels free to manifest only, as a rule, when dealing with friends and peers:

My friends Peter Berger et al. are quite incorrect in supposing that I take a different stand from that taken by *National Review.* I said on two separate television programs shown coast to coast that were I a resident of New Hampshire, I would vote for Buchanan in order to communicate to Mr. Bush the stamina of the protest vote, but that if the contest between the two were not for the nomination but for the Presidency, I would vote for Mr. Bush because of shortcomings I find in Mr. Buchanan's policies. On the matter of anti-Semitism, my conclusion in the essay was as quoted, but the sentence I wrote has been cropped. I wrote that the content of Mr. Buchanan's quoted remarks was indeed anti-Semitic, "whatever it was that drove him to say and do it: most probably, an iconoclastic temperament." In short, I communicated my own private guess that Buchanan is not anti-Semitic.

But it is as simple as this, that in my judgment Pat Buchanan made statements whose implications are indefensible, and perhaps one day he will agree, pending which people's feelings about him will be qualified.

Meanwhile, what on earth do the esteemed Dr. Berger et al. mean, "We pass over in silence the politics of the editors' recommendation"? What is going on in New Hampshire is political in nature, and they're not talking about racism in New Hampshire, they're talking about whether they want Mr. Bush to continue in the same direction or in a different direction. For *National Review* simply to ignore what the voters are being asked to consider in New Hampshire is an act not of moral discrimination, but of moral grandiosity.

Alongside the letter from the 13 came a private letter from a friend, the daughter of a very old friend (RIP)—of mine and of *National Review*'s. I will call her "Annabelle." She registered the same complaint as the 13, her point—their point—being that to encourage in any way someone who had erred as Buchanan had erred on the subject of ethnic and religious civility was not only wrong but contagiously wrong: If *National Review* and I did it, less sensitive people would do it, and the whole anti-anti-Semitic fabric would threaten to unweave. Her point, and theirs, comes down to the contaminating nexus: Anyone who had spoken as Pat Buchanan had spoken, as quoted in part one of this book, could not be trusted, must not be associated with, and should not be used as an instrument for anything at all.

I thought back to a lunch that had been given for me by Father Richard John Neuhaus, one of the 13 signers listed above, and the Religion Editor of *National Review*. The purpose of that lunch, to which a dozen prominent intellectuals and editors were invited, was to go over the ground I had taken in my original essay on anti-Semitism, and to review it alongside the Open Letter to William F. Buckley Jr. by Norman Podhoretz, which had been circulated to the luncheon guests, and is reproduced in part two.

At that lunch I began by reciting what in my judgment had been an important weakness in my own analysis; and what, in my judgment, was a weakness in Podhoretz's reply. I told them that one reader of my essay, a fellow editor whose judgment I respect, had remarked that he would himself, as an editor, feel very uncomfortable ruling as I had done in the case of Joe Sobran, explained above (Joe would not receive any assignments in *National Review* to editorialize on Mideast controversies, or to review books dealing with Israel or race relations). "That strikes me as just wrong," my friend said. "It seems to me that an editor has to agree to accept anything written by one of his editors, or nothing at all." I replied that I thought this unrealistic, that there are King Charles's heads from which many people suffer. For instance, I said, pursuing my own defense, might it not have been reasonable for an editor to decline to publish any columns by Westbrook Pegler that dealt with Mrs. Roosevelt? (Some readers of this book will remember—many of us with delight—the thirty-year-long obsession of Mr. Pegler with La Boca Grande, as he generally referred to her.) He was not swayed, and now I asked the lunch company their opinions on the question: Could an editor of scruple decline copy from a reviewer or columnist on a subject in which his judgment was simply not trusted, and maintain normal relations with him otherwise?

The opinion was divided. I then turned to one guest who inclined to agree with my critic. I asked him, knowing that he was pro-life on the abortion issue: Would you decline to accept an op-ed piece by Joe Sobran on abortion, on which subject he writes as eloquently as anyone else in America, because he is all messed up on the Israel question? To my surprise, he said, Yes: He would decline *any* contribution by Joe Sobran.

My second point focused on Russell Kirk. In my essay, I had flicked away his wisecrack about Tel Aviv being in effect the capital of the United States by summoning the tradition of the Tall Tale in America. Said I: In my essay, I defended Russell Kirk, insisting that what he had said was on an entirely different plane from what had been said by Joe Sobran and Pat Buchanan; and yet in his long answer to me in *Commentary*, Podhoretz renews his charge against Kirk, insisting that it carried the "stench" of racism. Is agreement between like-minded people on such a subject simply impossible?

The evolution was tantalizing. Here was I, responsible for bringing up the entire subject of Sobran and Buchanan for serious review, facing far sterner judgments against my targets than I thought reasonable. Several of the guests sided with Podhoretz on the Kirk statement, others with me.

Annabelle is the daughter of Catholic parents very active in their church. Although we had corresponded about many things, and even visited a few times, I had been surprised when I had from her the letter in February in which she spoke of herself as Jewish:

> . . . I thought surely you were aware that I'd become a Jew, because the event happened so many years ago, when I was 21 . . . . But since you weren't aware I will add a bit. I passed the rite in an Orthodox synagogue, and that was a matter requiring some three years' intensive study. You may be curious, and we can discuss things further if you like some time. Mine is a quiet observance; it has always been contemplative as opposed to ritualistic. With that as backdrop, I will tell you that I agonized for three days and nights before sending you and John O'Sullivan what I did finally send on the Buchanan matter. I do not say "agonized" lightly. I consulted several people, and . . . my husband and I talked late into those nights, debating. I really had to think things through. When the issue of anti-Semitism is involved and one is (how shall I say it?) an ecumenical Jew, one goes through a terrible self-doubt, questioning deeply and probing painfully whether one is overreacting because one is a Jew and the matter strikes home with such force. You know what I decided, and it still seems right to me.

That letter and two that followed it from her, together with several letters received after the second episode had been published in *National Review*, bring me to frame things a little differently in this closing chapter from the way I'd otherwise have done. Whether it was Annabelle's letter or the letter from the 13 scholars that moved me that evening in Switzerland I don't remember. But late one afternoon I picked up the phone and talked to one of my sisters, one of whose sons was playing an important administrative role in the Buchanan campaign. I said to my sister that I'd

like to try out on her, to be passed along to Pat Buchanan (he and I had not
been in touch since the publication of the essay), the text of a statement he
might make that would mollify those of his critics who worried about his
putative anti-Semitism. I wrote out the following:

> There has been a great deal of discussion in recent weeks of a controversy
> I was engaged in last fall.
>
> From what I said, some people have concluded that I am anti-Semitic. Of
> course I am nothing of the sort. Anti-Semitism is a violation of my religion,
> which I cherish above all other loyalties.
>
> Let me say this: that I understand, at this point, the intensity with which
> some Americans are concerned about this controversy. I said in the fall of
> 1990 that the impulse to resist Saddam Hussein by force of arms was almost
> exclusively generated by the Israeli lobby. I was wrong: that sentiment was
> quite general, and it included respectable voices of American conservatism,
> which is not a part of what I jocularly called the "amen corner" of the Israel
> lobby.
>
> I am sorry about this misrepresentation, as I am sorry that in naming
> important geopolitical strategists who favored such action against Saddam
> Hussein, I listed four important voices all of whom are Jewish Americans. I
> am especially sorry that I made the mistake of listing only non-Jewish names
> as probable military casualties of such action. I know, examining my own
> conscience in the matter, that I was not motivated by anti-Semitism. But I
> know also that many decent Americans, Jewish and non-Jewish, got that
> impression. Let me put this to rest by extending a sincere apology for any
> slurs against Jewish Americans. They are fellow Americans irrespective of
> any differences we had about the wisdom of President Bush's military action,
> which was ratified by the Senate. I will carefully and conscientiously avoid
> in the future any grounds for engendering prejudices I wish not to further,
> but to discourage and, as required, to do battle against, in the political and
> in the moral arenas.*

Within a few hours I was talking to my nephew, a member of the
Buchanan cadre. The text had been passed along, perused, and rejected.
The two reasons given were, one of them, obvious, the second less so. Pat
Buchanan felt that since he had never been motivated by anti-Semitism in

---

*Here is the initiative of the Reverend Jesse Jackson, as reported in the *New York Daily
News*, April 27, 1992—two months after my proposed statement to be authorized by Buchanan:

"And he [Jackson] again tried to put behind him the continuing impact of his nearly
decade-old reference to New York as 'Hymietown.'

"'People should forgive and move on,' he said. 'In my case, although I've continually
reached out . . . I'm being portrayed in a negative light. I fought with Jewish leaders against
David Duke, Patrick Buchanan and Ronald Reagan (when the ex-President visited a German
cemetery where SS troops were buried).

"'I am saying right now, if I've hurt anybody's feelings, I apologize. I have been reaching
out over and over. But right now, I am saying I do apologize.'"

making the remarks he had made and in taking the positions he had taken, there was no objective reason for him to issue an "apology." The second reason he gave was organically shrewd political reasoning: Up until then, he said, he had had to contend with a relatively small band of opinion-makers who were engaged in fussing & stewing over his alleged anti-Semitism. If he were now to make a broad statement one part of which acknowledged that he had offended Jews and all Americans concerned with anti-Semitism, then the entire country would be invited to focus on "Pat Buchanan: Anti-Semite?"—a question which up until that moment had been of parochial interest to a few moral fuss-budgets who suffered from the sin of scrupulosity. Let that whole question continue, was his political judgment, to play in a single tiny ring off in the zoo-section of the very large tent within which he was campaigning.

Reflecting on the question now, in hindsight, I conclude that Buchanan made the wrong ethical decision. I am not so sure that he made the wrong political decision.

The publication of the thirty-thousand-word section of commentary and criticism of the essay (part two) brought fresh reactions, among them several that stoutly applauded Joe Sobran's impressively resourceful self-defense. My own reaction to Joe's essay was forlorn: I knew, finally, that I was incapable of communicating to him what the whole subject was about. (He, of course, feels this frustration in reverse.) I am resigned to this failure, most rueful because of the respect and affection I feel for my colleague. I continue to hope that others might succeed in lodging with him the points I failed to score, but I doubt that will happen. More likely, only experience will teach him.

The mail brought in a quite extraordinary range of comments. I expected a few that would say simply that free speech must prevail, and even a few taking the contrary position—that free speech need not prevail when bomb-throwers submit editorial contributions to privately owned publications. But I heard also from Jews trembling from damaged sensibilities, and from Jews entirely insouciant, demanding to know why anybody had any right to think that they needed special protections in America; from those who wrote that Israel and especially Zionism were of tertiary interest to our foreign policy, and from those who believe that Israel's survival is a solemn American responsibility—the pursuit of anti-Semitism reveals considerable confusion, among Jews and non-Jews. The examples that follow suggest how wide is the spectrum of thought on the subject.

Mr. Alexei Marcoux of New Orleans began with a traditional point having to do with free speech.

Conservative thought is not monolithic. It is an evolving set of positions whose adherents strive to make them ever more consistent with the principles they hold are necessary to the survival of civil society. Your part two is itself evidence of this evolution, which has caused American conservatism to migrate from a reflexive anti-Semitism (characteristic of it at the turn of the century) to an enlightened anti-anti-Semitism. How does this evolution occur, save by vigorous debate within the conservative camp?

He then went on specifically to deplore the administrative measures we took.

> NR's treatment of Sobran is disturbing because it discourages the very process by which a body of thought is strengthened and extended. Sobran has, on conservative principles, taken issue with the prevailing conservative orthodoxy on a number of points. NR has countered his thoughtful and eloquent dissent not with debate, but with demotion. Part two is (to some extent) a debate, albeit one that takes place, as regards Sobran, *post verdictu*.

There were those who regarded our treatment of Sobran as evidencing a neo-Zionist keep-your-hands-off-Israel policy, choosing to ignore the evidence (some of it published in part two) which established NR's independence of thought on the subject. It is worth hearing exactly how the position can be stated. Mr. Michael Dilworth of Farmington Hills, Michigan, wrote,

> Throughout all of this anti-Semitic inquiry, I can determine no attack against anything Jewish except in relation to Israel. I see no personal attacks, but only arguments for and against certain foreign policies. . . .* Is Israel the Inspector General of what is right and wrong? Can't a person treat Israel with the same disdain that they might have used against Britain in, say, 1862? Or Germany in 1915?

He finished with a quotation:

> ". . . a passionate attachment of one nation for another produces a variety of evils. Sympathy for the favorite nation, facilitating the illusion of an imaginary common interest in cases where no real common interest exists, and infusing into one the enmities of the other, betrays the former into a participation in the quarrels and wars of the latter without adequate inducement or justification. It leads also to concessions to the favorite nation of privileges denied to others, which is apt doubly to injure the nation making the concessions, by unnecessarily parting with what ought to have been retained, and by exciting jealousy, ill-will, and disposition to retaliate in the parties from whom equal privileges are withheld. And it gives to ambitious, corrupted,

---

*This is not totally accurate. In a column accusing the Jews of trying to "repress candor," at the time of the mobilization for Desert Storm, Joe Sobran said that Jews "have become in a way psychically segregated from other Americans, separated by the nervousness that also gave them status and power. And when that separateness is broken down, as by Buchanan's mockery, some of them . . . can only understand it as a threat."

or deluded citizens (who devote themselves to the favorite nation) facility to betray or sacrifice the interests of their own country, without odium, sometimes even with popularity, gilding with the appearances of a virtuous sense of obligation, a commendable deference for public opinion, or a laudable zeal for public good, the base or foolish compliances of ambition, corruption, or infatuation."

The quotation is widely recognized as taken from George Washington's Farewell Address.

Still others focused on the differences between anti-Semitism, anti-Israelism, and anti-Zionism. Mr. Paul Hendrix of San Jose, California, was not engaged in letting Joe Sobran off the hook. He began by introducing himself and his interests—"I live in Switzerland but was born in Holland (1927) and call myself a conservative European. Because I am a Visiting Scholar at the Hoover Institution, where I do research for my book *The Great Oil Conspiracy—from Rockefeller to Saddam Hussein*, I spend regularly some time in California"—and then said,

> Though I agree with Mr. Buckley that, as the French say, *"c'est le ton qui fait la musique,"* I noted with regret that he overlooked the Red Herring aspect of anti-Semitism. The real issue is not whether we, as conservative Christians, must condemn anti-Semitism (of course we must) but whether we should (continue to) condone Zionism.
>
> For my book I have done considerable research on the Balfour Declaration and the Bevin–Truman dispute. I hold that Zionism (like Socialism) is a nineteenth-century, utopian illusion. It was Cecil Rhodes who inspired Herzel. Zionism has its roots in colonialism and racism, doctrines which Christian conservatives can not explicitly advocate nor implicitly condone.

Yet another criterion was elicited in an engaging letter by an attorney who identified himself as having served for several decades as counsel for the Grateful Dead rock group. He is siding with editorial permissiveness on interesting grounds:

> Whilst you and your magazine, in common with other conservative organs, incisively portray the "sensitivity" theme as censorship at best and a racket at worst, you, in dealing with Buchanan, seem to have given lip to that very hook: " . . . sensitive moral calibrators are likely to suspect, even if they cannot successfully reason, . . . that [Person] A is actively engaged in advocating invidious racial policies. The Buchanans need to understand the nature of sensibilities in an age that coexisted with Auschwitz."

It is the writer's position (he is Mr. Hal Kant of Reno, Nevada) that I emphasized the wrong virtue.

> With Jane Austen, it would have been far preferable had you opted for sense over sensibility; gadflies serve a purpose and needn't be condemned

while being opposed. Outside of economics, I do not agree with much of what Buchanan has to say, but he is always stimulating . . . and entertaining. "Tact and prudence" are advocated by Irving Kristol, whom you cite. Does that not include giving a little slack to your friends, as well as your enemies? Yes, this age is close to Auschwitz, but even more acutely, it is an age where civility is so lacking, and taking bitter and outlandish positions so prevalent, that the greater threat is not a revival of violent anti-Semitism (which we seem to agree is not imminent), but a more pandemic nonspecific meanness—even violence. People will not let others talk, will not listen, and will not put up with other points of view without pejorative labeling and uncivil behavior, all founded on the slimy slope of "sensitivity" laced with its parasitic mold, victimization. As a presidential candidate, Buchanan can be assailed for his positions, but as an agitator-journalist, he appears to be doing his job.

Perhaps I should establish that I was raised in an orthodox Jewish–activist Zionist family, and that a substantial part of my family was lost in the Holocaust, and that I personally have been the object of religious intolerance and prejudice. . . . Although apostate to both religious and ethnic affiliation, I have been blessed to have the opportunity to risk all directly to confront intolerance. I say "blessed" because it may be only when all is risked for love (in this case, love of constitutional democracy) that one truly appreciates the object.*

Yet another angle was that of the Totally Serene on the Question. Mr. Carl Engelhardt of Arlington, Virginia, began by asking,

First, how do intellectual journalists all manage to recognize who's a Jew and who's not? I sure can't figure it out. In this Noah's Ark called the United States, where we've got a horde of folks of every stripe from every corner of the globe, how in the hell do you tell the difference between Jews, Catholics, or Protestants, practicing or otherwise? . . . I submit that the issue of anti-Semitism is simply not an issue if for no other reason than Jews in America are nondistinguishable. They are a part of the whole cloth . . . nonrecognizable in an immigrant sea. Who's a Jew? Search me. What's anti-Semitism? Don't know what it is.

Is support for Israel, in the eyes of such as Mr. Engelhardt, in any sense a consuming Jewish question?

What *about* Israel? To me, Israel is a nation-state like any other. And since I can't distinguish what makes a Jew different from the rest of humanity, the fact that Israel is populated by large numbers of Jews means nothing to me.

---

*Mr. Kant closed with a graceful paragraph:

"Whether I am right or wrong, whether you care a fig or not for these observations, let me go on to say that your essay was one of the finest Christmas presents I have ever received. I spent the morning alone in the study listening to 'grace'-full music, and hanging on your every word. When I was young, holy-season gifts consisted of bright new pennies and trees planted in my name in Palestine. . . . Now that prosperity makes material gifts less fulfilling, intellectual and artistic treats such as you provide are a delight."

Therefore, supporting or not supporting Israel for me is in no way connected to the fact that many Jews happen to live there. The question becomes: Is supporting the nation of Israel in the best interests of the United States? For me, the answer is, Yes. Why? Because we have so many enemies in common: Iraq, Syria, Iran, Libya, to name a few.

My support for Israel does not mean necessarily that I favor propping up Israel's decrepit socialist economy with American tax dollars. It does mean that I believe that money given in the form of military aid by the USA to Israel is money well spent. But the bottom line again is (for those of us who can't tell a Jew from a Lutheran) that feelings for or against Israel cannot be used as a measure to indicate the existence of anti-Semitism. . . . My theory is that Jews in positions of authority in the United States need to keep the anti-Semitism drumbeat pounding because it offers one of the few ways that American Jews can remind themselves that they are still Jews. To clarify: except for certain Orthodox Jewish communities, Jews in America have become so secularized that they no longer know what it means to be a Jew. And, in fact, it doesn't mean much of anything anymore, especially to the vast majority of non-Jewish Americans who are under sixty.

Ivan Helfman of Royal Oak, Michigan, goes a step further, renouncing in effect offers of help in any effort against anti-Semitism.

I'd like to clean up some of the article's attitude problems. It was patronizing to me as a Jew; blind to Jewish Americans' diversity; and paranoid in its reckless exaggeration of anti-Semitism in America, a Jew-friendly country if there ever was one. In America, secular and assimilated Jews are welcome in just about any middle-class suburb or edge city. True Orthodox Jews, with their beards, fedoras, rituals, religious schools, and other signs of differentiation, raise more Gentile eyebrows. However, Orthodox Jews suffer no more prejudice than members of other distinctive subcultures, and they have formed strong happy communities from sea to shining sea. Why single the Jews from the cultural mosaic? Why can't Mr. Buckley view America, like the Jewish novelist Philip Roth?

. . . Instead, Mr. Buckley implies that Jews are too wimpy to be part of the drama because their "ethnic sensitivities vary," to the point where Jews are even off limits to WASP novelists. . . . In the real world, Jews require neither more nor less sensitivity than other groups.

Regrettably, the stereotype of the suffering Jew, "Jews as pale, sad people, persecuted for their insufferable virtues, like Isaac and Rebecca in *Ivanhoe*," as the Jewish writer A. J. Liebling put it, lingers, despite the Jews' demonstrated ability to thrive in America on their own abilities. Liebling, who was sent by *The New Yorker* to cover "trick assignments" on New York's East Side in the 1930s, discovered hundreds of thousands of "laughing Jews," and concluded that a history of the laughing Jew "would establish Noah, the bad kings of Israel, and Harpo Marx as the authentic leaders of Jewish thought and put the blast on people like Jeremiah and [New York Rabbi] Steven S. Wise . . ." and, logically, a double whammy on Robert Maxwell and Norman Podhoretz.

If American Jews have a problem, it's not anti-Semitism: it's sexy Gentiles. Apparently, interfaith marriages, which constitute over half of all Jewish marriages, are gutting the Jewish population to the point where one day it will be impossible to assemble ten male Jews to form a *minyan* (prayer group). You see, these marriages do not breed Jewish children. It's gotten to the point where to discourage Cohens from breeding with Bundys, some Jewish parents are being taught now to rear children that will turn off amorous Gentiles. Rabbi L. Moline, of Alexandria, Virginia, recently shared some ethnic purity tips with the *Wall Street Journal*. The trick is to keep Kosher homes, send the kids to Hebrew schools, and haul them to weekly Sabbath services.

The writer has very serious complaints, but they are not against either latent or explicit American anti-Semites.

Ironically, while Gentiles are loving American Jews to extinction, American Jewish wannabes are being flagrantly persecuted. The alleged villain is the Israel lobby. The situation was described by Christopher Hitchens in the January 1992 issue of Harpers. He wrote: "This is why in 1989 [the Bush] administration agreed, *under direct Israeli and AIPAC pressure,* to set actual quotas on the number of Soviet Jewish emigrants who could settle in the United States. This is why those emigrants were driven, often against their wishes, to Israel, and then—in the case of not a few—on to the West Bank, there to be used."

This discrimination has resulted in hideous degradation. On February 7, the *Today Show* broadcast pictures from Israel of an immigrant Russian-Jewish symphony conductor sweeping streets and a brain surgeon washing cars. If this sounds familiar, Jewish conductors and doctors got the jackboot when Hitler took power. . . .

Mr. Buckley ignores this outrage and the lobby's motives in perpetuating it, yet he finds it anti-Semitic when Mr. Buchanan states that many American Jews were not likely to die in a Gulf War: a logical statement that was based on the Vietnam War, where a disproportionate number of African-Americans died while many American Jews, myself included, sat it out with Clinton and Quayle . . . There are also American Jews patriotic enough to put the needs of American foreign policy above Israel, and smart enough to realize there are no simple answers in the Middle East, despite the lobby's ultimatums, anti-anti-Semitic posturing, and raid on the freedom of speech. Thank God there has been a backlash: the public has had it with the lobby and its greed. Americans oppose Israel's settlement policies and oppose loan guarantees to Israel by a 4–1 margin, according to a recent *Wall Street Journal*/NBC News poll. Consequently, the lobby has retreated and adopted more low-key tactics.

But some wrote in who were moved by the gravity of the indictments I made, did not consider them censorious, and went on to profess their disappointment with the behavior of the people I wrote about, as also about some of their defenders. They struck me as more plausible, more convincing, and certainly more moving. From Professor Robert Cohn of Stanford University:

> Where Sobran and Buchanan go off, from our standpoint, is in the realm of heart. A poet friend of mine wrote: "What is there to say/Of one who has turned away?" Pascal: *"Le coeur a ses raisons que la raison ne connaît pas."* One cannot judge a person who is not moved by the ancient bond that you allude to in your earlier essay, or by the humiliation you refer to in the later piece or the natural friendships that arose all along during our lives in this country. OK—but one can be very disappointed. It is sad to see very good people whom we need for a promising and meaningful alliance in the best of causes seize upon some passing and dubious event to question the whole undertaking.

Stanley Goldstein was for many years the accountant for *National Review* and remains a personal friend. He was elated by the appearance of the original essay and made despondent by part two, which collected criticism and commentary. I wrote to ask him why.

> Thanks for your letter . . . Your tone of warmth and friendship is evident when you are concerned with "exactly what it is that most irks you." This will be my attempt to answer that question but the task is more difficult than may appear on the surface.
>
> A simple and direct answer as to what irks me most is the fact that your monumental article did not do much to bring Joe Sobran and Pat Buchanan back into what I consider to be the conservative mainstream. The second most distressing aspect is that the wrong people supported you in part two. Last, I think that what is at stake here is the soul of the conservative movement and, although the good guys are winning, the margin is too small for comfort.

Mr. Goldstein went on to lament that Joe Sobran was "not only unrepentant, but somewhat belligerent," and he was disappointed that Buchanan chose not to reply. Above all, Stanley Goldstein was disappointed that a roster of star-level conservatives did not take the opportunity to make common cause with me—in contrast (come to think of it) with the disavowal of the John Birch Society thirty years ago, in which most conservative luminaries joined. And Goldstein brought up the point that hovers over this chapter of the essay, namely whether any linkage of any sort with Pat Buchanan endangers the movement.

> Allow me to expand on that:
> In 1961 you and Barry Goldwater convinced me that being a conservative was the best way to help America. I have thirty years invested in this cause, happily invested, and now I see danger. It is as though you and I belong to the same church on the corner and have a long history of praying together, putting up stained glass windows and monuments to relatives, serving on the

board of trustees to improve the church, and now we find that some of the fundamental ground rules are changing with the possibility, albeit remote, that we might not want to continue in the same church any more. It is a wrenching loss to walk across the street to begin a relationship with a new house of worship.

On a different level, more analytical, others wrote in to probe the performance of the principals. Don Pesci, a columnist based at the Manchester (Connecticut) *Journal Inquirer,* wrote me:

> Joe Sobran's argument turns on fair treatment: all points of view should be ventilated, and any point of view "has to be met on its own grounds." But then he adds ". . . it's irrelevant, and unfair, to accuse him [the person advancing a point of view] of ulterior motives." But ulterior motives *become* relevant when a point of view cannot be sustained and the person advancing it persists in willful idiocies. I [for instance] do not think Sobran's view on Israel—that the country's value to the U.S. as a "reliable ally" and "strategic asset" does not justify the support the United States has extended to Israel— is sustainable. Neither do I think Sobran should be silenced. If Sobran wants to say that "We have no stake in its [Israel's] feud with its Arab and Moslem neighbors," many of whom are anti-Jewish in the Hitlerian sense, let him say it. But he must not complain when others wish to dissociate themselves from his "we."
>
> One need not be a Jew to suppose that if the United States severs its "special" relationship with Israel, the Israeli state soon would be entirely at the mercy of its Arab and Moslem "neighbors." If Sobran has not yet urged the United States to sever its ties with Israel, it is simply because he lacks the courage of his own convictions. Sobran's idea, if implemented, will have consequences. And it is fear of the predictable consequences that has his opponents up in arms.

Pesci made other interesting points, among them:

> Hugh Kenner is wrong in insisting that a term that has no stable meaning is "not a profitable head for rational discussions." Athanasius would disagree with him. The purpose of rational discourse is to assign intelligible meanings to fluid concepts. Your essay is a noble attempt at clarification.

The author and novelist and long-time colleague in *National Review* Keith Mano touched on the same two points, though reaching different conclusions:

> . . . I must say Joe did a good job. Maybe he is an anti-Semite (I haven't read the *Instauration* stuff), but he created a *person* in his response. A Person "X," who should be allowed to express himself without fear. A person whose legitimate foreign policy doubts about Israel must not be squelched. Ulti-

mately I agree with Hugh Kenner—this is a major realignment of my thoughts on the subject. Podhoretz's condescending tone helped push me that way.

Mano agreed with Pesci that the essay had performed a useful service.

Of course you see the big picture. Strategically speaking, for the conservative movement your essay was essential. The syllogism—Sobran and Buchanan are conservative; S & B also are open to charges of anti-Semitism; therefore all conservatives are indictable—that syllogism is a killer. You took the wind out of that argument effectively. I'm glad you did. But I think some of our rights as free citizens were sacrificed.

Mano's closing point was reinforced by something of which he had no knowledge. Mano had complained that the subtitle of my *National Review* essay notwithstanding ("What Christians Provoke What Jews? Why? By Doing What?—And Vice Versa"), I had paid scant attention to the "Vice Versa." My reply to that charge is given above, in part two; and I thought it sufficient. But here was fresh evidence of irresponsible anti-anti-Semitism, namely a letter (dated March 19, 1992) addressed to the *Boston Jewish Times* by the National Director of the Anti-Defamation League and the Vice-Chairman of the New England Region of the ADL, respectively, Abraham Foxman and Richard Glovsky.

Close readers of the first part of this book will recall that I examine with some care the investigation of *The Dartmouth Review* made by the New England branch of the Anti-Defamation League at the request of the editors of the *Review*. On the important question—Who was it who in the dead of night inserted the quote from Adolf Hitler in the logo of the student newspaper?—I repeated that while it had not been officially established who was responsible for doing so, suspicions had in fact focused on one young editor who, unlike his seniors who also had access to the computer, refused to take a lie detector test. Moreover, the probable malefactor had no apparent motive other than to commit mischief. He had no record (nor had any of his seniors) of anti-Semitism. I went on: "The ADL Commission asserted that 'a staffer' was responsible, and the *Review*'s management no longer challenges that probability." Anti-Semitism was not involved. On the question, Had *The Dartmouth Review* been responsible for the destruction of the sukkah? I had written, "The [ADL] Commission found no evidence to link the sukkah destruction to [*The Dartmouth Review*]." And the chairman of New Hampshire's Human Rights Commission, conducting his own inquiry, had exonerated the *Review*.

In his long review of my essay, Norman Podhoretz is quoted above in part two as writing,

... it may perhaps strike you as more significant that I am with you all the way in your section exonerating *The Dartmouth Review* of the charge of anti-Semitism. Some people are always complaining that false charges of anti-Semitism are just as bad as anti-Semitism itself. I doubt it, but even stipulating that in certain circumstances it may be so, it remains the case that for these people, virtually all charges of anti-Semitism are false. . . . [Indeed,] for once, in *The Dartmouth Review*, we have a genuine example of false charges of anti-Semitism doing damage to innocent victims.

Yet early in March, the New England branch of the ADL honored the principal purveyor of the false allegation, the President of Dartmouth. I wrote a column on the subject:

The Anti-Defamation League really ought to make some effort to put its house in order. It is the veteran Jewish organization devoted to tracking down and exposing bigotry and to promoting civil rights. But in its search for opportunistic publicity it makes quite embarrassing errors. For instance, the award its Boston chapter made early in the month to Dartmouth President James Freedman. For what? A local newspaper reports that "Referring to the incident in which a Hitler quote appeared in the credo of *The Dartmouth Review*, ADL regional vice chairman Richard Glovsky, '69, described Freedman's response as "heroic." "Jim Freedman stood up to outrageous conduct," Glovsky told the room of alumni, college presidents, friends of Freedman, and supporters of the ADL. "Thanks to leaders like Jim Freedman there is hope."

Oh but that is exactly the opposite of the truth. Leaders like James Freedman give anti-anti-Semitism a bad name. For the very simple reason that he imputed anti-Semitism to a dozen Dartmouth student editors who had never waded in that mire, who were entirely innocent of the Hitler quote incident. Rather than investigate the incident where a mischievous—call him/her evil, if you wish—student managed secretly (he was never caught) to insert an anti-Semitic sentence from Adolf Hitler into the logo of the student newspaper, Freedman called a campus-wide rally to denounce the staff of *The Dartmouth Review* as racist and bigoted. His action, calling for a hysterical community response to the equivalent of one Swastika graffito in a student newspaper, was as inspiring to civil liberties as a lynch party in the South.

What is ironic is that Mr. Glovsky, who did the purring on the night in question praising Mr. Freedman, himself headed up the inquiry into *The Dartmouth Review* incident on behalf of the Boston ADL, invited to do so by the same editors denounced by Freedman. The report when issued quite explicitly denied that there were grounds for concluding that the Hitler quote represented racist attitudes of any responsible member of the *Review* (whose editor, by the way, was black). Sure, the Glovsky–ADL report reprimanded the *Review* on several counts for behaving this way or that way concerning this issue or that issue, but this pretty much amounted to denouncing sophomores when they are sophomoric. Suddenly he is at center stage honoring the greatest demagogue in the state, the president of the liberal-arts college who was so quick to find anti-Semitism when there was not a trace of it traceable to those he attacked.

What, then, were all those people in Boston doing, applauding someone (President Freedman) who had smeared young men and women with a false charge of racism? Mr. Abraham Foxman, who is the National Director of the Anti-Defamation League, reacting to my own essay, the same essay that prompted Mr. Podhoretz to exonerate *The Dartmouth Review*, wrote to the author that "The piece [including the exoneration of *The Dartmouth Review* editors] clearly reflects your well deserved reputation for . . . intellectual honesty and will enlighten all who take the opportunity—and show the good sense—to read it." But that apparently does not include Mr. Glovsky, the head of the ADL's Boston chapter.

Public organizations that need financial support and publicity are tempted from time to time to suspend their sense of discrimination for the limelight. Ten years ago the ADL gave a prize to Hugh Hefner of *Playboy*, I kid you not, for his contributions to civil liberty. The award cited "the empire he founded [which] has had a far-reaching impact, not only on the publishing industry, but on the mores of American society as well." To which this columnist responded at the time, "That is correct. Any serious disciple of Hugh Hefner would not hesitate to purr anti-Semitic lovelies into the ears of his bunny, if that was what was required to effect seduction. The invitation specifies 'black tie.' Well, if the guests arrive wearing only black ties, that will be more than some of the guests wear at Hef's other parties."

I have in my files a letter from the then National Director of the ADL confiding to me that his organization made a mistake. I feel free to reveal this since Mr. Perlmutter, RIP, is gone. It would be good to have an apology from Mr. Glovsky.

The ADL defended itself in a letter addressed to the *Boston Jewish Times*, signed by Messrs. Foxman and Glovsky. It is a sad example of the reluctance with which some people, in this case two gentlemen who head up organized Jewish groups, simply refuse on some subjects to be guided—even by evidence they themselves examined.

The ADL officials did not stop, in their letter, with a ritualistic defense of their award. "It is also difficult to understand," the letter continued, "how Mr. Buckley and other conservative figures could have failed to speak out against the Hitler quote when it appeared. To members of the Commission, this silence reflected a serious failure of leadership and understanding of the hurtful impact of this highly inflammatory act." That statement is beneath contempt. It would suggest that critics of a newspaper one of whose staffers had surreptitiously inserted into the logo a passage from the Marquis de Sade should begin their commentary on the episode by denouncing sadism.

But most incredible of all, "It is also noteworthy that Mr. Buckley chose not to mention that the *Review* pays 'special thanks' to him in each and every one of its issues. It is from this position that Mr. Buckley defends the *Review*." Readers who can remember all the way back to page 53 of this book will see there,

I should here record that *The Dartmouth Review*, from the first issue on, has included in one of its many tiers on the masthead, "Special Thanks to

William F. Buckley, Jr." I have never been told exactly why this practice originated, or at whose prompting. I have never been consulted by the editors about policy; I would as soon the *Review* ended the homage, but I continue to feel it would be ungrateful, even snotty, to say so. I say so now only under duress, in a document that requires me to specify my exact relationship to the *Review.*

One is entitled to wonder, at this point, whether Messrs. Foxman and Glovsky took the trouble to read their own report on *The Dartmouth Review* before deciding to lionize President Freedman.

The single most interesting analysis of the collection of commentary published in part two came from my colleague Jeffrey Hart, a senior editor of *National Review* for over twenty years, a distinguished author, and professor of English at Dartmouth. He got, I think, to the heart of the matter . . . .

Dear Bill:
I have read intensively part two.
This whole business is indeed a "cultural moment." The reactions are varied and often rich in substance.
I notice that almost everyone dealing with the subject starts with autobiography. A sentence or two in that vein from me. In 1942 I entered Stuyvesant High School, a high-powered school in lower Manhattan, ninety percent Jewish. They were fascinated with me, and I with them. The teachers and the students were naïvely shocked, and pleased, that someone from suburban and gentile Long Island could be, well, that intelligent. I became president of the Cancer Club and the Microscope Society.
The whole of part two is fascinating. I do have a strong desire to see an overall intellectual shape that makes sense of the whole.
I suggest that the shape is this.
I conclude that Israel is, literally, *sacred* to much or almost all [I have noted a specimen of the exceptions, above] Jewish opinion. And I mean *sacred* taking the term with full literalness.*
Sobran and Buchanan, on the other hand, have insisted on treating Israel as just another nation and interpreting U.S. policy toward it in an entirely secular sense. (I treasure Dean Rusk's remark [see page 158] that life would have been easier diplomatically if God had given them Nebraska instead.)

---

*I showed this chapter, in draft, to a very close friend, the writer and journalist Richard M. Clurman. His comment at this point is that "literally sacred" is exactly the wrong term, that Israel is "sacred" to most Jews as a secular not a sacred concern, and that this qualifier applies equally to Jews in Israel and in America (he and his wife are both Jewish). "It is sacred only in the sense that it is uniquely cherished, not in the sense, say, that the Vatican would be held 'sacred' to American Catholics, or Bethlehem to all Christians. It is unwise ever to suggest that the State of Israel is of theological concern to most Jews. It is not, even though it is a theocratic state."

I ran into this problem with Norman [Podhoretz] when he expressed great disappointment in my public support for Buchanan in New Hampshire. My response to him was that 1) this week we are talking about the record of George Bush, and 2) next week we can talk about anti-Semitism, protectionism, isolationism, and what-not.

No sirreee. I flunked for Norman on the sacred question.

Now, I can understand why Israel in fact has become sacred. The history of the twentieth century is, to put it mildly, unique. The Holocaust is a sort of hole in the cosmos, a guarantor of the existence of evil. It is an equivalent for Jews of the Crucifixion. Israel then became the equivalent of the Redemption. This is true even for relatively secular Jews. Judaism has never successfully separated God and Tribe. The People itself is the God carrier.

So, along comes Joe Sobran, rattling around in all of this, and discussing Israel as if it were a "policy" matter, just another country like, say, Belgium!

I think that from a full experience of the twentieth century I am willing to accept the sacredness of Israel as a religious fact. Hegel did not foresee this in his *Phenomenology of the Spirit*, but there it is, indubitably a fact.

In essence, Joe Sobran was secularizing all of this, separating Church and State without any invitation to do so. (Of course, Islam doesn't separate Church and State either, and its dominant tendency is now theocratic.)

So we have had Joe wandering around in this "minefield" as you call it, to all appearances invincibly ignorant of the religious and political realities he has been dealing with. Of course, Joe went on to add some little mischievousness about *Instauration,* Moses Maimonides, Jonathan Pollard, the ambiguous *Liberty* disaster, etc. etc.

Meanwhile, though surpassingly intelligent, MJS wanders around the minefield in a Candide-like posture of "Who me?" I find his posture unintelligible. Merely as an act of intelligence and understanding he ought to be able to imagine how his signals are being received. Is he the Complete Goyische Kopp?

The case of Pat Buchanan is rather different. Pat until quite recently was entirely pro-Israel. Indeed, our celebrations on your *Cyrano* [my schooner] over the Entebbe raid were so vigorous that it got us in trouble with the Bimini Harbor Police and assorted insurance companies. What outraged Pat were the two episodes of the Reagan visit to Bitburg and the Auschwitz nuns. In both cases he experienced at first hand in the White House the enormous pressure that was brought to bear by organized Jewish opinion. He undoubtedly thought the White House was being bullied. He has reacted by bullying back.

I myself am more firmly pro-Israel than I have been in the past, when I was pretty pro-Israel anyway. If I could not live in the U.S., I suppose I would choose to live in Switzerland, but I certainly can imagine living in Israel. I cannot imagine living in Baghdad or Teheran or Tripoli.

I also think that we have to take into account the sacredness of Israel, as I have put it, from a Jewish point of view. This is a fact of history and spirit, and it is nonsensical to behave as if it were not a fact.

2 · Epilogue

Bringing this essay to a close I find myself confronting three questions, morally related to one another, all of them directed to the question of the civil responsibilities of the ethical citizen in a democratic society.

A great deal of space has been given to Pat Buchanan in this book, notwithstanding that he was only one of the four actors subjected to probing in my original essay. It is obvious why this is so: he elected to run for President of the United States, and for that reason invited the fierce attention of his critics and his defenders. And as the story developed, the Bureau of Weights and Measures, so to speak, focused on the proper relationship of the ethically refined citizen to Buchanan, in weighing the question whether our defenses against anti-Semitism are as vigorous as they ought to be. This book is not about Pat Buchanan, but he serves us, *mutatis mutandis*, as Dreyfuss served, around whom a significant cultural quarrel, indeed evolutionizing into a historical movement of opinion, resulted.

Accordingly I begin my questions by asking:

Suppose that my conclusion, in reviewing the work of Pat Buchanan in respect of anti-Semitism, had been unqualified as to his bigotry? What course of action would I have urged on the voters of New Hampshire?

The critical sentence I see quoted more often than any other I ever wrote is here repeated for the fourth time: *"I find it impossible to defend Pat Buchanan against the charge that what he did and said during the period under examination amounted to anti-Semitism, whatever it was that drove him to say and do it: most probably, an iconoclastic temperament."* Suppose that the sentence had ended with the words, "anti-Semitism"? My answer to my own question: If that had been my conclusion—that he had been motivated by such a bias—I'd have disowned him, declining to endorse him as candidate for any public position, and I'd have assumed that his bigotry could not have escaped public attention during the campaign in New Hampshire.

The second question: Is it a highly visible public line, or only a line subjectively drawn?—that line beyond which a candidate for President is popularly rejected by the ethical community, resulting in his disqualification from contending for that office because of his trespass? Any attempt to draw that line intending to rally popular support for the process of political excommunication requires great care in definition and precision in fixing guilt, even as Gary Hart's delinquency was captured under klieg lights. There is a difference, as noted in part one, between the anti-Semite who doesn't want a Jew in his golf club and the anti-Semite who is explicitly or inferentially indifferent to the fate of the Jews in Israel.

Now almost any statement describing a broad political position runs the danger of reductionist formulations ("Give me liberty or give me death"). Anyone who believes in hampering trade imports however slightly is likely to be put down as a "protectionist."

Some readers, studying the evidence I surveyed, have pronounced Buchanan "an anti-Semite" pure and simple. Others, surveying the same evidence, stop short of such a conclusion, given that "anti-Semitism" is not as incandescently documented as the motel door, drawn closed on a man and a woman. If I had had confidence in a negative judgment, rather than in the qualified judgment I rendered, I'd have been entitled to state the case for disqualifying Buchanan from presidential consideration.

Suppose that the evidence against Buchanan bore exclusively on his attitude toward Israel. Could one then be serene in concluding, as unflinchingly as Mr. Podhoretz concludes, that Pat Buchanan had earned the designation "anti-Semite"? If so, should he then have been disqualified from political consideration for President by the ethical community? Is to be anti-Israel *qua* Israel—as distinguished from being critical of the policies of Israel's government—for all intents and purposes to be anti-Semitic? My answer to both these questions is: Yes: a) Yes, I'd oppose him for high public office, and b) Yes, I'd classify him as anti-Semitic.

Let us go on: Do we gain perspective by asking correlative questions? Suppose it were documented about a candidate that he was anti-Catholic. Most of us are familiar with the cliché that anti-Catholicism is the anti-Semitism of the highbrow, and most Catholics have experienced (if not, they are nevertheless aware of its practice) anti-Catholicism. Should all such candidates be excluded from office?

It is not as easy to answer this question affirmatively—because one needs to answer the question, What harm can reasonably be expected to come to Catholics by reason of the political ascendancy of an anti-Catholic in the United States?

There is no geographical promontory out there, populated by Catholics who are exposed to terminal persecution. Under the Communists persecution was so general—its victims were Christians and Jews, gypsies and kulaks, artists and poets—that it was never practical to mobilize Catholic sentiment in the United States for the specific purpose of bringing aid and relief to Catholics living behind the Iron Curtain.* Although in the history of America Catholics have been persecuted, that experience is remote (pretty much remote also for Jews; and, one day not too far distant, we must hope it will be remote also for blacks). There is no lowering threat against Catholics internally, though they are, as patrons of parochial schools, the primary victims of what I think of as First Amendment fanaticism. But (we repeat) there is no Catholic Israel out there, surrounded by Catholic-hating Moslems who have five times attempted to drive the Catholics to the sea, and into it.

I would hesitate, then, to endorse a blanket proscription against an anti-Catholic candidate. In other words, I am ready to concede that in our world, in our time, Jews have inherited distinctive immunities.

And a third question: For many years sexual regularity was expected of men who aspired to high office. This is now the case only in special circumstances of symbolic iconoclasm, Gary Hart's case being the obvious example. In part this is so because standards of sexual behavior are looser today; in part because persistent historical researches have penetrated the myths of other generations. We know now about the "other" Victorians, and we know now (in humiliating detail, for those who care) about the sexual and marital misbehavior of men who served as Presidents in this century, one of them a dead and lionized martyr about whom Leporello could have sung, without altering any of the lines, the aria that describes Don Giovanni.

But sexual promiscuity neutralized by abortion is quite another matter. A growing number of Americans, even if still a minority, believe that the removal and destruction of a live fetus is a form of infanticide. The question for them arises, as we seek to examine the moral compass of the modern American, Can someone who feels that abortion is infanticide tolerate (in the sense of voting for him, or of respecting others who do so) a presidential candidate who believes that the laws should permit any mother who desires to do so to abort her child? The question is glaringly relevant if the pursuit of anti-Semitism invokes the pursuit of the definitions of moral behavior an aspirant to high public office must not abuse, in a civilized country, in the perspective of the 1990s. What hangs in the balance in Israel is the possible extermination of a historical tribe, elect of God. There cannot be ambiguity about the moral question of jeopardizing their survival. But until a much larger number of citizens are persuaded to think of a fetus as a human being, even as it required the better part

---

*A case can be made that there was Christian exposure in Lebanon when the Syrians moved in in 1981.

of a century's agitation to promote a black from chattel to citizen, I would not disqualify a candidate solely because he is pro-choice. Such are the moral impositions of self-government, in deference to which Abraham Lincoln declined to move any faster than he did in the great moral question of his America. What some refer to as the sacredness of human life is not, for others, on the whole a bracing moral perception. Planned parenthood is unabashedly exercised through the device of abortion. And at the other end of life, euthanasia has a growing number of advocates.

The question of Israel is in two parts. The first asks, Isn't it possible to oppose Israel and yet still be free of the taint of anti-Semitism?

My own answer is deeply affected by commentary such as the letter that appears above from Mr. Engelhardt, which holds persuasively that in the absence of definitive military aid by the United States the probabilities are high that Israel would be extinguished. And we must suppose that in the years very soon ahead Israel's nuclear defense will be offset by counterpart weapons in Syria or Iraq or Iran—or, for that matter, Saudi Arabia—and that therefore a ground war would settle the question of Israel's survival. It would follow that any American President unwilling to support Israel militarily would be inviting the elimination of the Jewish state and its people.

An entirely different question asks whether to oppose Israeli policy at any given moment amounts to eviscerative anti-Israel activity—of a kind one could expect only from an anti-Semite. Language inviting just such a conclusion is now being used. Herewith Mr. Sidney Zion, a well-known author and journalist, writing in the *New York Observer*.

He begins by taking analytical short cuts, but without compelling summary rejection. First he gives us his "iron law," namely "that only a Jew can decide if a person is an anti-Semite." (Well . . . but okay—explain.) He proceeds to recite the burden of conversations he has recently had with Gentiles in which the consensus opposed the policies of Israel. "I have heard worse attacks on Israel, believe me. But always from other Jews." (Well . . . okay. Go ahead.) "And until fairly recently, it was almost invariably in an all-Jewish setting. The unwritten rule was that you didn't fight it out in front of Gentiles. This is known as a shonda for the goyim." (Some of us would have put it differently.)

Mr. Zion reveals now his ambush. One guest at a meeting he describes sought to ease the tension by saying, "Just because one criticizes Israel does not make one an anti-Semite."

Mr. Zion's response:

"My first answer to this is as follows: Just because you're anti-Israel doesn't mean you're *not* anti-Semitic."

He lets that sink in only for the time it takes the eye to descend to the next paragraph:

"But my real answer is that if you're anti-Israel, *I don't ask whether you're an anti-Semite*. Because if you are truly anti-Israel you are an enemy of the Jewish people. Therefore I don't need to calibrate the spit."

Mr. Zion has technically gone no further than we have gone in accepting the proposition that any failure to defend Israel militarily is an anti-Jewish act. But listen now to what we find ourselves up against:

"*You knew I was going to get to George Bush and James Baker, didn't you?*" (Mr. Zion is especially comfortable in the vernacular.)

"No American Administration has done more to legitimize anti-Israelism than this one, it's not even a close call. The reason is simple: They have conducted, from the outset, an anti-Israel policy."

It is carefree flights across such critical chasms that cause the moral narrative to break its bonds. Because *we have been talking about a moral question*, basically the question whether it is *morally* defensible to deal with the Jewish state with indifference. Suddenly we find ourselves dealing in *Realpolitik* (is it, e.g., correct policy to put pressure on Israel not to colonize the West Bank?), but to this question we are transporting arguments to intimidate the opposition that were generated by moral reasoning. The effect is to denature the moral arguments. A George Bush or a James Baker can respond to such as Sidney Zion by saying: *We know in our hearts and minds that we will defend the independence of Israel by any means necessary*. To imply other than this about our intentions is so to misread our policies as to earn disdain, if we are confronting ignorance; contempt, if we are confronting sophistry. If, Mr. Zion, to stand by the relevant United Nations Resolutions and the Camp David Accords is to be in effect anti-Semitic, then you and your followers may as well license the term anti-Semitism, even at the risk of forgetting that it was once a refuge of morally imperfect and dangerous men.

The May issue of *Commentary* carries an article by Norman Podhoretz entitled, "Buchanan and the Conservative Crackup." Here is where the article takes the reader:

Pat Buchanan in fact didn't do so very well advancing himself in the primaries. He won 30 per cent of the Republican voters in South Dakota, to be sure, but given that he didn't personally campaign there, these voters must be assumed to be the body of anti-Bush Republicans dissatisfied with their leader. To be sure, Buchanan energized the movement: but there is scant evidence that he accomplished much more than that, perhaps in part because the economies he advocated would have reduced the Bush budget by less than one per cent. The best that Buchanan was able to do by personally campaigning was to augment the anti-Bush vote by six or seven points.

My comment: I find this analysis plausible, though it does not fully account for the personal enthusiasm marshaled by Buchanan, or for his organizational skills, which include his mobilization of names and addresses of likely backers. And there isn't anything to be gained by ignoring Pat Buchanan's manifest forensic skills.

2. Pat Buchanan chose to go out under the banner of "America First." This reminds Norman Podhoretz that it was under this same banner that the isolationists fought to stay out of World War II. And that in an important campaign address, America First superstar Charles Lindbergh singled out 1) the Roosevelt Administration, 2) the British, and 3) American Jews as the three principal lobbies in favor of intervention; from which Podhoretz concludes that the assumption of that isolationist banner by Buchanan suggests that he is comfortable reviving a legendary movement contaminated by anti-Semitism.

My comment: The pro-Nazi movement was no more critical within America First than the Communist movement was critical within the movement to Aid the Allies. What Lindbergh said in Des Moines was quite simply correct, and why should it not have been? Even as German-Americans tended to oppose the war, Jewish Americans tended to favor it—for the best of reasons. They were, among other things, correct in their policy recommendations.

3. John O'Sullivan of *National Review* was initially persuaded by the fantasy that Buchanan might do so well in New Hampshire as to persuade George Bush to withdraw from the race; in which event *National Review* might find itself wonderfully situated to back a Republican candidate fully qualified by conservative standards, i.e., one who did not have the baggage Buchanan did as a protectionist, a nativist, and an isolationist.

My comment: John O'Sullivan entertained no idea that went beyond hypotheticals that could not be predicted. No one at *National Review* believed at any point that, as things would probably go, anyone other than Bush would be the Republican candidate. For the reasons given above, we backed Buchanan in New Hampshire.

4. By no means every conservative Republican backed Buchanan. (That is correct.)

5. WFB critically modified his conclusions about Buchanan when he went around stressing the second half of the sentence indicting him. His essay really said, pure and simple, that Buchanan *was* an anti-Semite.

My comment: That is not the case. One finds it odd how much ... happier some people are to believe that someone is really evil, when there is the alternative, intellectually respectable, of believing instead that that person misbehaved.

6. If Buchanan emerges as the leader of the American conservative movement, which is entirely possible, it will be a political disaster for that movement.

My comment: It is not going to happen. Pat Buchanan is happier, and better off, as a publicist than as a politician, and he is too proud to rectify mistakes which would prove disabling in any competition to lead the Republican Party. Meanwhile, his abilities and energy should be sought after by the responsible Right, which however is entitled to the necessary clarifications by him.

*   *   *

I conclude this book with a few sentences, set down in near telegraphic mode.

I begin by saying that the pain genuinely experienced by many American Jews when they feel even an emanation of anti-Semitism is—and ought to be—a major deterrent to those who insouciantly trip down that memory lane. Anyone who cares deeply how other human beings feel should care not to cause others to suffer on account of rhetorical carelessness, and that is a point Patrick Buchanan should accost, when he has time to draw breath.

Several critics and readers in the course of this exercise have made the effort to define "anti-Semitism." I don't find any definition conclusively satisfactory. The reason is that for different people, as abundantly illustrated above, the offensive word or deed differs in impact; so that what might strike one person as inoffensive to ethnic and religious loyalty or pride can wound others. The terms "conservatism" and "liberalism" have fluid definitions and Mr. Pesci is right that in such situations one can only labor toward crystallizations even knowing that they may never succeed.

Anyone who gives voice, especially if this is done repeatedly, to opinions distinctively, even uniquely, offensive to the security of settled Jewish sentiment involving religious or ethnic or tribal pride engages in anti-Semitic activity. Observers will disagree on the question at what point are that person's motives hostile to Jews. It is rarely safe to arrive cocksure at this conclusion ("So-and-so is an anti-Semite, pure and simple"), but even when charity is groping for alternative explanations for such behavior, the targets of such speech can be expected to act, so to speak, pre-emptively. This is how people behave. They take offense.

The anti-anti-Semitism of such as James Freedman, the guilty chapters of the Anti-Defamation League, and Sidney Zion actively foments hostility to organized Jewish objectives. The quickest way to lose a constituency nicely mobilized for right reason is to traduce right reason, thereby earning at first the demoralization of your constituency and, finally, its contempt. Those who hold up inter-religious civility to contempt run the risk of doing serious harm. Anti-Semitism should not run the risk of losing its august place among the gigantic malefactions in human history.

How will the events here chronicled play out in the years ahead?

After World War II there was time, and never a better opportunity to do so, to absorb the ultimate consequences of anti-Semitism. The details were gruesomely abundant. A reversal in public attitudes went forward so to speak in high gear. In the fashionable colleges and universities, where Jewish scholars had been denied tenure, there was sharp action designed to redress manifest wrongs. Complementary changes affected student life, and soon it was all but impossible to find a fraternity or a student society that denied membership to an undergraduate because he was Jewish. Meanwhile the older generation, which had grown up in a culture oriented toward anti-Semitism, drew back. I can't document it, but I have the feeling that there was a deep Christian fear that some would think of the Holocaust in terms of Christian eschatology. Clearly any such profanation worried those whose anti-Semitism was of a kind that centered on admissions policies in country clubs. And for others there was what I think of as simple fatigue with the question; that, together with manifest failure to deny the meritocratic claims of a generation of young Jews so conspicuously qualified to compete with the acculturated Christian in any activity. It sometimes amused me during those years (I speak of the 1950s) that here and there one could spot a flicker of the old anti-Semitism—in undeciphered protest against the super-achievements of the young Jewish generation. I don't have the figures, but I think that as many as thirty per cent of the matriculants at Harvard were by then Jewish.

Along with this integration came, of course, that growing indistinctiveness of the Jews remarked in one of the letters above. Establishing that a person was Jewish could not be done by trailing him on the Sabbath to see where it was that he worshiped; because, mostly, he worshiped nowhere at all, and in this sense was as commonplace as the American Protestant who attends church in order to be baptized, married, and buried, with occasional drop-ins on Easter Sunday and at Christmas.

With this elimination of the old cultural anti-Semitism something else began to happen. It came mostly in the Sixties, and what were then called Negroes were its principal agents. I remember learning of an affluent Jewish academic much given to radical politics who energetically backed what he considered an arm of the civil rights movements only to discover that a new hobgoblin had been discovered, someone other than the Southern Ku Kluxer: the Jew was running America, and had to be stopped! His crimes were his exploitation of the blacks in the cities and a foreign policy geared to the best interest of Israel. With respect to the first charge, this much was true, that the industrious Jew prevailed over competition that was comparatively listless. And that resentment was felt with special keenness by many who had once thought of themselves as brothers-in-distress. No longer. The Jews were now tenured professors at Harvard, with access to any position in America, and this notwithstanding that they composed only two per cent of the population. As for Israel, it was intuited by those black leaders who complained about whites that the Jews in America had attained singular powers in government: they had their own preserve—it was a nation-state called Israel. And no American politician with ambition dared to challenge its singular hold on American patronage. (As we have noted, there is some truth in this.)

It was during those years and after that the Left in America began to show signs of that disdain of Israel that is mentioned in part one. Israel had, for this generation of the Left, all those unattractive habits against which the Left railed. It was a garrison state; it indulged expansionist appetites; and its representatives were powerbrokers entirely comfortable sharing quarters with the Establishment and abiding by its mores and even its folkways.

The Left was not easily discouraged, in part because it had long since lost its capacity to shock. Hitler had been dead for eleven years before the Soviet leader got around to renouncing Stalin at the twentieth Congress, catching many American leftists, who had stoutly defended Stalin, by surprise. But there was plenty of swampland left to graze, and the Left repaired its fences. For a long while it was impossible, in their presence, to criticize Mao Tse-tung; or Ho Chi Minh. At home, Angela Davis was revered (and still is), and the enemy was the Right and, most bitterly, those who had come from the Left to make common fronts with the Right in the continuing struggle against Soviet imperialism and, at home, the overweening state. Creeping anti-Semitism (after all, an old bugbear of the Marxists) was simply one more aberration of a movement unharnessed by scruple or right reason.

It was not so with the Right, this immunity from effective criticism. In part because of a general aversion to old, discarded habits of mind: it was this that caused the special refractions from statements by Joe Sobran and Pat Buchanan, in contrast to the sameness of the emanations from such as *The Nation* magazine. Their animadversions on Israel and its "amen corner" attracted much attention at a time when conservatism appeared to be destabilizing, what with the political evanescence of Ronald Reagan and the disorientation of his successor. All of this was coincidental with the candidacy of Pat Buchanan and the self-anointment as conservative leader of a small organization called the John Randolph Society, membership in which is open to anyone, intellectual or moron, bizarre enough to endure one entire hour at the podium by its president, the anarchist Murray Rothbard. Professor Rothbard proclaimed himself in open opposition to any act of exclusion, as practiced by the conservative tablet-keepers of the past forty years, most specifically, *National Review*. In part one, Irving Kristol acknowledges at least the possibility that the conservative movement will be overtaken in the years directly ahead not by nostalgia (he approves of this) but by reaction; and here he has in mind a relapse into those discarded doctrines that defaced the movement for so long, most conspicuously the nativism within which anti-Semitism prospered.

My own view of it is that this is not in prospect, although I am puzzled by the apparent refusal of Pat Buchanan to, e.g., dissociate himself from the John Randolph Society. In 1996 the conservative movement will or will not be a healthy alternative to the inertial liberalism that so grudgingly relaxes its stranglehold on American political and philosophical thought. An index of the future health of American conservatism will be its resistance to the dulled sensibilities, moral and intellectual.

Index

"Abandonment of Israel, The" (Pod-
horetz), 121
Abortion, 18, 191–92
Abrams, Floyd, 62n, 63n, 66–67
Abzug, Bella, 62n
Acheson, Dean, 157
ACLU. *See* American Civil Liberties
Union
Adelman, Kenneth, 102
ADL Commission (Dartmouth), 46,
49–52, 53n, 57
report of, 46–48, 183, 184, 186
Ailes, Roger, 35n
AIPAC, 41, 43, 44, 80, 84, 85, 103, 104,
136, 138, 180
Allende Gossens, Salvador, 168n
Alterman, Eric, 41, 43–44, 93, 157–58
America First movement, 125, 126,
167, 168n, 194
American Civil Liberties Union, 82, 132
American Enterprise Institute, 30
American Israel Public Affairs Com-
mittee. *See* AIPAC
American Jewish Committee, 13, 35,
68, 157, 159, 170n
American Jewish Congress, 43
American Mercury, xii, 39, 112, 113
anti-Semitism of, xii, 12, 112
American Spectator, The, 32, 33, 40, 51,
58, 134
Anatomy of Melancholy, The (Burton),
158
Andretta, Patrick, 158
Anti-Christianism, 11, 81–82, 96, 104,
139

in Israel, 20, 21–22, 109
Anti-Defamation League, 31, 36, 39,
41, 46–47, 51, 56, 86, 103, 129–30,
183–85, 196
See also ADL Commission (Dartmouth)
Anti-feminism, accusations of, 46, 54,
55, 57
Anti-Semitism, xi, xii, 6, 12, 36, 76–78,
103, 112, 166
accusations of, 26–30, 33, 35–38, 46,
48–52, 54, 55, 57–58, 63–66, 99,
103, 114–15, 129–32, 164–75
passim, 189–90
and anti-Zionism, xiv, 12, 17, 47–49,
57, 60, 70–73, 121
among Arabs and Palestinians, xiii,
110, 111
among blacks, xiii, 50–51, 86, 166,
196–97
among Christians, 78–79, 86, 96
among conservatives, xii–xiii, 24,
112, 119, 120, 127, 132, 135, 142
definitions of, 4–6, 15–17, 31–32,
35–37, 59, 75, 92, 96–97, 137,
138
and editorial license, 48–51
among liberals, xiii, 11, 59, 62, 67,
68, 112, 115, 120, 127, 197
toleration of, xiii–xiv, 196
types of, 4–6, 42, 49, 131, 139
in universities, xiii, 6, 7–8, 10, 135,
196
See also under Buchanan, Patrick; Sobran, Joseph; Vidal, Gore

"Anti-Semitism Has Changed" (Perl-
    mutter), 36
Apartheid, 17, 49–50, 71, 101–2, 106
Arab American Institute, 43
Arafat, Yassir, 149
Arnold, Matthew, 142
Associated Press, 54
Atkins, Chester G., 55
Atlanta Constitution, 159
Atlantic, The, 102
Azana, Manuel, 168n

Baer, Andrew, 54
Baker, James, 193
Barnes, Fred, 35, 102
Barre (New Hampshire) *Times Argus*,
    52
Begin, Menachem, 80, 98, 106, 123–24,
    149
Bell, Daniel, 6
Ben Gurion, David, 44, 138
Bennett, William, 134, 165
Berger, Peter, 170, 171
Berns, Walter, 170
Bernstein, Leonard, 62n, 63n
Birnbaum, Norman, 62n, 63
Black Caucus, 86
black organizations, 50, 86
    anti-Semitism in, xiii, 86, 196–97
B'nai B'rith, 41, 46
    See also Anti-Defamation League
Boesky, Ivan, 42
Bond, Richard, 165
Bork, Robert, 170
Boston Globe, 46–48, 55
Boston Jewish Times, 183, 185
Bowles, Chester, 168n
Bradford, M. E., 77
Bradley, Bill, 62n, 63n
Branigin, William, 98n
Breindel, Eric, 102, 155
Brokaw, Tom, 102
Brown, Jerry, xiii–xiv
Brownfeld, Allan, 35–38, 41, 117
"Buchanan and the Conservative
    Crackup" (Podhoretz), 193–94

Buchanan, Patrick, xiii, xiv, xvi, xvii,
    25, 26–44, 53n, 55, 59, 65, 86, 91–
    95, 95n, 97, 102, 105, 112, 125–26,
    127–32, 134, 135, 136, 137, 139,
    140, 151, 152–57, 158, 163–78,
    180–81, 186–87, 189–90, 193–95,
    197–98
    accusations of anti-Semitism leveled
        against, xii, 26–30, 33, 35–38,
        76–77, 92, 111, 114–15, 119,
        129–32, 135, 139, 164–75 pas-
        sim, 183, 187, 194
    and Israel, criticism of, 26–27,
        35–36, 44, 134–35, 186, 197
    in the New Hampshire primary, xvi,
        xvii, 131, 163–71 passim, 187,
        189, 194
    newspaper columns of, xv, 33, 86,
        125, 134, 136, 166
    presidential candidacy of, xii, xvi,
        xvii, 44n, 91–92, 105, 126, 131,
        152–53, 156, 163–73 passim,
        187, 189–90, 193–94
    and A. M. Rosenthal, 25, 27–30,
        33–34, 37, 40–41, 65, 95, 95n,
        105, 114, 129–30, 131–32, 136,
        164, 165–67
Buckley, William F., Jr., xi–xvi, 14, 15,
    23–24, 28–30, 40, 75n, 109, 119,
    127–28, 134, 137, 142, 146–47, 151,
    154–56, 158, 159, 171–72, 177, 179,
    185
    and the *American Mercury*, xii, 12,
        39, 112, 113
    and Patrick Buchanan, xii, xvi, xvii,
        26–44 passim, 34n, 77, 128,
        131–32, 135, 136, 166, 168, 170,
        180, 194
    on the *Dartmouth Review* contro-
        versy, 53–57, 132
    on Israel, 104, 106–8, 124, 128, 136
    and A. M. Rosenthal, 25, 27, 28–30,
        129–32
    and Joseph Sobran, xii, 14–15,
        23–24, 28–30, 94, 96, 98, 99–102,
        103–6, 128

on Gore Vidal, 59–69
on Yale University, 6, 7–8, 127
Buckley, William F., Sr., 4, 5–6, 112, 147
Bundy, McGeorge, 5
Burnham, James, 39, 73, 77, 98, 101
Burton, Robert, 158
Bush, George, xvi, 31, 83–85, 99, 105, 126, 148, 163–69, 171, 187, 193–94, 198
Butterfield, Fox, 46, 56–58
Butz, Earl, 10
By Way of Deception: A Devastating Insider's Portrait of the Mossad (Ostrovsky), 20

"Can the PLO Play a Part in Peace?" (Dartmouth Review), 56
Capital Gang (CNN), 32
Carter, Arthur L., 62n
Castro, Fidel, 12
Catholicism, 7, 14, 78, 82, 83, 92, 104, 119, 120, 145–46, 190–91
Censorship, 107
"Certain Anxiety, A" (Podhoretz), 121
Chacour, Father, 110
Chafee, John, 85
Chamberlain, Houston Stewart, 92
Chambers, Whitaker, 39
Chan, Evans, 69
Cheever, John, 10
Chiang Kai-shek, 27
China: Alive in the Bitter Sea (Butterfield), 57
China Daily News, 69
Chomsky, Noam, 16
Christian Century, The, 127n
Christianity, 76, 77–80, 86, 151–52, 196
and anti-Semitism, 78–79, 86, 96
Christian Science Monitor, 36
Chronicles, 35, 37, 170n
Churchill, Winston, 19
Chutzpah (Dershowitz), 101
Clark, Ramsey, 62n
Cleveland, James, 53n
Clinton, Bill, 169, 180
Clurman, Richard M., 186n
Clymer, Adam, 83

Cockburn, Alexander, 118
Cohen, Eliot, 13, 93, 140
Cohen, Richard, 23, 25, 36, 52–53, 95, 105, 133, 165
Cohen, Theodore, 6
Cohn, Robert, 181
Cold war, 76
Columbia Journalism Review, 20, 109, 110–11
Coming Crisis in Israel (Zucker), 109
Commentary, xvi, 12–13, 14, 15, 17, 30, 33, 36, 59, 63, 68, 104, 113, 115, 117, 121, 122–23, 157, 173, 193
Committee for Palestinian Rights (Dartmouth), 50
Communism, 11, 31, 37, 50, 65, 116, 152, 190
Communist Manifesto, 38, 42
Coughlin, Father Charles E., 68
Cuddihy, Jack, 96

Daily News (New York), 35, 174n
D'Amato, Alfonse, 42
Danto, Arthur C., 62n
Dartmouth Review, The, xii, 45–59, 91, 111, 115–16, 132, 183–86
editors of, 46, 50, 53–54, 55, 56, 57
masthead of, 53n, 185–86
Davis, Angela, 50–51, 197
Dayan, Moshe, 74, 138
Dean, John, 10
Decter, Midge, 60–61, 62, 67, 68, 78, 99, 99n, 103, 122
Demjanjuk, John, 29
Dershowitz, Alan, 41, 44, 93, 101, 102, 104, 132, 133
Desert Storm. See Gulf War
De Toledano, Ralph, 78
Dilworth, Michael, 176–77
Dine, Thomas A., 43, 84
Dos Passos, John, 39
D'Souza, Dinesh, 56
Duke, David, 43, 44n, 95n, 105, 127, 147, 174n

Eastland, Terry, 170
Eastman, Max, 39, 77

Eban, Abba, 84, 135
Editorial license, 48–51
"Ein Reich, Ein Volk, Ein Freedmann"
  (Garrett, *Princeton Review*), 50–51,
  57
Einstein, Albert, 150
Eisenhower, Dwight D., 23, 152
Eliot, T. S., 126
Elliot, Osborn, 62
Elon, Amos, 4, 107
"Empire Lovers Strike Back, The"
  (Vidal), 60–61, 62–76 passim
Engelhardt, Carl, 178–79, 192
Epstein, Benjamin R., 36
Evans, Rowland, 36
Evans & Novak, 136

Falk, Richard, 62n, 63n
Falwell, Jerry, xii
Farrakhan, Louis, xiii, 23, 43
Feeney, Father Leonard, 21–22
Fitzgerald, Frances, 62n
Flynn, John T., 155
Folan, John E., 158
Forbes magazine, 165
Ford, Gerald, 67, 67n, 168n
Forrestal, James, 157
Forster, Arnold, 36
Fortas, Abe, 147
Fort Worth Star-Telegram, 52
Foxman, Abraham, 41, 183, 185–86
Francis, Samuel, 170n
Franco, Francisco, 168n
Freedman, James O., 6n, 45–47, 50–59
  passim, 87, 93, 104, 184
Friedman, Milton, 78
Friedman, Thomas, 20, 98n, 108–11
Friendly, Alfred, 36
Friendly, Fred, 62n
From Beirut to Jerusalem (Friedman),
  98n
Frum, David, 32, 33, 40, 93, 133, 134
Fundamentalists, 81, 104, 109–10
  philo-Semitism of, xii, 61

Gaffney, Frank, 28
Galbraith, John Kenneth, 74

Garrett, James, 50–51
Gelb, Leslie, 84–85
Genocide, 10, 11, 30, 47, 65, 131
Gentleman's Agreement, 7
Geyer, Georgie Anne, 95
Gilder, George, 53n
Gingrich, Newt, 165
Glovsky, Richard D., 46, 183–86
Glynn, Patrick, 170
Gobineau, Joseph Arthur de, 92
Goldstein, Stanley, 181–82
Goldwater, Barry, 154, 181
Gorbachev, Mikhail, 155
Gottfried, Paul, 24, 41, 78
Graham, Fred, 95
Gramm, Phil, 165
"Grin and Beirut" (*Dartmouth
  Review*), 47
Group characteristics, 8, 16, 36, 69, 87,
  121, 121n, 150–51
Grynberg, Henryk, 96
Gulf War, 16, 25, 26, 30, 31, 77, 84, 99,
  105, 115, 129, 135, 169, 176n, 180
  opposition to, 11, 16–17, 20, 23,
  25–26, 95, 99–100, 103, 113
  See also Hussein, Saddam

Hadar, Leon, 41
Haig, Alexander, 28
Hallow, Ralph, 34
Hamowy, Ronald, 41
Harpers, 180
Harris, David, 34
Harsch, Joseph, 36
Hart, Gary, 190, 191
Hart, Jeffrey, 12–14, 119, 186–87
"Hate That Dare Not Speak Its Name,
  The" (Podhoretz), 60, 113
Hauser, Rita, 107
Hawtin, Guy, 53n
Hazlitt, Henry, 77
Hefner, Hugh, 185
Hegel, G. W. F., 187
Helfman, Ivan, 179–80
Helms, Jesse, xii, 35n, 97
Hendrix, Paul, 177
Henry, William A., III, 32

Heritage (Los Angeles), 34
Hersh, Seymour, 23, 62n
Hertzberg, Rabbi Arthur, 51, 62n, 63n, 69, 145, 177
Hertzl, Theodor, 116
Hiss, Alger, 12
Hitchens, Christopher, 180
Hitler, Adolf, 17, 19, 34, 45–47, 50–55 passim, 65, 68, 123, 125, 135, 147, 149–50, 180, 183, 184, 185, 197
Ho Chi Minh, 197
Hoffman, Allison, 56
Holocaust, 5, 7, 50, 54, 60, 66, 76, 77, 81, 92, 96, 106, 134, 140, 141, 147, 151, 187, 196
    denial of, 32, 131, 166
"Holocaust Update" (Sobran), 105
Homophobia, 40, 46, 54, 55
Horan, Matthew, 3–4
Howe, Irving, 120
Huie, William Bradford, 39
Humor, 48–51, 58n
Hunter-Gault, Charlayne, 62n, 63n
Hussein, Saddam, 25, 26, 27, 28, 30, 31, 42, 105, 125, 131, 135, 163, 174
Hyde, Henry, 93, 157

Idler magazine, 133
In Re Sobran and The Problem, 3
In Search of Anti-Semitism (Buckley), xi–xii, xiv–xvii, 91, 93–106, 111, 113–18, 120, 130, 155
Instauration, 17–18, 19, 24, 105, 187
Intercollegiate Review, 78
International Herald-Tribune, 64
"Is He Villain or Victim?" (Barre Times Argus), 52
Israel, criticism of, 26–27, 35–36, 41–43, 60, 77, 96, 102–4, 122–24, 138, 176n, 182, 192–93
    equated with anti-Semitism, xiv, 5, 17, 35–38, 43–44, 49, 55, 63–66, 76, 95, 102, 116–18, 122, 125, 128, 134–37, 148, 176, 190
    by Patrick Buchanan, 26–27, 35–36, 44, 134–35, 186, 197

by Joseph Sobran, 11, 16–17, 20, 23, 25–26, 95, 99–100, 103, 113, 176n, 182, 186, 197
"Is the Romance Over? American Jews and the Left" (Dartmouth Review), 56

Jabotinsky Award, 110
"J'Accuse" (Podhoretz), 36, 42, 49, 60, 64, 75, 117–19, 121, 122
Jackson, Jesse, xiii–xiv, 23, 31, 174
Jefferson, Mildred Fay, 53n
Jeffries, Leonard, xiii, 86
Jennings, Peter, 62n, 63n
Jerusalem Post, 37, 117n
Jessup, Philip, 168n
John Birch Society, xi, 39, 40, 152, 155
John Randolph Club, 152, 153, 198
Johnson, Cecil, 52, 53
Johnson, Lyndon B., 5, 74, 163
Joining the Club (Oren), 8
Journal Inquirer (Manchester, Connecticut), 182
Joyce, Michael, 170
Judis, John, 6, 77–78, 158,

Kahane, Meir, 21–22, 108
Kant, Hal, 177–78
Kemp, Jack, 165
Kempton, Murray, 44
Kennedy, Edward, 47, 53, 62n, 63n
Kennedy, John F., 5, 48
Kennedy, Robert, 75
Kenner, Hugh, 93, 182, 183
Kiener, Ronald, 47
Kierkegaard, Søren, 151
Kifner, John, 21
Kiley, John, 156
Kilpatrick, James Jackson, 19, 28
King, Martin Luther, Jr., 49–50, 155
Kinsley, Michael, 42, 82–83, 87, 103, 139, 158, 169
Kirk, Russell, 53n, 78–79, 103, 115, 135, 173
Kirkpatrick, Jeane, 102, 120
Kissinger, Henry, 28
Knowland, William, 27

Koch, Edward, xiii, 62n, 63n, 85
Kochansky, Gerald E., 59
Kohn, Moshe, 37
Kollek, Teddy, 138
Kondracke, Morton, 192
Krauthammer, Charles, 28, 44, 102, 165, 167
Kristallnacht, 6, 52
Kristol, Irving, xv, xvii, 78–82, 86, 87, 93, 103, 128, 135, 158, 178, 198
Ku Klux Klan, 44n

Langer, Elinor, 62n
Lansky, Meyer, 97
Lapin, Daniel E., 25
Larkin, Philip, 126
Lazare, Daniel, 42
Lebanon, Israeli invasion of, 36, 37, 48, 75, 98, 112, 118, 138
Left wing, 59
    anti-Semitism in, xii–xiii, 11, 59, 62, 67, 68, 112, 115, 129
Lenin, Nikolai, 152
Lerner, Max, 102
Lerner, Michael, 42
Levenger, Rabbi Moshe, 150
Levin, Jeremy, 95
Levine, Dennis, 42
Levine, Irving M., 68
Lewis, Anthony, 36, 75
Liberty, sinking of, 136, 187
Liebling, A. J., 179
Lilienthal, Alfred, 41
Lincoln, Abraham, 192
Lindbergh, Charles, 194
Lippmann, Walter, 35n
London Times, 54n
Lupo, Alan, 55
Lyons, Eugene, 78

McCarthy, Eugene, 62n, 163
McCarthy, Joseph R., 19
Maccoby, Hyam, 96
McGovern, George, 73–74
MacGovern, John, 55
McLaughlin Group, The (NBC), 26, 41
McLaughlin, John, 26, 41

MacNeil, Lehrer (PBS), 110
Magid, Marion, 63
Maguire, Russell, 39
Maimonides, Moses, 22, 187
Makinson, Larry, 84
Malamud, Bernard, 147
Mano, Keith, 182–83
Mansfield, Harvey, 170
Mao Tse-tung, 74, 197
Marcos, Ferdinand, 104
Marcoux, Alexei, 175–76
Marshall, George, 23, 135, 157
Marshall, Thurgood, 104
Marx, Harpo, 179
Maurras, Charles, 77
Maxwell, Robert, 179
Mein Kampf (Hitler), 45–46
Metzenbaum, Howard M., 84
Meyer, Frank, 39, 77
Middle East Journal, 110
Mises, Ludwig Edler von, 101
Moline, Rabbi L., 180
Morgenbesser, Sidney, 62n, 63n
Morris, Roger, 109, 110–11
Morrison, Micah, 67
Moynihan, Daniel Patrick, 70–73
Muravchik, Joshua, 30–31, 32, 33, 37, 115

NAACP, 104
Nation, The, xii–xiii, 12, 41, 43, 58, 59–76, 86–87, 93, 113, 115, 122, 157, 168, 197
National Lampoon, The, 51
National Review, xi–xii, xv–xvi, xvii, 9, 12, 13–15, 24, 25, 29, 39, 77, 79, 86, 92, 98, 100, 103, 105, 106, 112–14, 119, 120, 127–28, 130, 132, 152, 154–56, 163, 165, 168, 169–73, 194
    and Patrick Buchanan, endorsement of, xvi, xvii
Nativism, 39
Navasky, Victor, 62, 157, 158
Naziism and Neo-Naziism, 24, 40, 43, 65

Near East Report (American Israel Public Affairs Committee), 41
Neier, Aryeh, 62n, 63n
Nelligan, Jeff, 93, 157
Neuhaus, Richard John, 104, 170, 172
New Anti-Semitism, The (Forster), 36
Newfield, Jack, 35
New Hampshire Human Rights Commission, 54, 183
New Republic, 13–14, 15, 17, 24, 31, 34, 35, 42, 77, 87, 102, 119, 125
News media, 36, 102, 165
 anti-Semitism in, xiii, 6, 36, 166
New York City Tribune, 24
New Yorker, The, 4, 179
New York Observer, 35, 42, 192
New York Post, 31, 33
New York Times, xv, xvi, 20, 21, 28, 33, 34, 36, 41, 42, 46, 54–58 passim, 80, 83–85, 98n, 101, 102, 104, 114, 118, 129, 137, 139, 155–56, 169
Nietzsche, Friedrich, 151
Nixon, Richard M., 9
Novak, Robert, xv, 32, 33, 36, 93, 95, 120, 134–37, 169, 170
Nuechterlein, James, 170

O'Connor, John J., 14
O'Hara, John, 10
"Open Letter to William F. Buckley, Jr." (Podhoretz), 93, 111–22
Oren, Dan A., 8
Ostrovsky, Victor, 20
O'Sullivan, John, xi–xvii, 94, 112, 127, 171, 173, 194
Oswald, Lee Harvey, 40

Pacifism, 26
Paley, Rabbi Michael, 47–48, 49
Palmer, Barry, 55
Pangle, Thomas, 170
Peck, Gregory, 7
Pegler, Westbrook, 44, 172
"Pensées" (Sobran), 25
Percy, Charles, 43
Peres, Shimon, 108

Peretz, Marty, 13–14, 15, 34, 102, 119, 120
Perle, Richard, 28
Perlmutter, Nathan, 36, 102, 103, 185
Pesci, Don, 182–83, 195
Petain, Marshal Henri Philippe, 139
Pfaff, William, 64, 65, 66, 93, 122–24, 169
Phenomenology of the Spirit (Hegel), 187
Philadelphia Society, 77
Philo-Semitism, xii, xiv, 34, 61
Pines, Burton, 77
Pinochet Ugarte, Augusto, 168n
Pinsker, Sanford, 133
Pius IX, 126
Podhoretz, Norman, xiv, xvi, 12–13, 14–15, 36–38, 44, 49, 59–65, 67, 68, 75, 87, 93, 94, 96, 97, 99, 102, 103, 111–22, 122–24, 138, 149, 151, 157, 158, 165, 172, 173, 179, 183, 185, 187, 190, 193–94
Pollard, Jonathan, 22, 110, 138, 140, 187
Pound, Ezra, 19, 105
Pressman, Gabe, 164, 167
Pritchett, Kevin, 52, 54
Private Eye, 51

Quayle, Dan, 180

Rabin, Yitzhak, 135
Racism, 18, 19, 70–71, 86, 87, 150, 166, 177
 accusations of, 40, 46, 49–50, 54, 55, 57, 104
 defined, 72–73
Rand, Ayn, 152, 155
Rather, Dan, 102
Reagan, Ronald, 23, 29, 98, 104, 126, 164, 174n, 197
 Bitburg visit of, 29, 174n, 187
Reasoner, Harry, 107
Religious practices, 47, 80–82, 87, 128–29, 141
 in Israel, 79–80, 109
Reswick, Murray, 138–39

"The *Review* Is Pro-Semitic and Pro-Israeli" (*Dartmouth Review*), 56
Revolt of Mamie Stover, The (Huie), 39
Rhodes, Cecil, 177
Richman, Sheldon, 41
Ricks, Christopher, 93, 156
Robertson, Wilmot, 17
Roche, John, 73–74, 93, 157
Roosevelt, Eleanor, 172
Roosevelt, Franklin Delano, 152
Roosevelt, Theodore, 45, 53
Rose, Charlie, 164
Rosenthal, A. M., xv, xvi, 27–30, 32–35, 37, 40–44, 93, 94, 97, 102, 110, 129–32, 137, 139, 147, 149, 151, 157, 164–70
    defenders of, 33–34
    and Patrick Buchanan, 25, 27–30, 33–34, 37, 40–41, 65, 95, 95n, 105, 114, 129–30, 131–32, 136, 164
Rosenzweig, Franz, 82
Roth, Philip, 179
Rothbard, Murray, 41, 152–56, 198
Rusher, William, 53n, 154
Rusk, Dean, 157, 186
Russell, Bertrand, 100

Sabrin, Murray, 41
Safire, William, 102
Salem, Lee, 95
Samson Option, The (Hersh), 23
Sartre, Jean-Paul, 144
Sayegh, Abdallah al-, 70
Schlamm, Willi, 77
Scranton, William, 9
Seymour, Charles, 7–8, 16, 69
Shamir, Yitzhak, 20, 21, 83, 106, 108, 138, 148, 149
Sharpton, Al, xiii
Shultz, George, 147
Siegman, Henry, 43
Silvers, Robert, 62n
Simon, Paul, 62n
Singer, Isaac Bashevis, 133
Six Day War, 73, 98
60 Minutes (CBS), 85

Smith, Gerald L. K., 40
Smith, Tom W., 159
Smith, William, 47
Sobran, Joseph, 3–4, 8–9, 11–26, 55, 59, 86, 91, 92, 93–103, 104–6, 108, 110, 118–20, 128, 137, 140, 151, 156, 158, 170n, 172–73, 175–77, 181–83, 186–87, 197
    accusations of anti-Semitism leveled against, xii, xiv–xv, 11, 13, 14, 35, 91, 111–14, 118–19, 175–83 passim, 187
    criticism of Israel by, 11, 16–17, 20, 23, 25–26, 95, 99–100, 103, 113, 176n, 182, 186, 197
    early career of, 8–9
    editorial note regarding, 9–12, 113
    opposition of, to Gulf War, 11, 16–17, 20, 23, 25–26, 95, 99–100, 103, 113
Solzhenitsyn, Alexander, 116–17
Soviet Union, 31, 69
Spain, expulsion of Jews from, 7, 135, 141
Stalin, Joseph, 19, 44n, 99, 197
Steinem, Gloria, 62n
Steiner, George, 123
Stern, Kenneth, 170
Stet (Princeton), 56
Stockton, Ronald R., 108–11
Strauss, Leo, 78
Styron, Rose, 62n
Susskind, David, 169
Syllabus of Errors (Piux IX), 126

Taft, Robert, 154
Tellechea, Manuel, 24
Thatcher, Margaret, 126
Theology, Jewish, 22
They Must Go (Kahane), 21
Thieu, Nguyen Van, 74
Thomas, Cal, 102
Thomas, Norman, 44, 168n
Tikkun, 42
Time magazine, 28, 32, 95
Today Show, 180
Tonkin, Humphrey, 58

Tonsor, Stephen, 77–79, 135
Topping, Seymour, 110
Truman, Harry S, 19
Tyrrell, Bob, 120, 134
Tyrrell, Father George, 18
Tyrrell, R. Emmett, 51–52, 53n, 58, 170

Union Leader (Manchester, N.H.), 55
Universities and colleges, 11, 45–59
    anti-Semitism in, xiii, 6, 7–8, 10, 135, 196
Updike, John, 10
U.S. News & World Report, 102

"Victory for Buchanan" (Rosenthal), 165
Vidal, Gore, 17, 59–69, 76, 87, 91, 93, 109, 115, 122–23, 138, 140, 157, 158
    accusations of anti-Semitism leveled against, xii–xiii, 12, 31, 59–69, 111, 113, 122, 127
Vietnam War, 59, 73, 74, 180
Village Voice, The (New York), 35
Von Hoffman, Nicholas, 36, 119

Waldheim, Kurt, 5
Walker, General Edwin, 39–40
Wall, James M., 127–29
Wallace, George, 19
Wallace, Mike, 62n, 63n
Wall Street Journal, 32, 46, 54, 165, 180
Walzer, Michael, 120
Wanderer, The, 157
Washington, Booker T., 5
Washington Jewish Week, 41
Washington Post, 23, 35, 36, 53, 102, 118

Washington Star, 138
Washington Times, 34, 170n
Waters, H. Franklin, 4n
Wattenberg, Ben, 102
Waugh, Evelyn, 126
Weber, Vin, 165
Weidhorn, Manfred, 93, 142–52
Weigel, George, 120, 170
Weisberg, Jacob, 31
West Bank policies, 48, 71, 75–76, 85, 106, 107, 125, 150, 180
Weyrich, Paul
Whelan, James, 53n
"Why National Review Is Wrong" (Sobran), 25
Wicker, Tom, 62n, 63, 65
Wiesel, Elie, 5, 135
    on Patrick Buchanan, 35
Wieseltier, Leon, 96
Wilkins, Roger, 62n, 63, 65
Will, George, 28, 35n, 41, 102, 111, 120
Williams, Walter, 53n
Wise, Steven S., 179
World Policy Institute, 41

Yeats, William Butler, 126
Yeltsin, Boris, 169
Yoder, Edwin M., Jr., 64, 65, 66, 93, 137, 169

Zion, Sidney, 56, 192–93, 196
Zionism, xiv, 9, 12, 17, 47–49, 57, 60, 69–73, 78, 101, 116–17, 121, 133, 150, 175–76, 177
Zogby, James, 43
Zoll, Allan, 152
Zuckerman, Mortimer, 102